SOCIAL
CAUSES
OF
ILLNESS

SOCIAL CAUSES OF ILLNESS

RICHARD TOTMAN

Pantheon Books, New York

LIBRARY OF CONGRESS CATALOGING IN PUBLICATION DATA
Totman, Richard.   Social causes of illness.
Includes bibliographical references and index.
1. Medicine, Psychosomatic.   I. Title.
RC49.T67   1979b 616.08   79-2307
ISBN 0-394-50856-4

Manufactured in the United States of America

FIRST AMERICAN EDITION

CONTENTS

To my father

In recollection of countless dissensions
and in anticipation of many more.

ACKNOWLEDGMENTS

I would like to thank:

Dr. Barbara Kugler, Dr. David Caudrey, Mr. Joe Kiff and Dr. Leslie Dunn, for their valuable comments on a draft of this book. Mr. Michael Clark, for a thorough critical appraisal of the drafted version. Mr. Raymond ffoulkes, conversations with whom spawned many of the ideas in this book. Mrs. Nicolette McGuire and Miss Rona Davies for their help with preparation of the manuscript. And my wife, Felicity-Ann, not only for providing wifely encouragement so unfailingly, but also for many helpful criticisms and suggestions.

I am also indebted to Dr. Norman Dixon, Dr. Grant Lee, Dr. Sylvia Reed and Dr. P. Heaf, the staff of the E.N.T. wards at the Radcliffe Infirmary Oxford, The British Heart Foundation, The Medical Research Council, Nuffield College Oxford, University College London, and all those who have helped with my research at several institutions.

For permission to reproduce copyright material I am grateful to:

British Medical Journal, (L. Rose, Some aspects of paranormal healing, 1954. Editorial, 1961); *Anaesthesia*, (A. A. Mason, Surgery under hypnosis, 1955); *Aldine Publishing Co.*, (M. Orne in Hypnosis: research developments and perspectives, Ed. Fromm & Shor, 1972); *The American Society Of Clinical Hypnosis*, (T. A. Clawson & R. H. Swade, The Hypnotic control of blood flow and pain, 1975); *Scientific American*, (A. Leaf, Getting Old, 1973. R. S. Morison, Dying, 1973); *Psychosomatic Medicine*, (A. Flarscheim, Ego mechanisms in three pulmonary tuberculosis patients, 1958); *Nature*, (J. Huxley *et al.*, Schizophrenia as a genetic morphism, 1964); *Journal of the American Medical Association*, (A. K. Shapiro, Etiological factors in the placebo effect, 1964); W. H. Auden, Collected Poems; Dr. L. Rose and Prof. R. H. Rahe.

'Doctor Thomas sat over his dinner,
Though his wife was waiting to ring,
Rolling his bread into pellets;
Said, "Cancer's a funny thing.

Nobody knows what the cause is,
Though some pretend they do;
It's like some hidden assassin
Waiting to strike at you.

"Childless women get it,
And men when they retire;
It's as if there had to be some outlet
For their foiled creative fire." '

W. H. AUDEN

INTRODUCTION

This book is written from the belief that the restricted view of illness and health which people in Western industrialized societies have come to hold, valuable though it has proved over the last half-century, has now more or less outrun its usefulness. If medicine is to advance from where it is at present, old ideas must change in a fundamental way. A new concept of health and illness is called for, and with it a new approach to care of the sick. Research and theory concerned with the influence of mental states on physical illness provides the starting point for such a change.

It is difficult to identify an exact point in history when medicine became established as a science. The transformation has been slow and cautious. It has come about, mainly over the last fifty or sixty years, not so much as a result of innovations within medicine itself as through the flowering of the natural sciences (physiology, pharmacology, genetics, etc.), and the acceptance and application by practising doctors of the knowledge accumulated in these fields. Medical undergraduates in almost all universities now train in a combination of natural science subjects before they first come into contact with patients.

One of the most profound consequences of this process is that our ideas about health and illness have been shaped in a very distinct way. These days, a person who goes to receive treatment is regarded strictly as a piece of hardware. His complaint is looked on as a mechanical business – as something wrong or out of balance with his tissues and organs. In the same way, good health is equated with proper bodily functioning. Moreover, it is not just those within the profession who have come to think exclusively along these lines. The huge public demand for medical services, the institutionalization of medical practice – in short, the success of medicine – is a measure of the widespread acceptance of a physical approach to illness and treatment.

To outsiders, what is more, the world of medicine is a closed community. Its workings are protected by a code of secrecy and surrounded by an aura calculated to induce in those being treated an attitude of submission, and to discourage questioning and resistance. Perhaps it is for this reason that until very recently medical policy and practice have escaped public scrutiny to an extent that is unique among the professions. Only over the last few years have some important questions been raised. Dr. Halfdan Mahler, director-general of the World Health Organization,[1] for instance was recently quoted as saying:

> The major – and most expensive – part of medical technology as applied today appears to be far more for the satisfaction of the health professions than for the benefit of the consumers of health care.

And Professor Thomas McKeown, head of the department of social medicine at Birmingham University, has made the challenging statement:

> Most people, including most medical people, are under the impression that health depends primarily on the treatment of the sick, through personal medical measures.... In fact, if we look back over what has brought about the improvement of health in the past, medical measures have made quite a marginal contribution.

Recently, a considerable body of evidence has accumulated which suggests that many serious illnesses, as well as being related to acknowledged physical causes, occur with some regularity following particular types of life experience. The

[1] *The Listener*, August 4, 1977, p. 130.

significance of this evidence is not to be underestimated. For if it is true that specific circumstances can render a person susceptible to illness, we are forced to recognize a degree of control over health prior to the point at which the accredited physical 'causes' can exert any influence. The physical aspects of a disease – the organic manifestations we have come to regard as the disease itself – may, in fact, represent a comparatively late stage in an 'underlying' dysfunction. If this is the case, then treating illness by conventional methods (with drugs, surgery, radiation, etc.) is merely scratching the surface of the problem. Physical intervention may be attending to the *symptoms* of the basic affliction rather than to the real cause.

Psychosomatic disease

Research into 'psychosomatic'[2] disease, as it has become known, is the study of ways in which a person's behaviour and inferred mental state relate to his chances of becoming ill. 'Psychosomatic' diseases must be distinguished from 'hypochondriacal' conditions. A hypochondriac is someone who claims to be ill, but shows no organic symptoms. A psychosomatic condition on the other hand, is one in which there is evidence of genuine organic pathology, but in which it is believed that this was, at least in part, brought on by psychological forces. People with psychosomatic diseases are not malingerers. Psychosomatic illness can be serious and may even be fatal.

Ideas about psychosomatic disease are changing. In the pioneer days of psychosomatic research it was believed that there were a handful of conditions, such as asthma, ulcers and high blood pressure, whose onset could be explained entirely on the basis of psychological influences. Since this early research, findings have made it clear that psychological factors affect many other conditions, including a large number of serious illnesses, even heart disease and cancer. While it used to be thought that there were just a few 'pure' psychosomatic con-

[2] Psyche – the mind, soma – the body.

ditions, now it is generally held that most, if not all, diseases have a psychosomatic component.

What does it mean to say that most diseases have a 'psycho-somatic component'? Certainly no one working in the field of psychosomatic research would want to claim that a person's psychological condition is the only thing governing whether or not he becomes ill. It is plain enough that other factors, such as the extent of his contact with infectious agents (viruses and bacteria), play an important part too. In fact, very few chronic diseases are now believed to have just one solitary cause. Rather, they are thought of as the product of a number of 'risk factors'. For example, heredity, high blood pressure, blood chemistry and smoking are all factors known to be related to the onset of heart disease.

But in addition to the various physical risk factors which have been discovered there is increasing recent evidence to suggest that psychological upheaval in people's lives may be influential, especially upheaval due to changes of a social nature. Moreover, it seems likely that the psychological or psychosomatic component in chronic diseases has been grossly underestimated in the past.

So most diseases are now recognized to be the product of not one but several contributory factors, each acting in combination with the others to influence the chance of symptoms appearing. If the concentration of a virus is extremely high, as it would be in an epidemic, this may be sufficient, on its own, to cause a person to become infected. If a person eats large quantities of animal fats and takes very little exercise so that the level of cholesterol in his blood rises, this, on its own, could be sufficient to provoke a heart attack. Similarly, the possibility must be entertained that under certain circumstances a person's mental condition can influence critical bodily balances so that normal functioning is impaired and illness results without any 'help' from outside agents. There is no reason why conditions such as arthritis and cancer could not be produced in this way. Indeed, some recent lines of research suggest they are.

Theories of psychosomatic disease

The idea that a person's mental condition affects his chances of becoming ill is not a new one. It has been alluded to by physicians at virtually every point in history. During the past thirty years many attempts have been made to explain the nature of the interaction scientifically – to specify exactly what is the psychological state which leads to lowered resistance. Surprisingly, not one of these attempts has really succeeded. Not one has achieved any general acceptance. It is important not to be misled by the now popular term 'psychological stress'. To say that a person succumbs to illness because of 'stress' is, of course, not an explanation in any sense. It is simply a re-phrasing of the problem. The fact that the term 'stress' has crept into the vernacular reflects the failure of attempts at explanation, not their success.

But a considerable number of psychosomatic theories have been put forward. One of my aims in this book is to account for why these have failed so conspicuously, and to spell out the snags with current concepts of psychosomatic influence.

Because many different categories of professional people have an interest in the psychosomatic issue (e.g. physiologists, psychoanalysts, experimental psychologists, sociologists), several different styles of theory can be identified. There are psychoanalytic theories, psychophysiological theories, sociological theories, ... etc, and the progression of thinking within each of these professional areas tends to go on more or less untouched by that within another. The result is a number of insulated and sometimes rather partisan schools of thought. I shall try to show that every one of these schools has its own built-in limitations, which, in the final analysis, render it incapable of providing a real explanation of psychosomatic influence.

While each style of psychosomatic theory is open to attack on different grounds, there is one deep-seated problem common to them all. This is the old one that philosophers have been arguing about for centuries, namely, how we are to conceive of the relation between body and mind.

The body–mind problem

What is the correct way of talking about 'mental' and 'physical'? Are we to say that mental events cause physiological ones, such as electrical activity in the brain? Or that electrical activity in the brain produces mental states? Or that mental events can cause brain activity as well as vice-versa? Or, alternatively, as some have suggested, that mental and brain events go on at the same time, as it were in parallel, but do not interact?[3] To many, these questions are no more than irritating philosophers' quibbles. But they lie at the very root of the problems with contemporary psychosomatic theory. Until we have sorted out just what it means to say that a person's mental state can influence his physical wellbeing how can we begin to construct theories, let alone go about evaluating them?

The body–mind problem is thus brought to a head in the study of psychosomatic influence in a way which it is not in any other subject. Close scrutiny reveals, plainly enough, that none of the existing schools of theory is able to get round it satisfactorily. It is primarily for this reason that psychosomatic research is regarded as something of a red herring by many natural scientists. So is the psychosomatic issue just a passing fashion which will never achieve respectability among the scientific community, and will eventually die out owing to its failure to produce proper theories? I believe this is not so, and that, in fact, the opposite is true. Viable theories can be constructed and there is a pressing need for them.

Aims of this book

My objective in writing this book is to do three things. First, to put the case that psychological factors do influence the onset

[3] So called 'psycho-physical parallelism', currently the most popular position among psychosomatic researchers.

and course of physical illness in an important way. Second, to outline a new frame of reference for conceiving psychosomatic influence which is free of the limitations of the old ones. And third, to suggest an answer to the question 'What are the psychological conditions which together with other factors contribute to a person's chances of becoming ill?' This third aim is therefore tentatively to put forward a new theory of psychosomatic influence – i.e. a new way of defining the psychological 'risk factor' (or 'psychological stress') itself. I am convinced, though, that this can be done only as the third stage in this threefold aim. The basic conceptual problems have to be faced first.

In a recent book, entitled *The explanation of social behaviour*, Harré and Secord have tried to point to what is wrong with social psychology, and why it does not seem to be getting anywhere very fast. They criticize the artificiality of traditional research in which one tiny fragment of social behaviour is taken and made the subject of controlled experiments in a 'laboratory'. In its place, they have suggested an entirely new approach. This is based on the principle that it is possible to construct a picture, or 'model' of what lies behind the things an individual does and says in his ordinary day-to-day existence. An individual's behaviour is seen as the product of an underlying 'structure' of rules. Harré and Secord believe these rules to be richly accessible in the accounts individuals themselves give of their own behaviour.

Several authors before Harré and Secord have recognized the force of so called 'structural' analyses in the study of human behaviour. The Swiss linguist, Saussure, was one of the first to point out that any study of meaning must invoke the notion of structure. Through the influential work of Lévi-Strauss, structural analyses have come to play a prominent part in anthropology. The psychologist and philosopher, Jean Piaget, one of the most highly regarded authorities on the development of thinking in children, has based his entire research programme on structuralist principles. In 1965, Chomsky revolutionized the study of language by proposing that structures underlie the understanding and production of grammatical statements.[4]

Research and common sense tell us that the study of psychosomatic influence is inseparable from the study of social meaning. If, on being told that my wife has eloped with my best friend, I feel sick, this reaction is not a consequence of the sounds of the words as they come over. Neither is it because the words signal imminent physical danger. It is a function of the social meaning of the act of unfaithfulness, as we understand it in our culture, and as I understand it in relation to my circles of friends and acquaintances, one of which is the 'group' consisting of my wife and myself.

Recent research has made it plain that the risk of becoming seriously ill is affected more profoundly by social factors than by physical wear and tear. It appears that events in people's lives influence health primarily on account of their social meaning to that person. Now, if one accepts the view that social meaning can be studied only by reference to underlying structure – and the arguments for doing so are basic, and strong, as I shall try to show – then this kind of perspective is unavoidable as we come to consider the psychosomatic component in illness. Our theory, or 'model' of the mental state predisposing a person to become ill has got to be cast in this mould. Moreover, there is an additional advantage in adopting this style of analysis which is that the logical snares presented by the body–mind problem can be circumvented.

The main idea which emerges from this line of thinking, and that which forms the central thesis of this book, can be summarized fairly simply. It is that people, in their dealings with others, follow social rules. When they stop following rules, for whatever reason, they are likely to become ill. 'Rules' is of course meant here in a slightly special sense. It refers to characteristic ways of relating to the social environment – styles of conversation and doing things, preferences, attitudes, values. Even the behaviour of eccentrics and immoralists exhibits

[4] Freud's theories have much in common with these approaches, although they cannot be called 'structural' in the strict sense.

consistency and therefore can be said to be governed by rules.

All kinds of circumstances can deprive a person of an opportunity for following the social rules he is accustomed to follow; for example the death of his wife, retirement, being socially ostracised. But research suggests that what is important is not one particular event. Neither is it that such events cause mental distress. It is purely that they cut a person off from being able to indulge in well practiced, habitual styles of activity and social interaction, and do not provide him with alternatives.

Another important factor is the nature of the rules themselves. If a particular individual holds rules which are very narrow in their application, or very rigid, it will be difficult for him to cope with social change when it comes, and to switch to new forms of rule-following which new situations demand.

I shall argue that enhanced susceptibility to illness occurs not as a by-product but as a direct result of this condition of social disorientation. The hypothesized sequence is therefore that certain (definable) circumstances in a person's life act on that person so as to induce in him a specific mental state. This mental state can be epitomised, or 'modelled', in psychological terms, but it is also a state of the brain which gives rise to neuro-hormonal activity with consequences for health.

The way I am proposing this happens is, of course, conjectural, and may be proved wrong by future research. Whatever the nature of a theory, whether it is a good one depends on how well it accounts for the facts, and whether any facts refute it. But a considerable amount of evidence exists consistent with the basic idea. An additional aim, and a very necessary one, is therefore to defend what is said by reference to studies which have been carried out in the past, and research currently underway.

Evidence is indeed by no means thin on the ground. We now have available the findings from many hundreds of studies consistent with the basic assumption that the capacity for recovery from illness, and for sustained resistance to disease, is there, latent, in the bodily resources of every individual, dependent for its ascendency on the right psychological conditions. Reflected in this evidence, and running through the arguments developed in this book, is the theme of *agency* – the view of man as an active decider, planner and doer, and the idea that it is precisely through sustained action and commitment that health is protected.

Pre-scientific medicine

Before the general adoption of controlled observation as a scientific standard around the middle of the nineteenth century and the rapid development of medical techniques which followed it, people's ideas about disease and healing in Europe as in most of the rest of the world, were steeped in religion, magic and superstition. Primitive ideas of how the evil spirit exerts its harmful effect on the body are unconcerned with physical causality as we know it. Explanations of why people became ill were grounded in complex, highly developed systems of prelogical beliefs and fantasy the description of which is inseparable from a description of the culture itself.

A method of diagnosis and treatment, for instance, in which the patient's belt is repeatedly measured, then cut into pieces and distributed and buried to the accompaniment of prayers, makes little sense to anyone who is ignorant of the associated beliefs. This particular medical ritual was practised throughout Europe until the end of the sixteenth century. As was, and still is, commonplace in pre-scientific societies, a disease was believed to result from invasion of the victim by an evil spirit, possession manifesting itself in minute to minute fluctuations in the dimensions of his clothes. The diagnosis of possession was arrived at by a series of dubious measurements, and treatment was aimed at exorcizing the evil influence by inducing in the patient a 'sympathetic' reaction to the purification or destruction of a particular garment.

The commonest primitive explanation of disease is that it is inflicted on the sufferer either as a result of another individual's curse, or as a punishment from a spirit for breaking a taboo. Often, mythical causes such as these are the only way of accounting for symptoms, and consequently the members of many cultures do not make any sharp distinction between the kinds of physical assault we would call disease and other forms of personal catastrophe.

The Kenyan Luo, for example, class together depression, hysteria, and cerebral malaria because they are all thought to be the work of spirits of possession. Some primitive concepts of 'illness' are so encompassing as to include, along with organic conditions, feelings of tiredness, dejection and apathy; incompetence in hunting, warfare and chiefship; and general adversities we would put down to simple 'bad luck'.[1]

Febrega and Manning [2] studied a group of Spanish speaking Mexicans in the Chapanis Highlands and found that these people hold a set of beliefs about illness which involve aspects of life that English speakers would regard as mental, bodily and social rather than medical. Outbursts of disease are taken as evidence that a person's general strength, stamina or *consistencia* is depleted: disease and wellbeing thus reflect the status of a person's adjustment and functioning in all areas of his life.

In cultures where beliefs such as these are held, treatment is not carried out by an expert-engineer whose job it is to get the body up to specification again, but by the shaman or witch doctor, whose administrations are steeped in religious and magical significance. His aim is not just to repair the affected organ but rather to revitalize the person as a complete unit – to inspire his hopes, reaffirm his self-esteem, revive his spirit; and all in one with these aims and quite inseparable from them, to reconstitute his physical health.

Scientific medicine

Over the past hundred years, in almost all the countries of the

---

[1] e.g. The Gonja of West Africa and several Central American tribes. (See, for example, the papers by Pitt-Rivers and Goody, in Douglas [1].)

world, medicine has undergone a profound change. Pre-scientific notions of disease, and the magic and intrigue surrounding them, have been steadily replaced by theories of physical causation. In industrialized societies, care of the sick is grounded in the conviction that disease can be understood only in terms of the physical and chemical properties of organs and tissue, and that the only way of treating pathological conditions is through physical intervention – procedures designed to interfere with the mechanical or chemical status quo. Poisons are countered with antidotes, pain with analgesic drugs, infections with antibiotics; while tumours are cut or burned out. Primitive, occult, transcendental and 'fringe' practices – in fact any system offering treatment not based on a physical manipulative technique – tend to be dismissed as the product of simple ignorance regarding how the body works.

Every year in Britain billions of pills are prescribed through the National Health Service alone, and many hundreds of thousands of operations are carried out. The escalating public demand for medicines has stimulated investment in pharmaceutical companies to such an extent that the manufacture of drugs and medical aids has become a major and highly competitive industry.

Few practices have survived into the 1970s where the doctor is able to carry on a friend-of-the-family relationship with his patients. The heavy demands placed on doctors inevitably mean that the average time available for individual consultation becomes less, and treatment, when eventually one's turn comes, often turns out to be cursory and impersonal. The present-day practitioner functions more like a pill-dispenser, and the surgeon more like a maintenance mechanic, than ever before in the history of the health service.

The contrast between theory and practice in primitive societies and that in industrialized societies is thus a far-reaching one.

At first sight it may seem misplaced, in view of the considerable distance which modern medicine has gone towards controlling disease, to question whether the development of sophisticated instrumentation should be its only concern. However, it is precisely because of medicine's success that the question should be asked. As an institution becomes inveterate, the complacent and authoritarian element within it gets stronger, more resistant to change, and increasingly reluctant to consider alternative ideas. So it is more than ever important for a full understanding of health and disease to keep track of the following questions:

1. Are the objectives and procedures of contemporary medicine still in line with what is acceptable from a moral, human and empathic point of view?

2. Even if modern medical treatments do counteract symptoms in a more effective and reliable manner than any other previous method or current alternative, should resources be concentrated exclusively on this project at the expense of exploring other possibilities? Because faith healing, witch doctoring, acupuncture and other fringe techniques do not contain procedures whose physiological basis is immediately discernible, is it right to dismiss these as ineffectual and file them away as 'not for serious consideration'? In particular, is there evidence that psychological and social factors are significant in the causation of organic disease?

The first question will be returned to at the end of this book. The second set of questions provides the starting point for the discussions in subsequent chapters.

Causes and effects in the scientific scheme

If someone we know suddenly becomes morose and irritable and complains of lack of energy, tiredness, and discomfort, we will probably attribute their behaviour to a bodily disorder. A doctor, by asking specific questions and making more informed guesses, may be able to pinpoint more precisely the nature of the dysfunction.

Suppose an individual says that he feels alternatively hot and cold, and that his muscles ache and his throat is sore. His doctor diagnoses 'flu. Implicit in this diagnosis is the belief that the patient is infected with a 'flu virus which has caused his immune system to react in a particular predictable manner, giving rise, in turn, to the symptoms which he feels. A chain of causes and effects, having several discrete stages, from entry of the virus to the experience and report of symptoms, is assumed to have taken place. This is represented in the simplest possible way in Figure 1.

invasion of virus —→   response of———→   symptoms (sore
                            immune system   throat, aches, etc.)

stage (1)   (2)   (3)

Figure 1   Cause and effect sequence implicit in the diagnosis of 'flu.

It is unlikely that a doctor will be able to reduce the level of virus in the blood directly, so he will probably prescribe a drug which acts on stage (3) of the sequence, in order to alleviate symptoms and lessen the patient's discomfort.

From the point of view of treating someone who has 'flu, and understanding why he reacts in the way he does, the crude sequence depicted in Figure 1 may be sufficient. But it is obviously not a full explanation. For instance, we could go on to ask why infection occurred at all in the first place. It may have been that the victim came into contact with a particularly high concentration of the virus, or a strain of virus against which he had very few antibodies. Alternatively, he may have inherited a proneness to becoming infected with 'flu viruses in general. Perhaps again, his immune response was slow to get going when the virus first entered his bloodstream.

It is likely, of course, that not one but several of these conditions prevailed at the time of his contact with the virus, and that each contributed to his becoming infected. They are not mutually exclusive, so each can be thought of as influencing the chance of disease occurring, in combination with the others.

Taking these considerations into account, a revised, slightly extended version of the causal sequence illustrated in Figure 1 could be constructed, such as that shown in Figure 2.

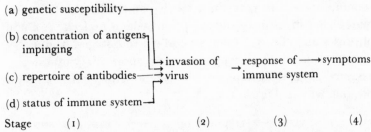

Stage   (1)   (2)   (3)   (4)

Figure 2 Extended sequence of causes and effects.

The initial stage, as shown in the revised version, involves several contributory factors. Since these are all historical and cannot be reversed, the doctor need not take them into account when he sees a patient. There is no point in his doing so.

The sequence can be expanded yet further, into a complex network of interacting causes and effects, and it is this expanded system, or parts of it, which scientists seek to elucidate by discovering the preconditions to organic states and changes, and then searching for the preconditions to these ... etc. For example, the state of the immune system at the time of infection can perhaps be attributed to short-term fluctuations in body metabolism, temperature, hormonal activity ... and so on.

To say that the main aim of modern medicine is to remove *the* cause of a disease is therefore misleading. The intention is that a treatment should interfere with the chain of interactions somewhere along the line, but it will be clear, even from the highly simplified representations of this in Figures 1 and 2, that there are many stages in the chain prior to the point at which intervention becomes possible. In fact, curative medicine tends to intervene at relatively late stages in the sequence. In the case of 'flu and other viral infections it is at a very late stage – the alleviation of discomfort from symptoms – this being kept up until the infection itself has been eliminated by the body's own natural defences. Preventive medicine (interestingly, the most recent development in the history of medicine) attempts to intervene at earlier stages: for example, by stipulating standards of hygiene, by insisting on universal innoculation, and by restricting the commercial and industrial use of specific toxins and drugs. Intervention early on in the sequence is also one of the long-term aims of geneticists via the selection and modification of genes themselves, opening up the possibility of preventing hereditary proneness to certain conditions.

The notion of a network of causes and effects, which I have illustrated taking 'flu as an example, but which underlies all scientific thinking about disease, betrays a fundamentally physicalistic, or mechanistic, orientation to the concept of illness. It treats the individual, the 'patient', as a biological black box; a complicated piece of machinery inside which events are assumed to take place in a law-like way. Many sections of the mechanism are still an enigma to scientists. But if some causes remain obscure at the present, there is always the tacit conviction that these are in principle discoverable and potentially able to be articulated in the overall superstructure of causes and effects, like unplaced pieces of a giant jigsaw.

Fitting psychosomatic influence into the causal scheme

In setting out the case that psychosomatic influence should be taken more seriously by the medical profession, two different approaches are possible. One is to concentrate solely on physical disease – organic illness as we, in a technology-dominated culture, know it – and to ask whether it is reasonable to suggest that a person's mental state can affect his bodily wellbeing.

The other is to press for a radical change in our mechanistic style of thinking and talking about illness, and for the adoption of a new concept of health and disease which is more encompassing than the one we have come to accept: perhaps one which is closer to that held in some of the primitive societies mentioned. By doing away with the sharp dividing lines between mental and physical which are so much a feature of our language, it would become easier to talk about psychosomatic effects.

The latter is the more difficult task. Fundamental shifts in the meanings of words, such as this would entail, do not happen overnight. So I shall approach the problem first in the former way, not attempting to bend the language, but focussing on physical disease as we know it, and looking for indications that organic symptoms are affected by psychological factors.

The question, 'Is it reasonable to suggest that a person's mental state can influence his bodily wellbeing?' can therefore be split up into about three subsidiary questions.

First of all, we can ask whether there are any 'ways in' for psychosomatic effects, considering what is known about the organic events leading up to the appearance of symptoms. The first sub-question, then, is, 'Is it reasonable from a physiological standpoint?'

Second, we can ask how much evidence there is to support the claim that psychological factors influence the onset and course of serious illnesses, and how sound this evidence is – i.e. 'Is it reasonable from a scientific standpoint?'

Third, we can ask whether the idea that mental states affect organic ones is reasonable from a logical standpoint. Is it a sensible and intelligible proposal to make? The importance of this question may not be immediately apparent. But of the three questions it is the one which gets swept under the carpet most often. Yet it is really the question to be faced first of all. So many attempts to explain the nature of psychosomatic influence have run aground, often after considerable effort has been put into researching them, on account of logical problems inherent in them right from the start. We shall return to this question later, in a discussion of psychosomatic theories. A primary aim of this book is to argue that psychosomatic influence *is* a sensible subject, even if we are focussing on disease in a purely physical sense; and furthermore, that magical and 'fringe' techniques of treatment *can* be looked at under the scientific microscope. But all this only if we adopt a new style of analysis.

To embark on a discussion of psychological influences on health without first some attention being given to the history of medicine would be ill-advised, and before turning to the question of whether psychosomatic influence is physiologically possible, it is instructive to examine some aspects of historical treatments from a psychological perspective. In fact, scientific medicine is scarcely a century old. Yet healing in some form has been in evidence for over 2,000 years. Could the art of healing have endured for this length of time and benefited no one? How are we to account for medicine's long ancestry?

Pre-scientific medicine

The proverbial belief the nastier the medicine the greater its power to heal would certainly appear to be borne out in the history of medicine. According to the records which exist of pre-scientific concoctions and devices which have been used to treat ailments at various times and in various places, a substantial number of these were unpleasant in some way. The belief common to many pre-scientific societies that illnesses were the result of demoniacal possession is undoubtedly connected with this widespread unpleasantness of treatments; remedies had to be noxious so as to drive away the invading demon.

Treatment consequent upon a diagnosis of possession would often consist in the application of a purulent substance which it was believed would repulse the demon, helped by incantations, charms and prayers. Ceremonies aimed at expelling spirits often involved elaborate and time-consuming ritual, and if, as was sometimes the case, the spirit was considered indestructible, some means might be sought for making it pass on into another person or object. A huge number of purgative remedies can be listed. Almost all of them were uncomfortable, and many downright painful. Herbs, fumigation, starvation, intense heat, intense cold, terrorizing, incisions, bloodletting, sacrifice and severe penances are some of the more common examples. Counter-productive though it may seem, animal and human sacrifices were also sometimes demanded by a witch doctor for a cure to be effective. And such sacrifices were frequently extravagant: the number of killings might be large and the ceremony protracted and involved. Generally, it was believed that the potency of a remedy was greatest if the victim of a sacrifice was someone significant to the person who was ill. Goody [1] recounts how the Gonja of West Africa ate human flesh as a medicine in itself, and how the efficacy of other medicines could be secured by the sacrifice of a kinsman, who had to be someone close and valued. This condition was stressed, and tests were made to confirm that the individual offered as a sacrifice was, in fact, such a kinsman.

The belief in spirit possession as the prime cause of disease was common in England until the decline of witchcraft in the late seventeenth century. But so deeply entrenched is this view, that the habit of calling in an exorcist as a last resort, when physical cures are finally seen to have failed, survived well into the nineteenth century, and is not unknown even today.

European techniques: some remedies of doctors and quacks

In medieval England there was little to distinguish between remedies prescribed by educated doctors and those offered by so-called quacks. The only difference between these two categories of practitioner was in their status; and this was for the most part self-attributed. There are records of more than the odd instance of a treatment being derided by the physicians of the day, only to be adopted by them at a later point in time (a habit not unheard of in contemporary medical circles).

When a treatment had gained a reputation for curing one

condition, quite often its therapeutic potential would be generalized by its proprietors, and it would be re-presented to the public as a cure-all. Hot irons applied to the skin, needles used to pierce the skin, and smoke inhalation, are examples of some generally acclaimed universal panaceas. Human tissue was comprehensively applied – nail parings as emetics, for example, and dried powdered human heart as a remedy for epilepsy (widely regarded for a long time as one of the most blatant forms of demoniacal possession).

Violence was characteristically associated with potency in medicines. The touch of a hanged man was supposed by some in the seventeenth and eighteenth centuries to have great healing power. Ointments were sold ostensibly prepared from 'usnea' – the moss scraped from the skull of someone who had died violently. It was also a familiar belief among many who practised folk medicine that the strength of a healthy wild animal could be transferred to a sick person in medicines containing the tissues or faeces of the animal. Paracelsus, a sixteenth-century champion of the movement in Europe to divorce medicine from religion, recommended ointments prepared from boars' brains and fat. The same idea of transferred strength lay behind the custom in ancient Rome of drinking the blood of newly slaughtered gladiators.

Exploitation of the public by charging enormous sums for treatments was rife throughout history; and large fortunes were made by those whose treatments became fashionable. For long periods, medicinal gold and gold solutions remained popular among those able to afford them. One eighteenth-century doctor is reported to have been prosecuted by the Royal College of Physicians for charging as much as £6 for a single pill.

Cures for mental disorders, when they were attempted, tended to be still more barbaric than those for physical symptoms. Unpleasant smells, loud sounds, blows and emetics were inflicted on patients. Blistering the head became popular during the seventeenth century as an ostensible means of restoring mental integrity.

The catalogue of bizarre, dangerous, and even fatal treatments which have been used at various stages throughout European history is almost endless. Preparations containing virtually every conceivable animal tissue, animal and human dung and urine, mummy flesh, eunuch fat, vipers, calcified worms, beetles, wood-lice, metals, pearls, precious stones, coral, religious relics, not to mention the extensive pharmacopoeia of herbs, often to be gathered under difficult magical conditions, are only a few examples of the mass of spurious medications which have at some time been prescribed in all seriousness.

The authenticity of historical cures

Shapiro [2] has pointed out that very few of the procedures and substances which made up historical treatments have been found to contain any specific organic effect for the condition being treated. According to Houston [3], no treatment with a physical basis can be found in all the pages of Hippocrates. To what extent historical treatments were effective by today's standards is very difficult to assess. Of course, extravagant claims were made by the physicians and quacks for their patent preparations, some in earnest and others not. Rival schools of medical opinion and quacks constantly condemned and ridiculed each others' prescriptions. In fact, the peddling of cures was the basis of such lively commercial activity and self-interest that it would not be wise to take any of the reports of the perpetrators themselves, positive or negative, at their face-value. As an alternative, we might adopt as our criterion patients' own reports of the success of treatments administered to them, and the reports of observers who were, so far as it is possible to gauge, relatively impartial in their attitude towards the remedy being applied. But this too is problematic, for we cannot necessarily equate patients' and observers' ideas about health and ill-health in the past with our own ideas today.

A fair number of harmful, even lethal, consequences of treatments, especially surgery, have been recorded, which is not surprising in view of the procedures these entailed. On the other hand, there are also plenty of reports of patients enjoying renewed health, and even of miraculous results. The authenticity of the latter is of course highly suspect, especially since opinions were often formed as a result of casually observing the patient immediately after he had received treatment. Follow-up studies were rare.

Nevertheless, it is important to keep sight of an important fact. Physicians in most countries were held in reasonably high esteem for extended periods of time throughout history, some achieving great eminence. Times and places can be cited which must count as exceptions to this, but there are many instances of quacks and local wise-women (the folk-cure experts) becoming famous for their cures, and being consulted regularly by a clientele from many sections of the community, including clergy and physicians themselves. Some treatments kept their reputations for centuries. Notable examples of these are bleeding by leeches, and contact with the body or garment of a royal person – the 'royal touch'.

The longevity of a historical treatment is therefore perhaps the best yardstick now available to us for assessing its efficacy. Given that a proportion of physicians and quacks used administrations which were repeatedly sought after, and given also that the reputations of these men often remained intact for a few decades at least, and sometimes much longer, it seems likely that some of their treatments met with some degree of favour among those treated. If this is accepted, the issue of the authenticity of historical cures really comes down to the question of whether these treatments merely induced people to say that they were effective, whether they affected only the subjective experience of discomfort from symptoms, or whether they genuinely altered the organic basis of complaints – and if so, how deep such influence went.

Faith healing

Of all the forms of attempted cures that have been written about, one of the most persistent throughout history, and one which we can feel sure does not often involve physical intervention, is faith healing. The administrations in this category need not have a religious connotation, and the term faith healing is taken here to include all forms of treatment where healing is assumed to come about by means of some invisible process, including touching, stroking, magnetism as well as exorcism, 'absent healing', spiritual purging and other procedures thought to require the mediation of a spiritual agent. Faith healers have existed in almost all parts of the world since classical times, and while their popularity has waxed and waned throughout history they have never disappeared. Buddha and Krishna were supposedly endowed with the power to heal, the mythologies concerning disease and health associated with them being closely bound up with the belief in reincarnation. Over fifty miracles are credited to Christ in the Gospels, and a few of these, we are told, relate to explicitly organic conditions. The apostles were also reported to have carried out a large number of cures and to have been copied by Christians and pagans subsequently.

What sort of people have been acclaimed as successful faith healers? Status, position or fame seem to be attributes common to many. The witch doctor in primitive societies is characteristically an individual of some esteem, and in the minority of instances where he is not respected, he is certainly feared. Chiefship often carries with it the role of healer, and it is not infrequent for this vested power to cure to be thought of as something which is inherited. The similar belief that a monarch is divinely endowed with a healing and cleansing potential, which he passes on to his children, has been widespread, and was firmly adhered to in England, lasting for several centuries after Edward the Confessor and probably predating him.

The notion that high status and power are assets to the would-be healer is reminiscent of a doctrine expressed by Freud and others after him: that a doctor's potential for influence is heightened if the patient sees him as a powerful figure of authority. But it is not clear that status is a necessary attribute of the successful faith healer. There are accounts of individuals originally living in poverty and obscurity whose power to heal suddenly became renowned. The reputation of Bridget Bostock, for example, a lowly Cheshire country dweller in the eighteenth century, became widespread only when she was in her seventies. It is also risky to infer too much from historical examples like this one, since patients attending for healing are rarely observed systematically, and the efficacy of cures is rarely publicized at all widely until after a healer has become well known. However humble the healer's origins, by the time he is attracting large numbers of patients and comes under public scrutiny he is already a comparatively notorious and prestigious figure. If status *is* important, this is not easy to prove or disprove through natural observation.

The history of faith healing to this day is replete with names of characters who gained enormous reputations (and sometimes enormous fortunes as well), who commanded large audiences and enjoyed large and constant clienteles. A much quoted example is Greatrakes, the seventeenth-century Irish 'stroker', whose style was to squeeze a person's complaint to an extremity of their body, and then coax it out by gentle caressing. However, Greatrakes was not a showman and rarely accepted payment. Boatloads of sufferers made the journey to Ireland in order to be cured, and records exist of his successfully treating all kinds of ailments, including blindness. Robert Boyle the chemist, and other contemporaries whose impartiality is held in high regard, have left on record their favourable impression of the results achieved by the practices of this modest and seemingly sincere Irishman.

A contrasting, altogether more flamboyant example is provided by Anton Mesmer, born in 1734, and originator of the doctrine of 'animal magnetism'. Mesmer was convinced that all diseases were the result of disturbances in magnetic fields surrounding the patient, and that by reversing these, the pathological process could itself be reversed, causing symptoms to disappear. His theories were wild and untestable, and were generally disregarded, although his critics conceded that there may have been an effect due to suggestion through the hypnotic technique he employed. This became known as 'mesmerism'.

Rose [4] described a typical setting in which mesmerism would be attempted:

> In a large room well supplied with mirrors, flowers, stained glass and incense, sufferers were put into a receptive frame of mind by soft music. In the centre was a tub, filled with iron filings, from which protruded rods: round this the patients sat in silent circles, holding either the ends of the rods or each other's hands. At the critical moment the 'magnetist' himself came in, dressed in a lilac silk robe and holding yet another iron rod. He then passed round the circle, staring into his patients' eyes, touching them or making passes over them. . . . (Rose, 1971, p. 54)

Faith healing continued to flourish in Victorian England, being given a new lease of life during the Revival, and it is still extensively practised in many countries today. The current resurgence of interest in 'alternative medicine' is reflected in the growing number of faith healing practices, and reports from established institutions of an increased demand for their services. Healing shrines throughout Europe admininster to a large influx of pilgrims every year.

Harry Edwards is probably the best known of contemporary faith healers. His meetings are typically well attended, and although he admits to carrying out a certain amount of bone manipulation, he believes each favourable outcome of his ministrations to be the result of spiritual and not physical intervention. He considers absent healing to be more effective than any form of contact between patient and healer. Absent healing may take place with or without a patient's knowledge, but usually consists of combined reflections and invocatory prayers at a pre-arranged time when patient and healer are apart from one another. The healing power is believed to come from a divine source, the job of the healer being simply to render a patient receptive to the healing influence. Harry Edwards claims to have treated a very large number of patients, and boasts a success rate of between eighty and ninety percent for improvements, and between thirty and forty percent for complete cures.

The authenticity of faith cures

In posing the question of whether a faith cure can actually produce organic changes, we are faced with the same problems as are encountered in trying to assess the validity of other styles of physically inert treatment. The publication of considerable numbers of ostensibly unbiased reports that are in reality nothing short of propaganda only adds to the confusion. However, a few seemingly impartial and better controlled investigations have been undertaken, and these are reviewed by Rose [4], in his book *Faith Healing*.

When the facts about faith healing and 'miracle cures' are scrutinized objectively, they are usually found to be a great deal less impressive than the initial publicity would have one believe. Closer inquiry into the nature of the improvement of patients who have received 'successful' faith healing administrations almost always reveals a greater degree of subjective improvement than improvement in physical signs and symptoms. Those who have made a study of large samples of faith healing clientele have consistently found it difficult to come up with more than a handful of instances where there is evidence that real and lasting benefit has resulted from a cure. And even this evidence tends to be weak.

Rose is a clinical psychiatrist with an interest in faith healing, whose own studies give no indication of any initial bias for or against faith cures. He systematically observed and follwed up a number of individuals who were receiving cures, and his reports confirm that there is often a wide discrepancy between the claims of healers and the truth about organic benefit. He has attended many of the meetings presided over by Harry Edwards, and, as a result of medical examinations carried out on patients following these sessions, has concluded that many of the dramatic and far-reaching cures claimed by the healer were in fact little more than short-term alleviations of discomfort from symptoms. Nevertheless he comments:

> ... the fact remains that many dozens of sufferers from arthritis and similar diseases – a high proportion of whom stated that their complaints had long resisted orthodox treatment – *did* appear to have their disability at least temporarily ameliorated as a result of Mr. Edwards' instructions and painless ministrations. (Rose, 1971, p. 147. Italics his)

In his search for cases which present strong, if not unequivocal, evidence for organic improvement from a faith cure, Rose finds none. But the case histories which he collected by obtaining from healers the names and addresses of 95 individuals considered to represent their most spectacular successes, are interesting and informative on several counts. Of the 37 cases where it was possible to obtain medical records, a substantial discrepancy between the information in these and the claims of the healer was found in 22 instances. Of the remainder – four people were discovered to be undergoing a course of medical treatment alongside the healing, so that it was impossible to disentangle the effects of each of these; four others gave an indication of improvement in function, but showed no organic change on re-examination after the healing; three improved, but relapsed again later; in two cases there was some 'suggestive' evidence that the healer had contributed to organic improvement; in one further case the disability was apparently completely relieved by the healer[1]; and in one case the condition continued to deteriorate.

A case history, as recorded by Rose [5], is given below to illustrate the sort of information on which his conclusions are based. This is one of the three cases where there was an indication of real relief from discomfort, but no evidence of any organic change:

---

[1] According to the reports of the patient himself, who happened to be a doctor.

Mrs. L. W. aged 60 had a fifteen-year history of 'rheumatism' with 'enormously swollen' knees causing great interference with walking, with no response to treatment at various hospitals and clinics and at the hands of an osteopath. She received absent healing, before and after treatment by a healer in January, 1951. Although immediately relieved, considerable pain remained, but gradually the patient could lift her feet painlessly. The healer had lifted her leg right up without causing suffering, which she 'couldn't possibly have stood if a hospital doctor (or she herself) had attempted it.' She continued to receive treatment from a healer 'for fear of slipping back.' One night she was awakened by the feeling that the door had opened and a presence was beside her bed; she felt herself turned over and there was something like a murmer of voices in the room. She fancied herself 'a little easier' next day. The hospital reported that since 1948 this lady had been attending for treatment of a non-toxic goitre, benign hypertension, obesity and osteoarthritis of both knees, the latter checked by x-ray examination. There was 'considerable symptomatic improvement' when last seen. The physician wrote in October, 1952, to say *she seems to have improved subjectively* a good deal since the laying on of hands of her spirit healer – *we can find little change* since before this operation ... *the angles of movement are about the same as they were at the time.*' (Rose, 1954)

From a scientific standpoint, the retrospective analysis of a small number of cases provides at best a shaky basis for making inferences. Information may have been lost, distorted, or collected in such a way as to lead to biased records. For example, a patient may have been examined by different physicians before and after the healing. Alternatively, if a single physician carried out both examinations and was aware that the patient had visited a faith healer, we cannot be certain that his report was not coloured, even unintentionally, by his own attitude to faith healing. Even if the correctness of the facts is guaranteed, it is certainly impossible to form any sure conclusions about the causes of improvement in a particular case. Changes in diet, exercise, smoking and drinking habits, or living conditions may have happened to coincide with the healing administration, or may even have been recommended by the healer. Any one of these factors by itself could have been sufficient to bring about an alleviation of symptoms. But although little can be concluded from reports of this nature, Rose's examples are informative, first because they illustrate how distorted cases become when they are the subject of sensationalist reporting, and second because they suggest that something is achieved by faith healing, even if this is only temporary improvement of a 'subjective' nature – short term alleviation of discomfort.

In attempting to assess its validity we are again returned to the most remarkable aspect of faith healing: the fact that its practice has endured, relatively unchanged, from the classical period onwards. Individual healers are remembered by their own esoteric styles of administering cures, but the general form healing takes has resisted any significant change. Very similar descriptions of faith healing ceremonies can be found at literally any point in history, right down to the present day when the practice is enjoying renewed popularity. Constancy of this order is not easy to account for if one assumes that faith healing has benefitted none, or only a small minority, of those submitting to it.

Consistent public demand for a service is a good but not an infallible index to the efficacy of that service. Nonetheless, this aspect of faith healing probably provides the strongest evidence we are likely to get that some positive effect accrues to some of those who receive it. 'Some positive effect' is admittedly a weak criterion against which to be assessing a method of treatment. It still remains difficult if not impossible to know just how extensive the effects of successful cures are, or indeed whether they reflect much more than lip-service on behalf of devotees. The question of whether faith cures can procure real and lasting organic benefit will remain unanswered for the moment and probably for some time to come. But it is not altogether unreasonable to conclude from the remarkable resilience of the practice of faith healing that benefit of some kind commonly derives from it.

A theme in historical treatments

I have argued in relation to primitive systems, faith healing and other practices in the history of medicine, that where a treatment has endured for any length of time, we have presumptive evidence for its efficacy in a weak sense. That is, we can conclude it was somehow beneficial to a significant proportion of those treated. Having confidence that such treatments influenced something, even if it was only the patient's attitude, we can move on to the problem of how such influence might have come about. What conditions must hold if a treatment which has no direct organic action is to produce a favourable result?

In trying to capture the essential elements in pre-scientific treatments, we are returned again to the impression that a very large proportion of them involved administrations which were characteristically nasty in some way: they were expensive, repugnant, sinister, uncomfortable or very difficult to procure. Many were even unsafe. Shapiro [6] reaches a similar conclusion when he says that 'Medical treatments were frequently elaborate, detailed, expensive, time-consuming, fashionable and at times dangerous.' (Shapiro, 1964)

Summarizing these attributes, it seems as if the majority of historical remedies were tailored so as to require the maximum possible commitment of time, resources and effort on the part of the would-be patient. This was especially so in regard to a healer whose methods were somewhat strange – and there was no shortage of strange practices. Even if the patient escaped pain or discomfort or extortionate charges, he would very likely have to spend a long time submitting to treatments that he would not normally be prepared to tolerate. Sometimes these would be bizarre enough to cause him embarrassment, and perhaps even put him at risk of criticism or ridicule from other people.

One must be wary, of course, of assuming that what is arduous by today's standards was equally arduous to, say, a seventeenth-century man. But notwithstanding this qualification, the history of medicine generally supports the claim that a large proportion of the available treatments at any period did involve a sacrifice or privation of some kind.

Now, it is well known to psychologists that the act of committing yourself to something which may turn out to be unpleasant or dangerous has certain specific consequences. These were first outlined by Festinger [7] in his 'theory of cognitive dissonance', and this theory provides us with one possible explanation of how treatments that are physically and chemically inactive can work.

Cognitive dissonance theory

Festinger published what is now widely referred to as 'dissonance theory' in 1957, since when it has generated a great deal of research and controversy among social psychologists. Its basic assumption is quite simple: after a person has made a decision he will tend to justify it. More exactly, he becomes the subject of a psychological state – a kind of tension[2] known as cognitive dissonance, which he seeks to reduce by finding or concocting reasons for what he did. In a way this is little more than common sense. It is familiar enough to encounter someone, who after spending a long time deliberating over whether to buy this or that car, decides on one and then talks of nothing else but the virtues of the chosen model and the disadvantages of the rejected one. He is going through the motions of generating reasons to justify his decision. Similarly, a person who is rebuked or criticized for having committed an immoral or undesirable action is likely to come up with excuses –

---

[2] It is not, in fact, necessary to invoke the concept of tension and tension-reduction in dissonance theory (Totman [8]), but it is used here as a convenient way of getting across the general ideas behind the theory.

reasons accounting for why he did it – in an attempt to get the action reclassified by his critics as 'normal' and socially acceptable. The inclination to justify one's actions to others and to oneself goes very deep. If an individual feels that his lines of defence are tenuous, and experiences guilt, he will often over-justify an action by supplying a large number of weak excuses for it.

To be able to pinpoint the circumstances in which a person finds it necessary to justify his behaviour, we must look at the society of which he is part, and at what that collection of people as a whole considers to be acceptable and unacceptable. Values differ widely between societies and between groups of people within the same society. Acts of spontaneous aggression directed against someone living in an adjacent village would engender widespread disapproval in England, but in warring primitive communities the same behaviour might be seen as not only excusable but brave and commendable. Justification is called for only in the first instance. It is incumbent only when an individual is seen (or sees himself) as having infringed a rule upheld by those in his own society. On a smaller scale, the same thing can be seen to hold within a particular society. A successful burglary which has the police fooled may be condemned by society at large, but it will be admired by the smaller group of criminals who make up the thieves' friends.

The inclination to justify one's own actions to oneself is both the most tenacious aspect of the justification process, and at the same time that branch of it which is hardest for us to recognize. Suppose a man visits a fairground fortune teller who forecasts that some dreadful catastrophe will happen to him in a year's time, but who also tells him that the spell can be broken and the catastrophe averted if he walks five miles along a specified country lane every Friday evening until the year is up. Suppose also that he has a healthy distrust of fortune tellers, but is nevertheless superstitious enough to worry over the prediction, with the result that he decides to play safe by carrying out the fortune teller's instructions. Because his friends and colleagues are rational down-to-earth types, he is reluctant to confess the real reason behind his new pastime and might explain it away on the grounds that he needs the exercise or that he has begun to enjoy walking for its own sake, and happens to like that particular stretch of countryside. He does so since he values their company and to some extent shares the same down-to-earth attitude. To walk five miles every Friday evening on account of something said by a fortune teller would be considered ridiculous by them (and by that part of him which share this attitude with them).

Let us examine the process of justification in this example more closely. When such an individual explains what he is doing on the grounds that he enjoys the walks, does he actually believe this, or is it merely a calculated deception which he keeps up? It would certainly be more convenient were he able to feel that the opinions he was expressing carried with them a degree of conviction – that is, it would be altogether less trouble if he really believed he was enjoying the walks. How could this be achieved? When a person justifies a decision to himself, this often involves the intervention of some unconscious activity – some mental workings out of which he is unaware. Put simply, what happens is something like this: some mechanism which I shall refer to as a controlling 'overseer', operating at a level below his awareness, works so as actually to alter his conscious experience, with the result that the evenings' walks really are rendered pleasurable. Moreover, this is done in a way that cannot be achieved voluntarily.[3]

It is well known that under hypnosis some people can be given suggestions which later, when they are awake, they find irresistible. If such a person is hypnotized and instructed to enter a certain chemist's shop and buy a bottle of aspirin at, say, 11.00 a.m., he may develop a headache at 10.30 a.m. in order to give himself a reason for carrying out the suggestion. The unconscious 'overseer' accepts that the suggestion is imperative, and generates a way of making the suggested action

[3] This idea requires a concept of the unconscious as an ordered, controlling entity. This is at variance with Freud's version. But it has been pointed out by several authors that the concept of an anarchic unconscious is problematical for logical reasons. (e.g. MacIntyre [9])

seem normal and reasonable so as to avoid any awkwardness, all without the awareness of the subject. In doing so, it can affect physiological processes in a direct and powerful manner – a degree of control quite outside the reaches of volition. In this case it produces a headache.

Returning again to the victim of the fortune teller's forecast, this man, regularly walking five miles every Friday evening, has to find a different reason for doing so from the real one. Unconsciously the stage is set for him genuinely to enjoy the walks (perhaps as a result of altered sensory thresholds relating to vision, hearing and smell). Thus his experiences, edifying in themselves, provide him with a means of justification which is free of the troubling suspicion that he might be deceiving others and deluding himself. He may even continue with the walks after the prescribed year is up, in order to reinforce this conviction.

These illustrations are not based on mere speculation. Research carried out in America by Zimbardo and his colleagues [10] supports the hypothesis that unconscious regulating mechanisms can be brought into play by the arousal of cognitive dissonance. In these experiments, student volunteers were required to go hungry or thirsty for a length of time, ostensibly as a part of an experiment concerned with the effects of hunger or thirst on perception. They were led to believe that at the end of the experimental period they would be given food or water. However, when this time came the same individuals were asked whether they would mind acting as subjects in a further experiment, involving an extended period of similar deprivation – i.e. they would have to go without food or drink for rather longer than they had anticipated. The real aim of the experiment was to study the effects on them of compliance with this request, and had nothing to do with perception, which was just a 'story' subjects were given to prevent them guessing what the real experiment was about. Subtle pressure was applied so that more or less everyone conformed with the request; but some people were given strong reasons as to why they should comply, and others were not. Those given strong reasons for instance were told that the experiment would provide especially valuable scientific information, or that they would be paid extra for their participation. The purpose of this was to build into the experiment justifications which could be used by these students to account for their compliance. When the experiment was over, they would be able to rationalize along the lines 'I didn't mind another period of hunger (or thirst) since this is such an important experiment'; or, 'I'm glad I chose to carry on without food (or drink) because now I have some extra money to show for it'. Some were given very strong reasons indeed for complying, being told that participation in the experiment was a necessary part of their undergraduate course in psychology. These subjects in a sense had no choice at all.

The individuals of interest, however, are those to whom no justifications at all were offered. It was reasoned that while most of them would go along with the request, which they did, they would be left in a state of cognitive dissonance, and would have to justify their decision to themselves by finding a reason for agreeing to what was in fact an unreasonable demand. It was also calculated that they would cope with this state of dissonance by imagining themselves not to be hungry or thirsty. They would then be able to rationalize thus: 'I didn't mind the extra period without food (or drink) because I wasn't really hungry (or thirsty) anyway.' Now, as in the previous examples, this rationalization would carry much more weight if the person making it was really convinced of its truth. So it might be conjectured that those in this group would genuinely feel less hungry or thirsty than those who were supplied with reasons or who had no choice. There is not much distinction between *feeling* hungry or thirsty and *being* hungry or thirsty, and so it was predicted that the students given no means of justification would actually show less evidence of being hungry or thirsty than the others. This was found to be the case. As predicted, they 'created' their own justification by unconsciously regulating their hunger or thirst – i.e. by 'reducing' its intensity. Differences were demonstrated between this group and the others both in the amount which they eventually ate (or drank) and in the level of plasma-free fatty acids in their blood – a measure known to be related to hunger.

In addition to modifying hunger and thirst, the same technique has been applied successfully to change people's appetites for unpalatable foods, and to reduce their experience of pain [10].

Historical treatments as arousing dissonance

The idea which I explored in connection with historical medical treatments was closely related to this research. Because a cure so often seemed to involve deprivation of one sort or another, I reasoned that it must have engendered resistance on the part of the would-be patient to committing himself to its procedures. Consequently, a person who eventually did decide to be treated would probably encounter cognitive dissonance as a result of his decision, and would unconsciously search for possible means of self-justification. Justification is cast iron if the treatment is perceived as successful: when asked 'Why on earth did you submit to that treatment?' the patient can reply 'I'm glad I did, since it has cured my complaint.'

Observations from history therefore give us the intriguing hypothesis that commitment to a medical procedure which is in some way privatory (e.g. effortful, expensive, painful) activates this justification process and mobilizes a person's unconscious mechanisms into effecting whatever therapeutic measures lie within their power. In this way the person can construe his treatment as effective, and his decision to receive it as a wise one.

If unconscious processes were limited in their power to produce a justification in the same way that conscious or voluntary processes are, this whole sequence would have very little significance. It is the capacity of the unconscious 'overseer' to intervene in a more direct and powerful way, and to bring about somatic changes which cannot be achieved through any amount of effort or willpower, that makes this sequence potentially interesting.[4] It is hardly realistic to suppose that the subjective and physiological effects found in Zimbardo's experiments, and those which I am suggesting have occurred throughout the history of medicine, could have been achieved voluntarily – for the simple reason that few people would hesitate to rid themselves of uncomfortable feelings or painful and debilitating symptoms if they were able to do so. What I am proposing therefore cannot be summarized by the catch phrase 'mind over matter', where 'mind' implies conscious effort. The point to be taken from Zimbardo's work is that it might be possible to exploit the justification tendency, along with the unconscious activity which it brings into play, to cause therapeutic changes that are effected by the individual's own bodily resources at a level below his awareness.

To test whether this idea is along the right lines and whether it does to some extent provide an explanation of how inert treatments can work, I designed two experiments: one at University College, London, the other at University College Hospital.

The first was concerned with the experience of pain, and like the experiments of Zimbardo and his colleagues was carried out in a laboratory using students as subjects. The procedures in this were intended to represent an analogue, if only an approximate one, to the actual situation of a patient undergoing treatment.

Students underwent a series of mildly painful stimulations, produced by a beam of light focussed through lenses on to a small area of skin on their forearms. This causes a momentary sharp sensation of discomfort without doing any physical damage to the skin. These heat stimulations represented the 'symptoms' of the complaint. In the middle of the series there was a break, and it was explained that one of the aims of the experiment was to study the action of a particular drug on the

---

[4] A good illustration of the ascendency of unconscious influence is provided by the phenomenon of subliminal perception, in which an individual's sensory threshold is altered by the nature of information 'registered' but not seen. Norman Dixon presents a reasoned account of this in his book *Subliminal perception: nature of a controversy* [11].

intensity of the discomfort produced by the heat (this was, of course, not one of the aims at all). It was made clear to everyone that there was a similar series of heat stimulations to follow, and each person was asked whether or not he wanted to be given an injection of this 'drug'. He was told that agreeing to this request was not essential to the experiment because individuals not receiving injections provided useful control (comparison) information against which to assess the drug's effect on others. But, as in Zimbardo's experiments, just enough oblique pressure was put on all subjects to ensure that almost everyone did in fact agree to be injected. The implication, although not actually voiced, was that the drug might reduce the discomfort from the forthcoming heat stimulations. In terms of the treatment analogy, the students in this experiment had been offered a possible 'cure' for the otherwise unavoidable heat stimulation 'symptoms'.

The 'drug', in reality, was nothing but water, the purpose of the experiment being to study the effects of making a commitment to receive it. It was reckoned that choosing to be injected with what was believed to be an unknown experimental drug constituted a decision which would cause the subjects concern, create dissonance, and thus engender the state of having to justify the commitment to oneself. The next step in the procedure was to supply a justification to some, but not all, individuals by offering them money for agreeing to be injected. It was anticipated that those given this financial incentive would rationalize along the following lines: 'I'm glad I chose to be injected because I now have some more money.' Those not offered money would of course not be able to say this. To achieve the same result – i.e. to resolve their dissonance – they would have to find or create some other rewarding consequence of opting for the injection, and it was calculated that they would do this by experiencing the bursts of heat after the injection as significantly less painful than those before it, so as to be able to rationalize thus: 'I'm glad I chose to be injected because the drug made the heat bursts much less painful.'

This is exactly what was found to happen. Those students

not supplied with a ready-made justification showed greater analgesia (reduced sensitivity to pain) following the injection procedure than those given the financial inducement or those not given a choice at all. This was indicated both by what they said, since everyone rated the painfulness of each of the heat bursts, and by the extent of changes in the electrical resistance of their skin, which was measured simultaneously with each stimulation. The amplitude of a person's galvanic skin response,[5] as it is known, is often used in conjunction with ratings to corroborate an interpretation that it is real pain and not just verbal reports that have been altered.

Thus, through this intricate and somewhat devious series of manoeuvres, it was demonstrated that a change in people's experience of pain could be brought about by an exclusively psychological (verbal) manipuation. Moreover, this type of change is not normally accessible to voluntary control. Here then is some preliminary evidence obtained under controlled conditions[6] consistent with the idea that the totally phoney administrations of quacks, and the more sincere but nevertheless equally inert methods of physicians and faith healers, can work by activating a mechanism in the individual's own psyche capable of modifying organic conditions in an authoritative manner. My speculation that many of these practices had persisted for extended periods in history precisely because they were to some extent effective is thus tentatively supported: by a similar sequence of conjuring tricks in the laboratory, people's experience of pain was reduced.

We can also surmise that if dissonance accompanied many historical treatments – and there are strong hints that it did – it was more that just the patient's attitude which was favourably influenced; it is possible that the pain from his condition was genuinely alleviated with the result that he really felt better. How long such an effect could last, and whether other conditions besides pain can be altered in the same way, are questions which still have to be answered.

[5] For details of galvanic skin response, see Christie [12].
[6] For a more detailed description of the experiment, see Totman [13].

There is an obvious artificiality about experiments such as this one, where manipulations are carried out in the rather strange setting of the psychologist's laboratory. We are left feeling not entirely confident that what has been observed is a true reflection of what goes on in the real world. In this experiment in particular the simulated 'symptoms' are unlike the symptoms of a real disease in that they are imposed on people 'from outside', rather than the result of an internal disorder.

A second study was therefore designed as the first step towards meeting this criticism. It was carried out at University College Hospital in London, and involved chest patients who were not seriously ill or scheduled for surgery, but who suffered disturbing insomnia in the hospital ward at night-time. Its aim was to see whether the dissonance technique could be put into practice to relieve their insomnia. Here again, exactly the same pattern of results was obtained. The favourable consequences of a (dummy) treatment were substantially increased if patients had to make a difficult decision concerning whether or not to receive it.[7] As in the experiments previously described, if the element of choice was absent, or the decision was experienced as too easy, this effect was measurably lessened. But where things were so arranged that the patient confronted a need to justify his decision, the therapeutic power of the dummy drug was enhanced, as predicted. Improvement in sleeping under these circumstances was significant. An average of about two hours per night extra sleep, as estimated by night nurses' observations and ratings, was enjoyed by those patients in whom dissonance was deliberately induced.

There were other indications besides nurses' reports that the 'drug' had worked for these patients. Most of them asked, quite unprompted, for the treatment to be continued in the ward after the experiment had ended. Some even requested a

[7] In this experiment the choice was between two ostensibly different 'drugs' in the form of tablets. Further details of the procedures can be found in Totman [14].

continued prescription of it after they had been discharged from hospital. Nor was it just mild or temporary insomnia which was relieved. One lady expressed extreme scepticism at the start of the experiment, doubting whether any sleeping tablets could be effective for her, since she claimed to have tried them all. She was one of those who, afterwards, asked for a continued prescription both in and out of the ward.

Here is evidence, then, that cognitive dissonance can be exploited to bring about favourable 'therapeutic' effects in the treatment of pain and of insomnia. How far this can be generalized to other symptoms and diseases must remain at present an open question. We have already found some evidence for its limits. From the results of an experiment carried out at the Common Cold Research Unit in Salisbury, the same effect does not appear to carry over to colds. [15].

Some practical and ethical considerations

The experiments I have described unavoidably involved some deception of the students, volunteers and patients who acted as subjects, and it would be ill-advised, not to say impractical, to suggest that the techniques developed and vindicated in them should be put into practice in any general way in the treatment of illness. So where do these experiments lead? First, they throw light on a phenomenon that has been puzzled over for a long time in relation to medical and fringe medical treatments – namely the power of organically inactive agents to heal. A second, more practical, consequence is that they provide us with knowledge about the gains which can accrue from actively involving a patient in his treatment so that he feels personally committed to it, which can be done in a thousand different ways during the course of ordinary clinical practice.

Where it is not possible to give subjects in a psychology experiment a full explanation of the aims and procedures in advance, it is standard policy to do so after the experiment has taken place. This was done in the experiments referred to here, in all but a very few cases where there was good reason to suppose that a particular individual might be distressed by such information.

Present day dummy treatments: the placebo

At the start of this chapter a number of historical treatments were described which it seems likely aroused dissonance in those submitting to them. Could this also be true of some modern practices? To what extent might contemporary treatments also have the same effect?

When evaluating a new drug, it is customary to test its effects against those of a dummy treatment, or 'placebo', as it is known. Scientifically, it is desirable for the placebo to be constructed so as to appear identical to the real drug, and for it to be administered under identical conditions. This is normally done using a 'double-blind' procedure, in which neither the patient nor the doctor administering a treatment knows whether it is the real drug or the placebo, so that their expectations and enthusiasms are the same for each. In these circumstances an effect of some sort is more often than not reported, even by those patients who receive placebos. In general, symptoms are favourably affected by placebos and sometimes the incidence of favourable effects is quite high.

In a study of over 17,000 British prescriptions in 1952, Dunlop et al. [16] concluded that about one third could be considered to be in the placebo category, where this was defined objectively to include preparations known to have no specific chemical effect on the condition being treated.

More recently [17], a controlled study was made of over-the-counter daytime sedatives used by patients attending a general practice in the USA. Placebos were found to be just as effective in treating anxiety and tension as both aspirin and 'compoz', the latter being America's best selling product of this nature.

As might perhaps be expected, the condition which placebos have alleviated more consistently than any other is pain, both chronic and acute. Beecher [18], reviewing a large number of studies, records that on average 35 percent of patients given placebos as analgesics in a clinical setting obtain relief from pain. In patients with psychiatric conditions, improvements from placebos were reported by Lowinger in as many as 75 percent of the patients treated [19]. In 1963, Haas [20] listed the conditions apart from pain whose successful treatment or management using a placebo had been reported in the medical literature up to that time. These included: headache, migraine, sea-sickness, insomnia, psychoses, neuroses, cerebral infarction, multiple sclerosis, epilepsy, Parkinsonism, alcoholism, mental reactiveness, tonic effects, asthma, hay fever, colds, coughs, angina pectoris, hypertension, intermittent claudication, arthritis, gastro-intestinal disorders, constipation, skin diseases and menopausal disturbances. Some subsequent additions to this list are: warts, allergy, acne, skeletal disease, smoking, senile brain disease, diabetes, obesity, chronic urticaria, enuresis, and optometric disorders [21–32]. This is an impressive list, and one which is continuing to expand as new studies are made. But widespread though its effects are, the placebo should not be thought of as the mythical 'elixir of life'. Most by far of the beneficial effects which have been produced by it consist in symptomatic improvement rather than the arresting or reversal of degenerative conditions.

In addition to their beneficial properties, placebos have also been found to mimic active drugs in their production of noxious side effects [33, 34], negative effects consisting in a worsening of the condition treated [35], and even dependence [36]. However, in general the beneficial outcomes of placebo treatment far outweigh undesirable ones and, as can be seen, extend to the 'successful' treatment of diseases which have a clearly organic origin.

There are very few experimental investigations of the placebo as a form of treatment in its own right, most reports of its action being incidental off-shoots from drug trials. The admonition renowned in medical literature that 'you should treat as many patients as possible with the new drugs while they still have the power to heal', has been credited to several famous physicians and is an indication of the widespread casual recognition of the placebo effect [e.g. 37–40]. Yet, even now there exists no formal acknowledgement within mainstream medicine of its potential, and consequently no systematic initiative to find out how and why a placebo works, and how the psychological mechanisms underlying it could be exploited to therapeutic advantage. This is a surprisingly negligent state of affairs, considering the wide range of disorders reported as having been helped by placebos. Even if it was found that the power of placebos went no further than the relief of discomfort, this would in itself be of considerable value.

It is not even certain that deceiving the patient is necessary for a placebo to work. In a study by Park and Covi [41], adult psychiatric outpatients (neurotics) were given a course of dummy pills; at the same time it was made clear to them that these were placebos and contained no active ingredient. It is interesting from the point of view of the analysis developed in this chapter that an explicit choice was introduced into the situation, patients being asked 'Are you willing to try this (sugar) pill?' After a week of such treatment a patient's improvement was assessed by means of a clinical examination and his own ratings. The 14 out of 15 patients who returned to the clinic all showed significant improvement in symptoms. This is a very high success rate indeed.

So here is an example of a favourable outcome from a placebo administration which is clearly not attributable to 'suggestion'. In this study, by freely and knowingly choosing to take an inactive substance, patients made a commitment which could well be construed as 'silly' or 'pointless', and was thus likely to have aroused dissonance in them and activated the need for justification. It is possible that the observed improvement in symptoms was a function of this. There is a hint that the choice put to patients probably did arouse dissonance, in that the one patient who resigned from the study did so on account of ridicule from her husband.

In that almost all pre-scientific treatments have been shown to have no direct organic effect on the condition being treated the history of medicine is, in a sense, the history of the placebo effect. Are there any other indications from more recent and contemporary medical practice that effects due to dissonance might be at work?

Placebo tablets themselves tend to be optimally effective if they are expensive, bitter tasting or unpleasant in some other way [42]. And there is also evidence that greater improvement follows a course of inert injections than a course of inert pills in the treatment of obesity [28], and hypertension [43].

A contemporary procedure which qualifies *par excellence* as requiring a heavy commitment on the part of the patient, and which rivals some of the more colourful historical practices in the degree of ritual involved, is surgery. A patient probably has to wait for a bed, is formally admitted, deprived of all vestige of status, is administered to in a number of technologically sophisticated and alarming ways, has to sign a form exempting the hospital from responsibility for his life, and is systematically rendered unconscious. Many reports of unexpected cures resulting from surgical procedures which were entirely investigatory, especially in relation to ulcers and low back pain, can be found in the medical literature.

The placebo effect of surgery was discussed in an editorial in the *British Medical Journal* in 1961. The following extract contains a strong hint that cognitive dissonance may be involved. The author is discussing first the effects, not directly attributable to the operation, of a lumbar sympathectomy[8]:

Has there been some indirect, obscure, but nonetheless objective change resulting from sympathectomy? ... Must we admit a psychosomatic element? Or is it just that the patient is anxious to be helpful, anxious to justify in his own mind his decision to submit to operation ...

Perhaps the most fruitful field for placebo effects is the surgery of peptic ulcer. Here is a disease liable to spontaneous and quite unpredictable variations, where the symptoms and indeed the activity of the ulcer itself are conditioned largely by muscle tone and spasm. And here is a patient, often

[8] The severance of a sympathetic nerve fibre.

introspective and suggestible, who has suffered much and long, has tried many treatments, and been a sore trial to many doctors. At last after much mental turmoil he agrees to confide his health, his very life, to a surgeon. If the surgeon plays his part properly in the consulting room the battle is half won long before the scalpel is brought to use.... (*British Medical Journal*, 1961, p. 1627)

Other explanations of these examples are of course possible. Incidental organic effects of surgery, or of substances injected, could conceivably have been responsible for the remedial effects noted. These findings are therefore suggestive but not conclusive in relation to the dissonance explanation.

Some comments made by Janet in 1925 about faith healing are also relevant here. Janet remarked that among the conditions predisposing to a cure at Lourdes are a long and arduous pilgrimage to the shrine, and periods of tedious waiting once one has arrived. Miracle cures are rare for the local inhabitants [44].

Frank [45] draws a parallel between faith healing initiation ceremonies and the administrations surrounding patients who come to American clinics for psychotherapy. Traditionally, this intake procedure involves the patient in interviews with a social worker, the purpose of which is to determine a person's eligibility for psychotherapy and to prepare him for it ... 'appearing like a probationary period to determine his worthiness to receive this form of treatment.' (Frank, 1972, p. 160). Other writers also have conjectured that placebo effects might occur in psychotherapy (e.g. [46, 47]).

There are no grounds for supposing treatments that are physically active to be exempt from this analysis. If the dissonance effect is as pervasive as these findings and illustrations suggest, it may compromise the organic component in physically effective surgery and medication, given the right conditions.

Many more examples can be found which suggest that cognitive dissonance is at work in medical treatments. The experimental evidence, and the numerous less formal indications, past and present, combine to make a strong case that this is how many historical treatments survived so long. But how general is the dissonance effect in treatment? Can it explain *all* improvements with a psychological origin? The next question we must turn to is whether there are treatments which appear to work through their psychological influence on the patient, but which cannot be explained in this way.

As we have seen, many pre-scientific treatments offered the would-be patient unpleasantness and privation. But this is by no means the whole story. Also recurrent throughout history has been a style of treatment which appears to rely on precisely opposite methods: cures being associated with soothing techniques and requiring a much more passive, relaxed state of mind.

Treatments based on relaxing and meditative administrations are as old and enduring in history as those demanding an active involvement and conscious investment on the part of the patient. Sleep temples were used in ancient Greece and Egypt. Charms were often set to melodies, and practices based on the belief that music in itself possessed healing powers were common among ancient civilizations and pre-scientific societies. The lullaby reputedly has its origin in songs sung to a sick child by the mother in anticipation that their soothing effect would set the stage for restored health. Eastern medicine, especially that connected with Yoga and Zen, has for centuries placed importance on altering a person's state of consciousness so as to relax his body and mind in order to facilitate 'curative' meditation. Such techniques have endured until the present day. In China they exist little altered, and function as a complement to physical medicine. In the West they are currently enjoying a revival of interest and publicity.

The strange and tranquil states of mind which these strategies appear to induce in at least some people are epitomized in the state of hypnosis. In Europe, interest in hypnosis was awakened in the late eighteenth century as a consequence of the publicity surrounding the notorious Anton Mesmer.

The large volume of case studies subsequently recorded by nineteenth-century physicians, mainly in France, bears witness to this. The methods of hypnotists – whether quacks, theatrical performers or doctors – are based on the claim that the vigilance which defines a person's rational waking state can be temporarily suspended so that he enters a trance-like condition, similar to sleep. However, this condition is unlike sleep in that the ability to understand, act on, and store instructions is retained. In contrast to his response to persuasion – when arguments or directives are critically assessed in full consciousness – a person's reception of information from the hypnotist is supposedly uncritical. The rational censors, filters, and barriers which operate during normal wakefulness are not brought into play. A hypnotized subject accepts the statements made by the hypnotist as authoritative and binding, without putting up any resistance to them.

How authentic are reports of hypnotism?

Travelling stage hypnotists have lent to the practice of hypnotism an aura of charlatanism, and to this day scepticism remains a commonplace public reaction. But what is really behind hypnotism? Is the whole scenario simply a rehearsed fraud? Or is the hypnotist really able to exercise some special control over his subject?

It is now well known that in psychology experiments, the subject will often do whatever he can to conform to the experimenter's wishes and expectations, especially when the experimenter is a figure of some authority, such as a tutor or doctor [1]. One of the main challenges levied at those claiming extraordinary effects from hypnosis has been to prove that the same kind of calculated acquiescence does not take place during hypnotic sessions. How are we to be certain that the 'hypnotized' subject is not simply acting out what he thinks is expected of him because this is the easiest way to avoid embarrassment and please the hypnotist? Examples can be found where this explanation seems to hold up very well.

According to the 'old school' proponents of hypnosis, the classic distinguishing features of the hypnotized state consist in the power of the hypnotist:

(1) To exercise control over the subject's limbs and actions while he is under hypnosis.

(2) To produce in the subject analgesia (reduced sensitivity to pain) as a result of a verbal suggestion while he is under hypnosis.

(3) To implant post-hypnotic suggestions (PHS's). These are directions to be carried out later by the waking subject, usually at a specified time.

(4) To extract information from the subject (for example, about a distressing past event) which it is not possible to do if the subject is in his normal waking state, either because he is reluctant to divulge this information, or because details are repressed and therefore not accessible to conscious recall.

(5) To produce hallucinations, either causing a subject to perceive objects which are not there, or causing him not to perceive objects which are there.

(6) To produce post-hypnotic amnesia in a subject so that when he 'awakes', he remembers nothing about the hypnosis session.

On the face of it, these criteria would seem to be straightforward enough. But problems arise on two counts. First, by no means everyone can be hypnotized, and those who can be exhibit varying degrees of conformity to these standards. PHS's, for example, are not inevitably carried out – they are enacted with varying reliability depending on the subject, the hypnotist, the nature of the PHS itself, and other conditions which still remain obscure. Again, it is not always the case that a person will divulge information concerning past traumatic events. In relation to the fifth criterion, only the minority of hypnotized subjects can be consistently made to generate a full-blooded, stable hallucination of a suggested object. In other words, people's experiences and reactions under hypnosis differ widely.

Analgesia – a test for hypnosis?

Notwithstanding the variability of these effects under hypnosis, there still remains the thorny problem of fraudulence. How are we to be sure that the hypnotic subject is not faking? Considering the list given above, it would seem that the second criterion – the one relating to analgesia (reduced sensitivity to pain) – would be able to provide the strongest test. A person is unlikely to deny experiencing pain, one might think, especially when doing so could lead to further more painful tests.

Before chemical anaesthetics became available, there were many thousands of reports of the hypnotic induction of pain relief in dentistry, obstetrics and surgery. More recent cases of surgery being conducted under hypnotic analgesia have been published. One such is recounted by Mason [2]. The patient was a woman having cosmetic surgery carried out on her breasts. It was decided to use hypnosis instead of chemical anaesthetics for the second of two operations, since she had reacted to the anaesthetic previously administered with fear and a variety of other unfavourable symptoms. She had accepted the idea that the second operation might be carried out under hypnosis, and had proved to be a good hypnotic subject in several preliminary sessions. Mason describes the operation itself:

> She was then hypnotized and told that the chest wall from thyroid notch to xiphisternum including both breasts would become numb and insensitive to pain, and also that the numbness would extend inwards to her ribs. She was then tested again with pinpricks and was seen to be quite insensitive to pain. There was also diminished sensation to touch.
>
> She was then informed that she would hear only the

hypnotist's voice during the operation and all other sounds and voices would not be noticed.

The chest wall was swabbed with spirit and the patient immediately said it was cold. At this time, a small drop of spirit splashed on to the patient's eye and stung her. She immediately winced and remarked, 'My mascara has run.' This inadvertently served to illustrate an advantage of hypnosis, that the patient retains all normal protective reflexes except those which have been specifically negatived for operative purposes. Thus accidents such as ulna pressure, root traction, burning or slipping from the table will be brought to the notice of the anaesthetist by the patient himself before producing irreparable harm.

The operation was commenced on the right breast. The scars were excised a considerable distance on either side and T shaped incisions about five inches long and three inches across were made. The incision extended completely round the lower half of the breast and from the centre of this another incision extended upwards to the nipples. The patient did not flinch or move in any way. She remarked once that she felt a prick when the surgeon went too far laterally, apparently beyond the area of suggested anaesthesia. This indicated the importance of defining the areas of suggested anaesthesia accurately and making sure they extend well beyond the operational site. She was immediately reassured and told that her sides would become numb. Throughout the operation which consisted of excision of scars, skin, a wedge of breast tissue and fat, and complete re-shaping of the breasts, the patient never showed signs of pain or seemed distressed. She spoke often and light-heartedly, once asking if her skin was tough. Her pulse rate stabilized at 96 and respiratory rate at 24 per minute. There were no signs of shock. On one occasion she remarked that she was thirsty and was given a drink with a feeding cup while the operation continued.

The left breast was treated in a similar manner and this operation passed as uneventfully as the first. The whole procedure took seventy minutes. The patient was then told the operation was over, and said, 'good show'. She was asked to sit up and did so unaided while being bandaged.

Suggestions that she would suffer no post-operative pain were given and she was then awakened. She smiled and said she had felt nothing and remembered nothing. If there was any fear or apprehension it was felt by the operators rather than the patient. (Mason, 1955)

There are many recorded case histories similar to this one, as well as accounts of how hypnosis has been used in wartime military hospitals and prison camps, where analgesic drugs were unavailable or in limited supply.

For hypnotic analgesia to become established as a scientific fact, we must be able to observe it reliably, under controlled experimental conditions in the laboratory. The controversy as to whether or not people do in fact experience a reduction in pain under these circumstances is closely bound up with the issue of whether the verbal reporting of pain, or of its absence, can be taken at its face value. This might seem to be something of a quibble, but there is plenty of evidence showing that subjects will submit to an amazing amount of discomfort in psychology experiments before registering any complaint, presumably on account of the desire to project a favourable impression to the experimenter by not appearing squeamish. The feeling that verbal reports cannot be relied on has led to a voracious search for physiological indices of pain that are less open to falsification. Heart rate, breathing regularity, muscle potential and blood pressure have all been tried out as possible indicators. Unfortunately, it has been very difficult to find even a single measure which shows anything like a one-to-one correlation with pain reports. According to the Stanford Laboratory of Hypnosis, where some of the most highly regarded research on hypnosis is carried out, the best physiological correlate of reported analgesia is blood pressure. But even this is not without its weaknesses.[1,2]

[1] For a review of the research on analgesic effects in hypnosis, see Bowers [3].
[2] The work of the Stanford group is described by Hilgard [4].

Hypnosis deliberately simulated

Some ingeneious attempts at finding out whether or not hypnosis is a 'genuine' phenomenon have been made by Orne.[3] Orne used an experimental design in which a proportion of individuals about to be hypnotized were instructed that when the time for the hypnosis session arrived, rather than allow themselves to enter a trance they were to remain alert and try to fake the behaviour of 'real' hypnotized subjects so as to fool the hypnotist, who did not know in advance which individuals were 'simulators' and which had not received the faking instruction. So as to prevent those told to fake hypnotic behaviour from becoming inadvertently hypnotized, only individuals who were not susceptible to hypnosis were used as the simulators. The question asked was whether there were any reliable differences between simulators and 'real' hypnotic subjects.

It was discovered that those asked to fake the hypnotic state were surprisingly successful. The behaviour of simulators mirrored that of real hypnotic subjects so closely that even professional hypnotists were unable to tell them apart. Not one of the six criteria listed earlier, supposedly representing the classic defining qualities of the hypnotic state, could be used as a basis for discrimination. However, one unexpected reaction was seen to be unique to 'real' subjects: a remarkable tolerance of logical incongruities.

This was brought out in the following way. A co-experimenter was seated well within the subject's range of vision, and some time during the course of the session the hypnotized subject would be instructed to close his eyes while the co-experimenter moved quietly to a position behind him. The subject was told that on opening his eyes he would still see the co-experimenter sitting in his original place – i.e. he was given the suggestion to hallucinate the figure who was no longer there, this being facilitated by the earlier impression. Naturally, all subjects, both real and fake, reported that they still saw the

[3] See Fromm and Shor [5].

co-experimenter in front of them. But when instructed to turn round so that the co-experimenter could be seen where he was now standing, and asked, 'Who is that behind you?', the two groups reacted quite differently. The difference lay in the type of explanation offered to account for the apparent contradiction. 'Real' subjects were generally less perturbed and showed much less of an inclination to offer any explanation of the anomaly than did 'fake' subjects. Orne writes:

> After looking back and forth between the hallucinated and the 'real' associate, the (non-faking) subjects indicated verbally that they were perceiving two images of the same person. When asked about this, they tended to give bland responses such as 'mirrors' or a 'trick'. Though they seemed somewhat confused, they did not become seriously disturbed.

On the other hand:

> The 'fake' group, in most cases, either refused to see anyone behind them, or claimed that they could not recognize the person. Occasionally, they admitted recognizing the associate behind them and then claimed that the hallucination had vanished.
>
> This finding appears to represent a valid and significant difference. The 'real' subject responds to a subjectively real image of the associate in the chair. When asked about an objectively real image of the same individual, he is able to perceive this as well. He can respond to perceptions that are subjectively real and determined by the suggested environment, as well as to this actual perception of the real world, without attempting to satisfy a possible need to make them logically compatible. The absence of expression of a need for logical consistency seems, at this point, to be one of the major characteristics of hypnosis. (In Fromm and Shor (Eds) 1972, p. 119)

It is important to point out that the suspension of logical

explanation which is described in this passage was not invariably a feature of the reactions of hypnotized subjects,
although it was found in many, especially those who were able
to enter a deep trance. The significant point is that this
phenomenon was observed in *none* of the subjects simulating a
trance.

Conflicting reports under hypnosis

In studies and case descriptions not primarily concerned with
the question of what defines hypnosis, several authors have
remarked on the peculiar character of a person's explanations
while under hypnosis, and their comments correspond in an
intriguing way to this description given by Orne of 'trance
logic'. There are accounts of hypnotized subjects being asked to
distinguish between a real and hallucinated object, and being
able to do so successfully, without this causing the hallucinated
object to disappear.

This capacity to hold simultaneously two apparently conflicting 'attitudes' to experience while in a hypnotic state is
nicely illustrated in an example cited by Sutcliffe, who
describes the reactions of one particular subject during an
experiment on hypnotic analgesia. This person consistently
reported no pain from electric shocks being administered,
although she showed a noticeable physiological reaction,[4] and
was seen to jump sharply each time. When asked about this she
replied, 'I don't feel anything but *she* seems uncomfortable.' [6]
Seemingly reflected in this reply are both a subjective
experience and a reaction as if from an outside observer, side
by side, but in apparent contradiction to one another.

Other examples of the same thing are cited by Bowers [3]
in connection with 'automatic writing' and 'automatic talking'.
Some individuals when in a hypnotic trance demonstrate a
capacity to say or write in a fluid and intelligible manner things
which they are apparently quite unaware of revealing. Again

[4] Galvanic skin response (see Chapter 2).

this is done as if some outside observer, rather than the person himself, is divulging the information by way of a secret 'behind the scenes' commentary. This has been termed an 'automatic' response, and is considered to be a kind of direct line from some level of registration and control within the person that is not immediately accessible, even under hypnosis.[5]

When individuals capable of producing this 'automatic' style of output are given the suggestion of analgesia under hypnosis, and are subjected to what would normally be very painful stimuli, they typically report no pain if asked about it directly. But – and this is the interesting point – they are capable of indicating, at the same time, by means of the automatic writing or automatic talking that the stimulus is painful. For example, one subject, while denying the painfulness of pin-pricks to the left hand, 'automatically' wrote with her right hand, 'Ouch, dammit, you're hurting me.'

In a recent investigation of this paradoxical duality of reporting, Hilgard actually managed to get hypnotized subjects to supply two different ratings of the pain 'experienced' as a result of one arm being submerged in circulating water at 0° C (an extremely painful experience under normal waking conditions). An 'open' and a 'hidden' report was elicited from each individual, and these differed greatly from one another in terms of the amount of pain signified. For example, where the subject's report of pain was based on a scale stretching from 0 (no pain) to 10 (exceedingly painful), 'open' reports of pain following suggested analgesia averaged a score of 1, while 'hidden' reports averaged a score of 8 [7].

A similar ability to produce more than one assessment of pain is found among patients who have undergone a form of brain surgery known as frontal lobotomy. This involves severance of the connections between the prefrontal lobes and other areas of the brain, and may be carried out in cases of severe and per-

---

[5] It would be misleading to talk about the 'unconscious' in this context, because this is precisely what many authors would like to refer to as that which becomes accessible through hypnosis. This point is discussed later in this chapter.

sistent pain which has proved intractable by other means. Following the operation, these patients frequently report that the pain itself is still present and undiminished, but that it is no longer bothersome – it has lost its unpleasantness [e.g. 8].

Are the wrong questions being asked about the hypnotic state?

It is these facts, rather than attempts to verify any of the previously listed 'classic criteria' of hypnosis, which encourage the belief that the hypnotic state is a 'genuine' phenomenon. Thus to gain a true understanding of what is involved in hypnosis it would seem to be more fruitful to concentrate on these obviously remarkable phenomena, than to stay with the other now well-worn questions that are turning out to be emptier than they at first seemed.

The reluctance of some scientists to think of hypnosis as an altered state of consciousness stems from exactly this predicament. The questions which have been posed in order to prove or disprove the 'authenticity' of the hypnotic state turn out to be largely unanswerable. The final blame for this lies with the language in which these questions are couched. Most psychological and psychiatric terminology is borrowed from ordinary everyday language. This borrowing has its dangers and ultimately its limitations, especially when words are needed to describe mental activity that is unavailable to awareness. Ordinary language is rooted in and constructed around 'attended-to' experience – i.e. situations and events of which we are sufficiently well aware to want to describe and communicate them. It is not equipped to handle the kinds of distinctions that are called for when describing what happens during hypnosis. For instance, in discussing hypnotic analgesia, are we to say that a person is not experiencing pain on the basis of what he says? If so, when someone gives two opposite reports we are forced into concluding both that he experiences and that he does not experience pain. Can we even say that he 'registers' pain but does not feel it? If so, what is the 'he' that is doing the registering if it is not the feeling 'he'? And so on. The very concept of analgesia, defined as 'reduced sensitivity to pain', turns out to be too impoverished for the state of affairs it becomes necessary to describe. Even the old distinction between conscious and unconscious is found seriously lacking when it comes to attempting to describe what lies behind the analgesia paradox. Hypnosis itself has traditionally been understood as providing direct access to unconscious drives and motivation. If we are now to revise this and say that even in deeply hypnotized subjects there remains a level of 'experience' which is 'hidden' – in what terms is it going to be possible to represent this?

The analgesia paradox is not the only instance where conventional description and explanation runs aground. There are many other facets of what is said by hypnotized subjects which suffer from inadequate portrayal. Attempts to represent in language what is going on suffer in the same way as does a stained glass window when photographed by a primitive camera and reduced to a poor quality monochrome print. The conclusion we are forced into is that no conceivable answer to these traditional questions is going to have the power to represent anything like adequately the condition of a hypnotized person.

Indeed, these remarks about the limitations of 'borrowed' ordinary language terminology apply not only to the characterization of hypnotic phenomena, but also to understanding intentional behaviour. It is unlikely that what happens in hypnosis will be properly understood in the absence of a general theory of voluntary action.

Cures by hypnotic suggestion: skin disorders

Other conditions besides pain have reportedly been helped by suggestions given under hypnosis. Migraine, asthma, skin disorders, blood pressure, blood loss, menstrual disturbances and peptic ulcers are some examples. Two of the more blatantly 'physical' of these – skin disorders and asthma – illustrate the kinds of effects which have been claimed.

Let us first consider inflammatory skin conditions and warts. Here we are at an advantage since the presence or absence of these conditions, and any fluctuations in them, are relatively easy to detect. A number of papers in medical and psychological journals describe cases in which warts have been successfully removed by hypnotic suggestion. The suggestion itself can be direct – the hypnotist simply stating that a condition will vanish – or it can be embedded in a sensory fantasy: for example, the idea that the affected area is being irrigated by a cleansing liquid. Suggested bodily control has also been used successfully. One psychiatrist, for example, gave his patients the suggestion that the area surrounding their warts was warm, and it was implied that the dilation of blood vessels which caused the warm sensation enabled that area to be saturated with infection-fighting white blood cells [9]. Others have treated patients using the opposite idea – that the blood supply to the affected area should be cut off so that the warts would be starved. Both techniques were effective, showing that it does not matter too much what 'story' a hypnotized subject is given.

Use of the wart-starvation suggestion has been described by Clawson and Swade [10]:

A leading dermatologist of Salt Lake City called me and said that he had been treating an 18-year-old girl for the past five years for flat and common warts and was getting no actual results, as the warts increased faster than he could do away with them. I was asked to try hypnosis on her. I agreed to do so, and the girl came to my office for hypnosis. I have never seen so many warts on one individual in my life. Her face and body were literally covered with pinhead warts. There were hundreds of them, including five large ones on her arms. Her mother was very sceptical when I said that it was possible to remove the warts with hypnosis. I induced hypnosis by the relaxation method and deepened the hypnotic state by the escalator method previously described.

When the depth of hypnosis was sufficient ... I said, 'Catherine, your subconscious mind has the ability to control the blood supply to any part of the body. Now I want you to stop the blood supply to each wart on your body.' This was repeated three times, and she was brought out of hypnosis feeling fine. She was advised to come once a week for hypnosis.

On each successive week the number of warts had markedly decreased and her mother was so thrilled that she had the neighbours viewing the results each week. In two months' time the last of the warts were gone. To date, three and one half years later, there has not been a recurrence of a single wart. (Clawson and Swade, 1975)

In an imaginative study reported by Sinclair-Gieben and Chalmers [11], fourteen patients were given the suggestion that only those warts covering one side of their body would disappear. Out of ten successfully hypnotized subjects, nine were free from warts a few weeks after the start of treatment, but only on that side of the body relating to the suggestion.

This finding has proved difficult to replicate, other researchers either failing to produce a localized effect or having more limited success. Indeed, some investigators have not managed to achieve any effects at all using hypnosis to treat warts. Warts are believed to be caused by a virus and it is well known that they appear and disappear spontaneously, that is, in a way that defies explanation at the present. Presumably, in order for them to thrive certain biological conditions of the skin must obtain, and it is not unreasonable to speculate that these conditions vary with a person's mental and emotional state. There is some indication [12] that individuals most susceptible to effects from hypnotic suggestions are those whose skin shows a characteristic high level of fluctuation in response to psychological stimuli.

There have been claims that all sorts of other skin conditions, including itching, eczema, acne, blisters, burns and wheals, can be alleviated by hypnosis, and that certain of these may even be induced experimentally by a hypnotic suggestion.[6] This research has been the arena of much controversy. However, enough positive findings have come from studies to support the conclusion that some but not all hypnotizable individuals show clear evidence of skin changes as a result of suggestions given to them under hypnosis.

But, as usual, a qualification must be added. It is not yet absolutely clear from the experiments carried out whether the state of hypnosis is in fact a necessary pre-condition for the occurrence of these effects. While it seems likely that the hypnotic state is characterized by enhanced suggestibility, similar effects have been known to happen outside hypnosis and the fact that some people are suggestible in the waking state is well known. Hellier [14] conducted an experiment in which non-hypnotized patients believed both of their wart-covered hands to have received a dose of X-rays. Only one hand had been in reality exposed to a very mild dose of X-rays, but nevertheless the warts disappeared on both the hands of almost all those who were cured. This kind of suggestion (Bowers calls it *implicit* suggestion) in the waking state reminds us of the effects which can be achieved with placebos.

Asthma

Hypnotherapy has been tried and developed with some success in the treatment of asthma, and objective as well as subjective indications of improvement have been used in its assessment. Control groups in these studies (against which the effects attributable to hypnosis are assessed) often consist of patients given instruction in relaxation. Here again the effectiveness of hypnotic suggestions varies from one study to another, but a technique recently developed by Maher-Loughlan and his associates called hypno-autohypnosis has reliably produced

[6] It is necessary to be cautious before drawing any firm conclusions from studies purporting to demonstrate the production of skin conditions, as these studies have often been methodologically unsound, and the import of their findings somewhat diluted by negative results [13].

lasting therapeutic results [15]. The method used consists in experienced hypnotic subjects being given the post-hypnotic suggestion (PHS), during an ordinary session of hypnosis, that they will subsequently be able to re-enter the hypnotic trance at a signal given at will by themselves. For instance, it might be suggested that a patient will be able to enter hypnosis voluntarily by counting down from 10 to 0, and that he will then remain in a trance for an exact period of time (usually 10–30 minutes). Other suggestions are given during the initial hypnotic sessions to encourage deep relaxation and an optimistic attitude about recovery. The goal of autohypnosis is to enable patients to re-experience the same sensation of relaxation and confidence when they are on their own. 'Topping up' episodes of hypnosis by the therapist are interspersed among the autohypnosis sessions, in order to recharge the original PHS for autonomous trance entry, but these are increasingly spaced out to avoid the patient becoming dependent on the physician – a real problem is psychotherapy, and to some extent in physical therapy as well.

Hypno-autohypnosis meets with considerable success, and the results from it are significantly better than from the control procedure of relaxation instruction. It is notable that in one trial those patients whose asthma was known to be the result of an infection, an allergy, or some other physical agent such as fog or humidity, benefited just as much from this form of treatment as did those whose symptoms were attributed to psychological factors. But with asthma, as with skin disorders, it is not easy to know whether the therapeutic effects reported are the result of straight suggestion, or of suggestion while under hypnosis. Here again, significant effects which can override those of chemical preparations have been produced by simple verbal suggestions directed at fully alert patients [16].

Suggestion

Overall, research has supported the claim that waking suggestion does occur, and that there is a relation between a person's waking suggestibility and his suggestibility under hypnosis [17]. As a general rule, people responsive to waking suggestion are those most responsive to hypnotic suggestion. Furthermore, the effects of waking suggestion are sometimes surprising. This being so, can it in fact be maintained that hypnosis induces a state of heightened suggestibility? The pattern of evidence bearing on this point provides a reasonably clear answer. A person's suggestibility *is* significantly heightened during hypnosis but not very much, on average [3]. Moreover, recent evidence, especially that coming from the Stanford Laboratory [4], favours the idea that hypnotic and waking suggestion are closely related phenomena and may well be manifestations of the same psychological disposition. Moderately high correlations hold between a person's suggestibility in and out of hypnosis.

Optimal conditions for influence through suggestion

Ullman [18], in a perceptive article reviewing the treatment of warts by suggestion, reaches certain conclusions about the conditions that are favourable for a suggestion to be effective. His comments exemplify those made by several other authors writing on the subject. Ullman proposes that an important precondition for effective suggestion is an authoritarian attitude on the part of the therapist towards the patient. The same point has been made by Freud, who considered it important for successful psychotherapy in many cases that the therapist be regarded by the patient as a high status figure. To corroborate this, we only have to recall the numerous historical examples of powerful and renowned men and women being credited with the power to heal. This makes sense considering the definition of suggestion as a form of influence where what is said 'gets straight through' normal rational filters without being evaluated or criticized. The higher the attributed authority of a source of information or instruction, the less likely the recipient is to adopt a sceptical or suspicious attitude, and the more inclined he will be to take what is said at face value.

Vacchina and Strauss [19] have recently added to our knowledge on this point. Their evidence confirms that the hypnotist's perceived authority is an important factor in influencing a subject's susceptibility to hypnosis. But they also show that this holds only for 'dogmatic' subjects – people who score high on a measure of personality known as 'dogmatism', characterized by a general dependency on figures of authority, and on authoritarian or 'straitlaced' ways of life.

Suggestion and cognitive dissonance

Two main conclusions can be drawn from the preceding discussion. First, whatever other psychological devices are active in making chemically inactive treatments work, suggestion (waking or hypnotic) must be recognized as an important influence in itself. And second, the fact that an attitude of deference on the part of the patient seems to be conducive to his heightened suggestibility strikingly contrast the operation of suggestion with that of cognitive dissonance. This particular contrast is only one of many. On reflection, several lines of evidence become apparent which show that the conditions necessary and conducive to the operation of the one process are the antithesis of those optimal for the other. Table 1 illustrates this by listing some of the characteristics of each process and some of the conditions governing whether influence is likely to be effective in each case.

(1) **Active involvement vs. passive submission**

As we have seen, cognitive dissonance is a psychological state which obtains after a person has made a decision about something important. Dissonance is resolved when he has justified his commitment to himself. If the course of action he takes is determined for him; that is, if the decision is effectively taken by someone else, dissonance will not occur. Suggestion, on the other hand, depends for its operation on the exact opposite of this: the subject must be the passive recipient of information, making no decisions, responding mechanically to the directives he receives.

Cognitive dissonance	*Suggestion*

Necessary characteristics of subject's behaviour

(1)	Active involvement	Passive submission
(2)	Experience of intention	Absence of experienced intention
(3)	Mobilization of rationalization and justification	Suppression of rationalization and justification: uncritical acceptance

Conducive conditions

(4)	Health, alertness and vigilance	Ill health and tiredness
(5)	Effortful decision-making	Relaxation: if possible hypnosis
(6)	Low-status administrator	High status administrator

Table 1   The process of influence by suggestion and cognitive dissonance. Characteristics of each and the contrasting conditions which must hold for influence to be effective in each case.

(2) **Experience of intention vs. absence of experienced intention**

This is closely related to, but not identical with, (1). Dissonance will not occur unless a person considers his action to have been the result of his own free choice. If he sees himself as having been forced into committing the action he avoids any need to produce a justification on the grounds that he was not the responsible agent. Many court cases are argued along the lines that the defendant cannot be held responsible for a criminal act, because his doing it was the result of forces or circumstances beyond his control (e.g. his deprived childhood, or mentally deranged condition, or excessive exposure to television violence).

Of course, a person may do something as a result of coercion from others (e.g. social pressure) without being aware that he is responding to coercion (how often do we gently coax someone to do something and then allow them to think they are acting on their own initiative?). When this happens, the important factor is the way the person himself construes things – whether or not he *thinks* his action was voluntary. So long as he fails to recognize that he was being pressed by others, and continues to believe that he freely chose to act in the way he did (even if he is deluding himself), then dissonance, and the need to justify, will be aroused.[7] Contrastingly, actions which are the result of suggestion, such as those carried out under hypnosis, are not accompanied by the same conviction of agency.

(3) **Mobilization vs. suppression of rationalization**

Cognitive dissonance makes a person try to account for something he has done by justifying or rationalizing it. We have seen how this involves categorizing the action as acceptable by identifying it as consistent with a socially upheld rule or value. Now to justify is to explain. Accounting for anomalies in the physical world – the world of things – relies on the same kind of explaining process as does accounting for deviations in one's own behaviour.[8] In Orne's experiments on hypnosis, it was observed that the inclination to explain apparent anomalies was much less prevalent among 'real' hypnotic subjects than among those faking a trance. In fact, Orne cites this as the main difference between the two groups.

Not only does the general tendency to rationalize and explain things seem to be temporarily suspended in hypnosis, it is also the very thing that has to be by-passed for a waking suggestion to be effective. The instruction must be received uncritically.

[7] This is quite a complicated point and is discussed at greater length by Totman [20].

[8] The psychological term 'cognitive dissonance' refers to the *general* tendency to explain anomalous events, whether the instance in question is one's own action or whether it is something observed and external to the observer. (e.g. [20], [21]) For the sake of clarity it has been illustrated in this book only by examples concerned with the former – the case of one's own actions.

Its sense and likelihood must not be weighed up, as they characteristically are in the contrasting process of persuasion.

(4) Health, alertness and vigilance vs. ill-health and tiredness.

When an individual commits himself on an important issue, he arrives at a decision by carefully considering all the pros and cons. This necessitates an active and focussed mind. Russian investigators [22] have found evidence that verbal suggestions are likely to have a greater impact if the organism is tired, ill or in some way psychologically depleted. This is presumably because his critical faculty is temporarily diminished, permitting freer entry of unquestioned information.

(5) Effortful decision-making vs. relaxation

For a decision to evoke dissonance, it must be difficult and effortful. As we have seen, treatments which place heavy demands on the individual can be interpreted as being unwittingly geared to creating dissonance by making the commitment of the would-be patient hard and privatory. Setting the stage for suggestion effects involves the exact opposite to this – mental and physical relaxation on the part of the subject being necessary for entry into a hypnotic trance and the optimum condition for receptivity to suggestions.

(6) Low-status administrator vs. high-status administrator

A number of psychological studies (e.g. [23, 24]) have shown that cognitive dissonance is more effectively aroused by a low-status experimenter than by a high-status experimenter. This makes sense, since doing something in compliance with the requests of a lowly person is more likely to require self-justification than doing something for an important person.

Counter to this we noted earlier how a high-status source of information can encourage suggestion.

So where do all these contrasts and comparisons lead us? Paradoxically, I believe, it is towards accounting for the effects of suggestion and cognitive dissonance under the same umbrella.

In several passages I have talked about a person's 'critical faculty', and the 'rational censors', 'filters' and 'barriers' which operate in all of us during normal wakefulness. Normally, we do not respond automatically to everything we are told. When someone says this carpet is more hardwearing than that, or this car is more reliable than that, we do not go out straight away and act on this information, like machines. First of all, we weigh it up carefully, and think about whether it is likely to be true. If it fits in with what we already know and expect, or if it is said by someone we trust absolutely, it may be accepted without too many more questions being asked. If not, more information will probably be sought, not only about the thing under consideration, but also, perhaps, about the person who is the source of the information. Man is naturally sceptical. Information is sifted and assessed before he responds to it. Much of it gets rejected.

But there are occasions when this constant vigilance is relaxed. It will be relaxed a little if the speaker is someone we trust, or if he is an accepted authority. It will also be relaxed if we ourselves are very tired, or drunk, or ill.

The mechanism in us responsible for assessing information and letting only some of it through functions rather like a guard who stands at a checkpoint in a military precinct. Normally, individuals are required to show their passes before they are allowed in. (Normally, we require some knowledge of a person's credentials before we will believe what he says.) People whose faces are familiar to the guard stand a good chance of being able to get past the checkpoint without having to show their passes. (People we know and trust are more readily believed than strangers.) A diplomat is allowed in without being recognized by the guard because he carries a special pass. (The special pass is like the knowledge that the speaker is a great expert on his subject.) If a foreign agent wishes to gain entry, he knows that his best chance will be towards the end of the guard's shift, when the guard is feeling most tired.

Nevertheless, our critical faculty performs like an inefficient guard, for it is known that a certain amount of information does get through, unnoticed, to influence our behaviour and our experience at a later time. This has become known as the 'subliminal' entry of information. Pictures or words can be flashed at a person, using very short exposures, so that he is unable to discriminate anything at the time, but some time later his behaviour shows clear evidence that he has been affected by what he subliminally perceived (but did not *see*). The same thing happens if words are spoken through head-phones at a level well below a person's threshold for hearing. Very often, themes from the subliminal stimulus appear later in his fantasies and dreams. It is as if there is a secret way into the military camp, round the back, of which the authorities and the guard are unaware, and through which a steady trickle of illegal entries are made [see 25].

Subliminal material can influence more than just a person's fantasies and dreams. Instructions can be subliminally com-municated too. In one experiment, some students were about to write essays. Before they did so, half were shown the sub-liminal instruction, 'Write more', and half were shown 'Don't write' (none of the students were actually aware of seeing these messages – they were flashed too fast). The essays of those shown 'Don't write' turned out to be significantly shorter than the essays of those students shown 'Write more' [26].

This kind of direct, machine-like influence of an instruction on the organism (I have deliberately avoided saying 'the person' here, because 'the person' is, in a sense, exactly the thing which is by-passed) seems very like the influence of the hypnotist on a hypnotized subject. Post-hypnotic suggestions are carried out apparently without any knowledge on the part of the subject of having been given the instruction.

Direct suggestions aimed at altering bodily functioning, such as suggestions that a skin condition will clear up, at first sight do not seem quite the same as suggestions to carry out actions. Yet they are in a sense the same, because it is not the 'person' who is responding in each case, but rather some more primitive level of control within the organism, which seems able to exercise a much more direct and powerful kind of control.

How do the effects discussed in connection with cognitive dissonance relate to this analysis? We have seen how directives from other people are normally filtered and assessed. Cognitive dissonance, on the other hand, results from one's *own* decisions. One might reasonably suppose one's own decisions and commitments to be exempt from the assessment procedures that are automatically applied to information from 'outside'. Logically, this must be so, otherwise it would be impossible for individuals to act at all.

When a person decides to do something and firmly commits himself to a course of action such as going to receive treatment for an illness, the implications of what he does will be free of the critical procedures that are normally applied to directives from others. Returning to the military analogy, this is like the guard himself entering the camp. In this circumstance, the normal checking procedures are simply not applicable. He has a unique and unchallengeable authority to enter because he is both checker and checked.

Similarly, in the case of an individual committing himself to a course of action, the thing which enables him to decide which alternative to take is exactly the thing which normally assesses and filters directives from others: the individual's critical faculty or rational power. This is why deeds done by a person, *providing the person sees himself as freely choosing to do them*, carry a unique authority. The *same* kind of authority therefore attaches to them as to suggestions from an all-powerful hypnotist – an authority which incorporates the power to regulate organic processes in a direct and immediate fashion.

The more difficult the decision to receive treatment, the greater the choice and commitment involved, and the greater the dissonance which follows. So when our patient chooses, after much deliberation, to go to the acupuncture clinic, or to make an expedition to Lourdes, the implication (or suggestion) which automatically attaches to this decision is that it is a sensible and wise one, and that it is likely to have a favourable outcome. As soon as he has made the decision to commit himself, he has a psychological investment in the chosen treatment.

Looked at in this way, we see that the processes of influence through suggestion and through cognitive dissonance are not so dissimilar after all.

It must not be forgotten, also, that in submitting to a hypnotist in the first place the subject makes a blanket commitment to subordinate his own will to that of another person for the duration of the coming sessions. Contrary to popular belief, a person has to be willing before he can be hypnotized. This decision itself cannot be without a certain amount of resultant dissonance, and therefore cannot be ignored in explaining what happens subsequently, under hypnosis. In a sense, all the things done at the hypnotist's request thereafter carry the subject's own higher-order 'stamp of approval'. Ultimate control still rests with the subject because it is he who chose to give the hypnotist special licence in the first place. The same thing can be said of a patient seeking help from a psychoanalyst: the consequences of the initial decision to invest the analyst, perhaps above all other people, with one's confidence and trust, must be taken into consideration in explaining the results of psychotherapy.

4 THE PHYSIOLOGICAL BASIS OF PSYCHOSOMATIC DISEASE

The history of medicine provides some provocative leads regarding the possibility of psychological influence on the outcome of a treatment. Before going any further into an analysis of psychosomatic effects, it is necessary to examine the question of how feasible is the notion of psychosomatic disease from a physiological angle? Is there any direct evidence that a person's psychological reactions to his environment influence the bodily conditions responsible for whether or not a disease gets going? If not, are there, at least, some known channels through which such effects could come about? Or is the opposite true? Does what is known about the workings of the human organism rule out the possibility of psychosomatic influence altogether?

What is immediately clear is that as yet there is no physiological *proof* of the psychosomatic hypothesis. No one has yet demonstrated the complete sequence, from psychologically significant event to onset of symptoms.

Nevertheless, sufficient convincing evidence has been obtained for us to be confident of the existence of various channels through which psychosomatic effects could be transmitted. In talking about psychological influence on disease we do not need to stretch scientific credulity. Unlike accounting for extra-sensory perception, metal bending, and other parapsychological happenings, it is not necessary to look round for completely new systems of explanation. Although the teasing out of many unknown details in the process will take time, there is nothing to indicate that psychosomatic influence is mysterious in the sense that it poses a challenge to conventional scientific systems of explanation.

The aim of this chapter is therefore to make it clear that psychosomatic influence is highly plausible from a physiological point of view, even if it is not yet a proven fact.

Challenging situations and their effect on the body

It is not necessary to turn to experimental evidence to know that threatening situations consistently produce a number of involuntary bodily reactions. Everyday observation of ourselves and others enables us to list many of the more prominent changes that take place when a person is alarmed. His mouth goes dry, he experiences palpitations, he pales and perhaps freezes for a short time. These reactions form part of a general automatic response, and serve an important function for survival by preparing the organism for 'fight' or 'flight'. The changes that take place mobilize the resources of the body so that the individual is especially well equipped for one or other of these courses of action.

This group of involuntary bodily reactions is controlled by a mechanism known as the sympathetic nervous system (SNS), which is stimulated following the appraisal of danger. During the instant of confrontation, activation of the SNS has the following effects. Saliva flow is inhibited; peripheral blood vessels are constricted; and heart beat is accelerated, enabling blood to be channelled to the brain and muscles. In addition, the bronchioles (passages to the lungs) are dilated, thereby stepping up oxygen intake; bladder contraction is inhibited; and eye pupils are dilated. Adrenalin is also pumped into the bloodstream, which aids and abets these changes and inhibits digestion. The increased supply of adrenalin also stimulates the conversion of glycogen (stored sugar) to glucose (readily usable sugar) in the blood so as to make extra energy readily available should it be needed. It is not difficult to see how all these changes act in concert to alert the organism and prepare it for a defensive or aggressive stand. A similar but milder form of the same reaction has been referred to as the 'orientation reflex' – elicited by the perception of something unfamiliar. This involves not so much the appraisal of danger as awareness of an 'unknown quantity', which may or may not constitute a threat, and which provokes a characteristic cautious approach and exploration [1]. Closely related to these reactions is another biological function known as 'arousal' or 'activation' [2]. This is controlled by specialized structures in the brain and is responsible for wakefulness and alertness. It is assumed that a certain basic level of arousal is a necessary condition for occurrence of the orientation and fight/flight reactions.

In normal circumstances the organism is able to cope with and remove a source of threat in one of three possible ways. He can investigate it and recognize that it is not threatening after all. He can place some distance between it and himself by making it go away, or by fleeing himself. Or he can destroy it. Occasionally, however, none of these things happens and the initial strong reaction, rather than being allayed, persists and goes through a series of identifiable changes. This sequence has been described by Selye [3], and named by him the 'General Adaptation Syndrome'. One of the main components of the General Adaptation Syndrome is the prolonged pro-duction and secretion of chemicals by the adrenal glands, among which is a group known as corticosteroids.

Researchers interested in the environmental conditions which trigger these reactions have shown that various of them can be elicited by experimentally presented 'stimuli' such as electric shocks and thermal pain; also by working at insoluble problems, and by watching films of Australian Aboriginal rites involving circumcisions. Similar and related physiological reactions have been recorded in real life situations intuitively believed to be stressful, including parachute jumping, speaking before large audiences, and taking exams.[1]

Aspects of social interaction which psychologists are fond of investigating, such as conformity, deviation, leadership, and the cohesion or 'togetherness' of groups, have also been linked with SNS related reactions. Leiderman and Shapiro [4] have reviewed some studies in which hormonal products in subjects' blood and urine and electrical properties of their skin were measured and related to various social factors. Unfortunately, the results of experiments like these, in 'psychophysiology' or 'psychobiology', as it is known, do not give us a set of nice clear

[1] Some references to these studies are alluded to in Chapter 7.

relationships between psychological circumstances on the one hand, and physiological states on the other. The many attempts to discover a physiological pattern corresponding to each of the emotions as they are experienced and reported by people have been unsuccessful, with the result that this objective has now been more or less abandoned. Even on a less ambitious scale the same precipitating agent or 'stimulus', when repeatedly applied in the laboratory under precisely the same conditions, has been found to evoke quite different physiological reactions from different individuals. For example, one person may show a marked increase in heart rate, but only a slight alteration in breathing, following an electric shock; while another's breathing is the factor most affected. Furthermore, the consistency with which one reaction dominates is itself known to vary between people, complicating the picture still further.

However, a great deal is currently being discovered about what governs the physiological responses of organisms to features of the environment [e.g. 5]. In general, psychophysiologists view an organism's response to any given environment as the result of the following three classes of influence:

(1) The nature and strength of the impinging 'stimulus' – part of the organism's immediate sensory environment (what he sees, hears, feels);

(2) Dispositional characteristics of the organism – the result of genetic endowment in interaction with past experience;

and (3) Temporary fluctuations in bodily states (e.g. rate of metabolism, degree of tiredness).

These three categories are assumed to embrace the sum total of the influences acting on an individual at any time. It is believed that in principle, even if not in practice,[2] it is thus possible to arrive at an exhaustive 'blueprint' of every human

[2] The practical limitations on being able to control, perfectly, all the relevant features being almost certainly insuperable.

organism so that its response to any given environment at any given moment is totally predictable.

However, there is a special problem with the first class of influence which does not arise in the case of the second and third. Both the latter (dispositions to respond in a specific way and cyclic bodily fluctuations) are conceived as internal states of the organism. But in dealing with impinging 'stimuli' it becomes necessary to get outside the organism and find a way of describing its environment in a meaningful manner – i.e. in terms of what is already known and expected. For instance, the noise of a passing car may not stimulate adrenalin secretion to anything like the same extent that the sound of a ringing telephone does, although the two sounds may be equivalent in their physical intensity.

So it is not enough to describe someone's environment in terms of those attributes which might be of interest to a physicist – i.e. to fix, arbitrarily, on some feature and adopt it as the thing of interest (or 'stimulus'). The environment has to be split up into its component parts according to what is significant to the individual. This must, of course, involve taking into account genetic factors as well as past experience. The first class of influence, therefore, cannot be divorced from the second.

Prolonged hormonal response: too much of a good thing

Prolonged physiological reactions to a physically stressful or a psychologically threatening environment, in particular the excessive secretion of corticosteroids, can aggravate or initiate diseases such as ulcers, hypertension and heart disease [6, 7]. Having said this, two cautionary notes must immediately be added. First, it is not always clear, from the experiments on which this conclusion is based, exactly what sort of stress is most effective in producing these damaging effects. Comparatively high intensities of physical stimulation that one would consider, intuitively, to be harmful to the organism – such as electric shock – have frequently failed to produce any clear organic consequences at all. And there is some evidence to suggest that situations of conflict, uncertainty and in particular helplessness produce signs of anxiety more consistently than sheer physical assault [7–9]. Seligman [9] has described a number of animal experiments concerned with the effects of helplessness. In these experiments, animals are given unpleasant stimuli such as electric shocks. Some animals learn to terminate the shocks by making a required response such as pressing a lever, while others, who receive shocks of identical intensity and duration, are unable to control them. Generally, the helpless animals develop more ulcers and exhibit more extreme signs of anxiety than do the animals able to exercise control.

Second, this conclusion is based almost exclusively on the findings of experiments with animals, and there are good grounds for being sceptical about how far findings from the animal laboratory can be generalized to man. Experimentally contrived 'stressful' environments are often highly artificial, even for the unfortunate species being subjected to them. Whether it is possible to say with any confidence that they represent analogues to human encounters remains a very moot point. It is a focal argument of this book that the uniquely human capacity for language and symbolic representation demands a whole new approach to defining what is 'stressful' to man, and to a particular individual, and necessitates a style of analysis which gets right away from comparisons with lower animals.

Selye has made a number of studies which show that damage to the heart, kidneys, liver, blood vessels, bones, and skin can occur as a result of injections of adrenal hormones which are natural, or 'adaptive', under normal circumstances, and that such damage is intensified by simultaneous exposure to physical stress. His experiments have been criticized on the grounds that abnormally large doses of hormones were often administered. This calls into question the equivalence of the experimentally induced states to the natural bodily reactions they were presumed to emulate. But clinical experience with the side effects of cortisone and other related treatments generally leaves little doubt that an excess of these hormones can be harmful.

There is a strong suggestion too that the depletion in corti-costeroid resources which follows a period of their intense secretion (or administration) can exacerbate or cause arthritis and similar conditions [10]. In fact, it would seem that no bodily organ is sacrosanct, for we shall see how the systems protecting against infection and even cancer can be put at jeopardy by sustained high levels of these hormones.

The sequence leading up to the prolonged and excessive release of corticosteroids

The adrenal gland is stimulated to manufacture and release corticosteroids by another hormone – adrenocorticotropic hormone (ACTH) – which is itself released by the pituitary gland, situated in the brain. A part of the brain near the centre (see Figure 3), the hypothalamus, has been found to be the controller of ACTH release. Cells of the hypothalamus contain a substance known as corticotropin, which when liberated stimulates the release of ACTH into the bloodstream, where it is carried down to the adrenal glands. This system of trans-mission has become known as the hypothalamic-pituitary-adrenal axis.

Recent research enables us to trace back this sequence a stage further, and it is now clear that the area of the hypothalamus responsible for the release of the ACTH receives its instructions in turn from other 'higher' centres in the brain. These 'higher' centres consist in a complex of cells called the limbic system, which although dispersed is functionally related. When certain areas of this system are removed, damaged or stimulated electrically, the fight/flight reaction is affected. For example, fearlike behaviour and rage can be provoked by electrical stimulation to a part of the limbic system known as the amygdala [11]. Two distinct sites have been isolated within the limbic system such that the removal of one produces a condition in which the fight/flight reaction will occur at the slightest provocation, and the removal of the other leads to a virtual absence of the fight/flight reaction even under extreme

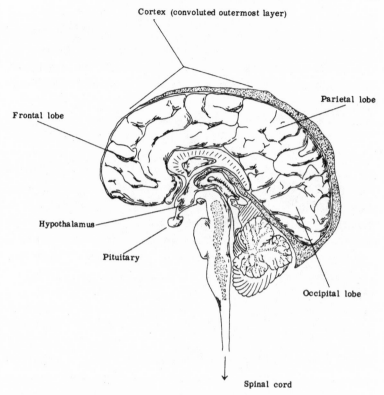

Figure 3   The human brain cut lengthwise between the two cerebral hemispheres. (Adapted from J. W. KIMBALL, *Biology*, Addison-Wesley, 1965)

provocation. Gray [12] has concluded, on the basis of these and other findings, that there are two competing systems which control the hypothalamic-pituitary-adrenal axis. One of these acts so as to excite, and the other so as to inhibit, the sequence subserving fight/flight which starts in the hypothalamus. The balance between the two determines the threshold of the reaction. Also, Fonberg [13] has discovered that the removal of a section of the amygdala leads to the loss of normal orienting responses and exploratory behaviours in animals. In humans, tumors in the same regions have been noticed to produce a similar state of apathy, non-responsiveness and withdrawal [14].

It is also instructive to look at these psychophysiological interactions the other way round, that is, to focus on the psychological situations that give rise to activity in this complex of brain centres, and in the hypothalamic-pituitary-adrenal axis. It is known, for instance, that almost any environmental event which produces signs of an 'emotional state' increases corticosteroid output. The limbic areas which control hypothalamic activity appear to be activated by pain and other forms of biological stress. Many kinds of physical and psychological assault are followed by activity in the hypothalamus itself. The situations which provoke activity in the hypothalamus most effectively and most reliably are ones involving novelty, conflict, unpredictability or the frustration of behaviour that had previously been adequate in coping with environmental demands [15].

Effects on the immune system

Evidence is beginning to accumulate which suggests that high blood levels of chemicals connected with the release of corticosteroids from the adrenal glands[3] can inhibit the response which the normal healthy body makes to antigens. Antigens are foreign substances which enter the body from outside. They can be bacteria or viruses, and are 'recognized' by antibodies – ever-present cells which the body continuously manufactures and which circulate in the bloodstream. There are a very large number (10^{20}) of antibodies present in the blood at any particular time, although this includes some duplicates. Consequently, millions of different types of antigen can be recognized. The relation between the different antibodies and antigens is rather like that between lots of different keys and locks. Each type of antibody can recognize only one type of antigen. Thus for each of the many existing strains of virus or bacteria, there is likely to be an antibody that recognizes

[3] Including ACTH and adrenocorticosteroids themselves.

it. Specific antigen cells are marked by a distinctive pattern on their surface. An antibody recognizes its corresponding antigen by means of this pattern, and when recognition occurs the antibody responds by combining with the antigen and in this way ear-marking it for destruction or removal by other bodily mechanisms. The cells which manufacture antibodies are called lymphocytes. Each lymphocyte manufactures many identical antibodies, some of which adhere to its surface and circulate, attached to it, serving as 'samples' of the progeny of that particular lymphocyte. When one of these antibodies recognizes and combines with an antigen, its parent lymphocyte becomes stimulated to do two things: it begins to produce and secrete antibodies, and at the same time it divides to create another cell identical to itself. These two cells then continue to divide, into four cells, then eight, then sixteen, and so on, giving rise to a colony of cells manufacturing and secreting one species of antibody which eventually eliminates the invading antigen.

If the invading antigen is a virus or bacteria also dividing and multiplying within the bloodstream, the speed at which the antibody response gets off the ground, and the rate at which it proceeds, are crucial factors in determining whether the infection will be eliminated before it kills or damages the host. Occasionally, when an antibody adhering to the outside of a lymphocyte encounters an antigen it recognizes, the parent lymphocyte, instead of entering the stimulated state in which it creates more of that antibody and starts dividing, reacts in the completely opposite way. It becomes inhibited so that its antibody-producing response is suppressed. There are at least two ways in which this can come about.

A lymphocyte which does not become stimulated may become paralysed – which is to say that no further encounters between its adhering antibodies and matching antigens can activate it. Very low or very high concentrations of antigen are two conditions which have been shown to result in the paralysis of a lymphocyte.

Quite apart from the possibility of paralysis, a special kind of lymphocyte is known to exist which does not make and secrete antibodies. Its function is to kill foreign cells and tissue, including cancer cells, and to act as a kind of catalyst either by helping or by antagonizing the antibody-producing lymphocytes in their task of eliminating antigens.[4]

There are many gaps in our knowledge about what controls these complex processes, and what determines the response of a lymphocyte encountering a recognized antigen. However, it is clear that these, and perhaps other similar mechanisms, in no way rule out the possibility of psychosomatic influence. Psychological states, through their impact on the higher centres of the brain and the limbic-hypothalamic-pituitary-adrenal pathway, could tip some of the sensitive balances which govern the body's response to a vast number of diseases in which the immune system is involved. These range from infections and allergies to arthritis, auto-immune diseases and cancer, and include numerous other degenerative complaints associated with ageing. There would thus seem to be no shortage of potential 'ways in' for psychological influences in the causation of such conditions.

The evidence bearing directly on this issue is highly suggestive but by no means clear of snags and complications. Various forms of experimentally contrived 'stress' have been shown to lower the body's resistance to infection in rodents. Corticosteroids are known to depress antibody formation in some animals, under some conditions, and there is evidence that corticosteroids and ACTH given before or during an injection of antigen, suppress circulating antibodies [10, 17].

Korneva [18] has presented findings which indicate that the destruction of a small area of the hypothalamus suppresses the antibody response of the rabbit to foreign proteins. Moreover, electrical stimulation of this same region of the hypothalamus was found to lead to one or more of the following effects: (1) earlier onset of the antibody response, (2) a greater magnitude of antibody response, and (3) a longer duration of antibody response. The discovery of these highly complex features of the immune system is mainly based on experiments with

[4] These and other related processes are described by Jerne [16].

rats, rabbits and mice. Once again, the situation must be infinitely more complex in man. Nevertheless, research has shown not only that there are numerous mechanisms by which brain activity could ultimately suppress the immune response, but also that this is a highly probable eventuality.

Cancer

Cancers are groups of abnormally proliferating cells that fail to differentiate themselves into tissues and organs. They can arise in any part of the body. Those that remain localized and do not invade surrounding tissue are called benign tumors. Most growths are benign but a few grow quickly, spread from their original site, find their way into the bloodstream, and are transported to other parts of the body which they invade. This process of spreading is known as metastasis, and these tumors are said to be malignant. The incapacitating illnesses and deaths caused by cancer are almost always the result of metastasis. Benign tumors are rarely fatal [19].

The main problem in preventing serious illness and death from cancer is therefore more one of preventing the spread of abnormal cells than one of controlling the abnormal growth in the first place. One special attribute of cancer cells is that they display unusual surface characteristics, and this is the feature of cells which antibodies use to recognize them as 'foreign'. As might be expected, many different types of cancer cell have been found to evoke a limited reaction from the immune system, both in animals and man. Prehn [20] has presented several lines of evidence supporting the idea that a primary function of the immune system is to maintain a constant surveillance within the body, and to destroy cancer cells, regardless of origin, at a stage before they amass into tumors. Whether or not tumors develop and grow can therefore be regarded as the result of the balance between immune system competence (speed of reaction etc.), and the growth potential of a particular embryo-tumor. There is some evidence that if the immune system fails to destroy cancer cells, it can act to slow their propagation.

A metastasizing tumor must come into contact with the immune system on its journey through the bloodstream to a new site, and there is evidence to suggest that its encounters with antibodies and lymphocytes can determine its survival. The interplay between cancer cell and immune system is thus an attractive possibility if we are searching for ways in which psychosomatic influence could be realized. The likelihood that the immune response is suppressed by hormones, in particular by corticosteroids, brings well within the bounds of credibility the prospect of influence on cancer formation from higher centres in the brain. Southam [21] broaches several other possible mechanisms besides this one, including the idea that corticosteroids, through their tendency to coagulate the blood, could increase the chances of a circulating cancer cell adhering to and penetrating the walls of capillary blood vessels in organs distant from their site of origin.

Although each of these effects is well documented, psychological influence on cancer is not yet a proven fact, since we still lack any demonstration of the entire chain of events, starting with a psychologically significant encounter and culminating in a malignant growth. Once more, we can conclude that, notwithstanding the present state of relative ignorance about the mechanisms controlling the growth of cancers, this kind of influence does appear to be possible, even likely.

A finding that bears passing mention at this point is one reported by Katz *et al.* [22], who investigated various attributes of women with breast cancer. In this study it was found that a high level of corticosteroids relative to the hormone androgen was associated with the psychological characteristics of apprehension, worry, fear and despair. A high corticosteroid–androgen ratio is a pattern known from previous research to be related to poor prognosis in such cases. (A low corticosteroid–androgen ratio on the other hand was associated with hope, faith in God or fate, and pride.)

Higher cortical functions

The cortex, or outermost crust (see Figure 3), is considered to be the most recently evolved part of the brain. It is responsible for the most sophisticated and least understood aspects of an animal's activities, and is highly developed in man. The human cortex analyses and interprets incoming information from the sense organs, and contains large areas devoted to the categorizing, associative, symbolic and linguistic activities that are related to thinking, recognizing and recalling – the so called 'higher' functions. It used to be thought that the cortex could be neatly divided into sections, each having a mappable boundary, and each being involved in one and only one specialist activity, such as trunk movement, recognition of colour, memory of place, sentence construction, etc. Now it is realized that such theories of localization, as they were known, are far from adequate representations of the true way in which the brain works. The modern view is that the central nervous system, which includes the brain, constitutes a very much more complex and adaptable mechanism. Systems of communicating cells can be identified, but these are not necessarily linked on grounds of proximity. Rather, they are considered to be related because they form part of an assembly serving a definable function. Indeed, their component parts may well be dispersed. The essential relation is thus a functional and not a spatial one, each cell complex being a unit because of the job it performs.

Moreover, a great number of changes in the organization of these assemblies are known to take place during the brain's development – a process not completed until the age of 15. It is often possible that if a system serving a particular function is damaged, causing that function to be lost or impaired, then by means of the appropriate practice and training the lost function can be taken over by other systems which were not previously involved in its control.[5] Indeed, the cortex seems to be capable of so much flexibility and compensation that is has

[5] Or, at any rate, not obviously so.

been characterized as an organ capable of forming functional organs.

Patients who have suffered brain damage to a particular area of their cortex provide us with valuable information about the workings of the brain and central nervous system. Roughly speaking, destruction of the cortex results in an uncontrolled proliferation of the more basic activities necessary for survival (such as eating, drinking, and the fight/flight reaction) which are known to be controlled by other more primitive areas of the brain. This would imply that the cortex exerts a constant general restraining influence on other parts of the brain, which is lost when it is removed or destroyed.

Many of the disturbances in function resulting from confined damage seem somewhat extraordinary on first consideration. For example, when patients with damage to one particular region (Broca's area), are asked to pronounce a word or phrase, they are often unable to get beyond the first syllable, which is simply reiterated with minor variations over and over again. An analogous difficulty is experienced when these patients try to write. Again, they fail to progress beyond an individual letter, or part of a letter, which is compulsively re-written a large number of times. Patients with damage to another area (the temporal region), while retaining the ability to recall a sequence of words or syllables, cannot do this in the correct order, even when only four or five words are spoken and repeated to them many times. Damage to certain divisions of the cortex concerned with vision (the occipitoparietal zones) can result in an inability to identify correctly an object represented in a picture. Instead of integrating parts of the object in the picture into a whole, as is normal, these patients characteristically focus on a single contour, then break off their inspection after forming premature conclusions about the identity of the object. For example, Luria [23] has described how in relatively severe cases a pair of spectacles may be identified as a bicycle, the patient extrapolating from the image of two circles and a line.

Openminded accounts of the nature of disturbances in brain damaged patients, such as Luria gives, show up the inadequacies of localization approaches – where some dimension of human functioning or performance is arbitrarily described in advance and allocated to a specific place in the brain. Arbitrary definitions of dimensions of mental activity encounter exactly the same kind of difficulty as experiments designed to study physiological reactions to arbitrarily selected aspects of the physical environment. The nature of the disturbances seen in patients with brain damage, and the difficulties so often encountered in trying to express them in language (on the part of both patient and doctor) show us that it is possible initially to learn more about the workings of the brain by naïve observation of such patients, than by premeditated theories involving concepts taken from everyday usage.

It is interesting to note that damage to the frontal lobes of the brain, an area believed to be involved in the more abstract functions – such as intellectual activities, planning and volition – almost always results in a marked loss of the individual's critical faculty [23]. As has already been suggested, the by-passing of this faculty, or of something very similar to it, might conceivably account for the effects attributable to waking and hypnotic suggestion. Moreover, we have seen how central the notions of rationalizing, planning and volition are in relation to cognitive dissonance.

The brain, then, is highly active in its interpretation and synthesis of incoming information. When signals are received from sensory receptors, they do not filter through mechanically as if travelling through a torpid network of passages or conducting wires. Input is actively and constructively worked on, and this entails elaborating it, setting up and testing hypotheses (guesses) about it, and eventually categorizing and perhaps storing it – at which stage it 'makes sense', 'is recognized', 'is understood' etc., [24].

Now, not only is this true of the perception of objects (the physical world), it also applies to the perception of people's actions (the social world). When we watch someone doing something, his action does not appear to us like a meaningless succession of arm and leg movements. It is seen as a coordinated attempt to achieve some goal. We understand the action and its purpose by recognizing the social significance of the goal towards which it is directed. Our interpretation of events in the social world is therefore every bit as 'constructive' as our interpretation of events in the world of objects. In both cases, it has to be said that there exists a constant coded representation in the brain of how things, physical and social, 'ought to be'. This representation determines what we expect to perceive, and our reaction when we do perceive something. Whether or not what we perceive makes sense depends on whether or not it can be assimilated to the existing coded representation. Removing part of the cortex interferes not only with 'input' and 'output' – how incoming information is received and how performance is affected – but also with how 'input' is ordered (interpreted), and how we select and assemble a response to it.

The relevance of these considerations to psychosomatic influence is this. If it is true that a person's social experiences can influence his susceptibility to disease, we need to ask how something as vague-sounding as 'social experiences' could start off a chain of causes and effects ending in a reaction having critical consequences for health (such as the secretion of adrenal hormones). The initial stage of this process must be regarded as activity in the higher centres of the brain: the centres that contain the coded representation of the individual's social world; the centres responsible for regulating and interpreting his interactions with other people.

Exactly the same thing can be said about social (verbal) communications which result in the alleviation of symptoms – the cures and remissions which can arise as a consequence of suggestion or cognitive dissonance. To consider this incoming information in isolation is missing the point. It has to be viewed in context of the representations of the social world which are already there, somehow encoded in the structure and activity of the cortex. What determines whether incoming information will ultimately cause hormonal or other organic reactions affecting health, depends not so much on its nature 'in the raw' –

i.e. whether it is a loud noise, the hysterical ravings of a demented spouse or the furious outbursts of an employer – but on its significance to the person. Needless to say, this is not the same for all. It is quite possible for an individual to become accustomed to any of these occurrences, even to the extent of expecting them regularly. The way a person handles 'input', whether physical or social in origin, is therefore traceable back to his past experience. For it is his past experience which has determined the coded representations – the structure – in terms of which he understands and reacts to his present environment.

The processing of social information by the cortex is the stage in the psychosomatic causal sequence about which least is known. As we consider the route from the higher centres of the cortex through the limbic–hypothalamic–pituitary–adrenal pathway, interactions become progressively easier to elucidate and describe, although large gaps still exist in our knowledge of all the various stages. Nevertheless, by far the most important problem the researcher interested in psychosomatic disease faces is how to represent, or 'model', this initial stage.

What the foregoing brief discussions do make plain is that there is no case for thinking of psychosomatic influence as in any way mysterious, occult, unscientific or requiring 'parapsychological'[6] explanation. In searching for physiological mechanisms that could provide the basis for subliminal perception, Dixon [25] concludes that we do not have to scrape around for sketchy and speculative possibilities, for the situation is one of an *embarras de richesses*. Exactly the same is true of mechanisms that could underlie psychosomatic influence – there is no shortage of these.[7]

---

[6] At least at present. There is also no case for ruling out parapsychological phenomena as a possible explanation sometime in the future, if and when more is known about such things.

[7] For an up-to-date discussion of findings in this area, see the section, *Intermediate mechanisms: from psychological response to physiological reaction*. In Lipowski *et al.* [26].

In the first half of this book I have tried to establish that therapeutic psychological intervention in physical disease is possible. However, many 'hard line' experimentalists will still be left with the impression that the evidence for this is inconclusive. But to expect cut and dried proof of psychosomatic influence in studies of man is simply misguided. The obstructions to testing hypotheses using closely controlled experimental designs are enormous. No medical authority is prepared to risk assigning seriously ill patients to research whose aim is to try out psychological ways of alleviating symptoms when this entails the *withholding* of medication.

New drugs are, of course, frequently evaluated on a group of patients, but normally this happens only after a preliminary series of investigations with animals has given a strong indication that the drug in question is likely to be beneficial and has no negative side-effects. The preceding discussions of psychological ways in which symptoms can be alleviated, however, and the ensuing review of psychological and social factors associated with the onset and course of disease, make it plain that the concept of man as a linguistic creature with a unique capacity for symbolic representation is one which the psychosomatic researcher is unable to do without. For this reason, few of the questions which present themselves as the important ones can be translated into hypotheses capable of being tested in experiments with animals.

It is true that a few therapeutic techniques involving conditioning[1] have been developed as a direct consequence of

[1] The operant conditioning of somatic activity such as heart rate [1] and respiration [2]. See also [3].

studies with animals, but it now seems certain that major advances will not be made in any theoretical 'language' that accounts for animal and human behaviour in the same way. Any system in which the social meaning of situations is reckoned to be an important factor must be applied in the first instance to man himself.

If we turn from experimentation to a more 'naturalistic' style of collecting facts, as Rose[2] did in his attempts to assess the outcome of faith healing, difficulties are by no means at an end. Consider studies of faith healing clientele, for example. Most people going to a faith healer have already tried conventional treatment. Many are suffering from conditions already diagnosed as intractable, some from terminal conditions, and a fair proportion may be turning to faith healing as a last resort. Such individuals are by no means representative of a normal patient population. A number will be simultaneously receiving prescriptions from their doctors, and any hope of being able to control, or take into account, these and other possible concurrent influences is an overly optimistic one.

When it comes to researching psychological or social conditions which might be active in the causation of diseases, even more serious problems arise. An 'experiment', in the traditional scientific sense of holding all other conditions constant and varying one single factor so that its effects can be studied *in vacuo*, is effectively ruled out. It is neither ethically desirable nor practically feasible to contrive, experimentally, complicated psychological settings hypothesized to interfere with health. The upshot is that, like it or not, we have to make do with 'descriptive' research – studies demonstrating an association between disease and some aspect of the physical or social environment, or the subject's personality. There are many such studies from many different disciplines, in the form of psychiatric case reports, demographic[3] and anthropological observations, and correlative data from psychologists and sociologists. But as in the study of 'fringe' medical treatments, a descriptive

[2] See Chapter 2.
[3] Statistical studies of populations.

study does not have the power to establish or confirm causal interactions, owing to the fact that alternative interpretations of the observed relations are always possible. For example, changes in eating habits, smoking or exercise might reasonably be said to accompany many of the social changes which have been related to the onset of disease.

But although the findings of studies remain weak in their causal implications when considered individually, this applies to a far lesser extent when they are considered *en masse*. Moreover, there is a very large amount of this descriptive information. I believe it is the themes and consistencies which emerge when sifting through this proliferation of descriptive data which provide the most valuable insights into the psychology of becoming ill.

In assessing theories, hypotheses, and ideas about psychosomatic influence, whether from the standpoint of factors that improve or factors that worsen a condition, one is therefore compelled to play a quite different game to that of progressing logically, step by step, from one clearcut experimental test to the next. The task is much more complicated and difficult. It is to deduce what is going on from a welter of suggestive and insinuating data, because these, as opposed to the facts which the 'hard line' experimentalist deals in, are virtually the only kind of data available.

We shall now turn to evidence bearing on the question of whether psychological and social circumstances can produce or exacerbate illness. No attempt will be made to include all such data, as this would be a very large task in itself and several comprehensive reviews already exist [4–8]. Instead, what follows is intended to be a reasonably representative sample of the kinds of finding which have encouraged those researching into psychosomatic disease to carry on looking.

The topics which have interested investigators can be split into three main categories:

1. Circumstances, or 'life events', in an individual's life preceding the onset or worsening of a disease.

2. Personality traits linked to susceptibility.
3. Emotional states preceding and concurrent with a disease.

In this chapter we shall concentrate on studies in the first of these categories – those concerned with stressful life events and their effect on health. In the following chapter, studies linking personality types and emotional states to illness susceptibility will be discussed.

'Life events' and disease onset

The idea that upsetting or threatening 'life events' can affect health is not new. Allusions to it have been made by many physicians at many points in the history of medicine. The past decade, however, has witnessed an unprecedented intensification of scientific interest in this possibility. A large number of current research initiatives are directed towards trying to measure changes in an individual's environment (especially changes having social significance) and their effects on physiology and health. Indeed, it is probably fair to say that this particular limb of research is beginning to claim the attention of researchers more than any other.

Bereavement and loss

The 'broken heart' syndrome, the idea that separation from a close friend or relative increases the risk of becoming ill, is entrenched in Western literature. In the 1950s, researchers set out to see if they could establish it as a scientific fact. Higher than average disease rates were recorded among recently bereaved people [9, 10]. Le Shan and Worthington [11] found that cancer mortality rates were higher among widows, widowers and divorcees than among married and single people, taking into account the effect of age. Cancer patients as a group were also studied [12, 13], and it was found that among them there was an above average incidence of recent loss of an important relationship, the individuals concerned having failed to form alternative attachments.

During this time, many psychiatrists published case histories and other findings which appeared to support the loss-disease hypothesis. Their ideas about what constituted a 'loss' experience were not necessarily restricted to bereavement or marital separations. Green and others [14, 15] reported that very high percentages of patients with leukaemia and lymphoma had developed symptoms in the wake of experiences which could be characterized as traumatic losses reacted to with feelings of despair. The types of experience listed include predominantly the death or serious illness of a close relative or friend, but also divorce, change in residence or school, menopause, the advent of a sibling viewed as a rival, and the threat of separation from the mother. Litz [16] studied patients with hyperthyroidism, and identified similar types of event prior to the onset of symptoms, including deaths of close family, separations, infidelity and desertion. Chambers and Reiser [17] observed patients with congestive heart failure, and defined the 'precipitant' as 'loss of security through rejection by some key figure upon whom the patient was dependent'. Again, this included mainly deaths, as well as desertions, rejections and evictions. Similar conclusions, giving almost identical descriptions of the precursors to disease, have been drawn in connection with pulmonary tuberculosis, pernicious anaemia, multiple sclerosis, ulcerative colitis, disseminated lupus erythematosus, Raynaud's disease, asthma, and various other serious illnesses [18–26]. Reports that the losses encountered were reacted to with feelings of hopelessness and despair were frequent.

There is, however, a serious snag in drawing conclusions from these studies.

It can be argued that if a researcher looks hard enough for a 'loss experience' in the recent life of someone, especially where this is loosely defined, there is a good chance he will discover one. Assessment of life events preceding the onset of symptoms was most often made by interviewing patients. There are a variety of reasons why people might respond to the questions they are asked in an interview by overplaying their recent distress – perhaps because they want sympathy from the doctor, perhaps because they feel the need to give positive answers to his probing questions, or perhaps simply because they generalize the suffering experienced on account of their illness to the preceding months. Unfortunately there is no way of deciding between these possibilities. If an equivalent group of healthy people, or patients who were not chronically ill, had been interviewed in exactly the same way, and a difference found between their reported experiences and those of the chronically ill sample, the conclusions reached would be on much firmer ground. But no such comparison or 'control' groups were included in these studies, with the result that we lack this vital information on the 'base rate' of people's reporting loss experiences.

To interpret the findings from these studies is therefore not easy. The most valuable information to come from them is perhaps that contained in the documentaries which a few authors give on individual patients and the course of their symptoms over time in relation to changes in their social environment. In several studies, cases have been described in which symptoms initially appeared in the wake of a separation experience, disappeared on re-establishment of the lost person or advent of a substitute, and reappeared again on a second separation or its threat [14, 17, 18, 20, 22, 23, 27]. Especially interesting are those accounts of instances in which the doctor himself came to function as a replacement for the lost person. There are reports of symptoms improving under conditions of regular contact between patient and doctor, worsening on severance of this contact or the threat of severance (e.g. the patient about to be discharged), and improving again on renewed contact – these changes not being attributable to any concurrent treatment [17, 28, 29].

Other investigations have incorporated some form of comparison group into their design. Lombard and Potter [30], in a survey of 523 cases of cervical cancer, and a similar number of matched disease-free controls, found that 20.7 percent of subjects with cancer had been separated or divorced at some time during their lives, contrasted to 6.7 percent of the control group. Schmale and Iker [31] successfully predicted cervical cancer in suspected cases, on the hypothesis that malignancies would be diagnosed more frequently in women who reported that they had reacted to a life event in the six months prior to their presentation at the clinic with feelings of hopelessness. It is noteworthy that objectively defined losses were found to be similarly distributed among those with and those without malignancies, even though most of the predictive life events can be unambiguously characterized as involving loss or the threat of loss. These were: major illness of a family member, husband unfaithful, husband rejected patient's goals, and the loss of a friend. The authors emphasize that the key factor in predicting malignancies was not the occurrence of one of these events so much as the reaction to it with feelings of hopelessness.

The experience of loss 'actual or threatened' was found by Mutter and Schleifer [26] to differentiate children aged six to twelve, with infectious and other diseases common to a paediatric setting, from healthy children of the same age group. Unfortunately examples of the types of experience included in this category are not given by the authors.

Using several interview scales Parens et al. [32] assessed student nurses after their first six weeks, and found that scores on an 'object loss' scale were able to predict general illness over the subsequent eight months. Loss was assessed predominantly in terms of the recent death or illness of a major relation. The diseases observed included respiratory, gastrointestinal, head, skin and other complaints.

Thiel et al. [33] compared fifty men, aged 40–60, who had just had a heart attack with a matched group of healthy control subjects. A significantly higher incidence of divorce was identified among heart patients than among the controls, and there was also a tendency for heart patients to report more frequent losses of friends over recent years than was the case for controls.

Kasl and Cobb [34] recorded sustained high blood pressure among people who were losing their jobs, and Cobb [35] has described differences between men going through the process of being made redundant, and a control group, in terms of several physiological measures obtained by sampling blood serum and urine.[4]

A negative finding was obtained by Imboden *et al.* [36]. Reports of losses over the previous year were elicited from 455 employees. 26 percent reported some kind of separation, which underlines the need for control groups in these studies. Separation experiences were not found to be associated with visits to the dispensary over the subsequent 18 months.

This last study is widely quoted as providing the definitive verdict on the loss-disease issue. This is odd, for while highlighting some very important points concerning the planning of this kind of research, an extremely narrow view was taken by the authors of what constituted a 'loss'. An individual was classed as having experienced a loss if he reported instances of marital separation, divorce, or death or illness in the family in response to six standard yes/no questions. No proviso was made for losses outside the family, and no account was taken of the context, and thus the meaning, of a separation to a person. The diseases suffered by the subjects in this experiment over the 18-month follow-up period are not described, but they were measured by number of visits to the dispensary 'in the event of any kind of illness or medical complaint regardless of its nature'. As such, they are unlikely to be comparable in severity with conditions of the patients who have been studied in other investigations.

Evidence linking loss with breast cancer would appear to be weaker than that relating to other diseases [37–40]. Typically, patients with breast lumps are seen and their recent history of loss experiences assessed at a stage before their diagnostic biopsy has been carried out. Reports from patients subsequently discovered to have malignant tumors are then compared with those from patients whose tumors are found to be benign. In considering these studies, a query arises concerning the use of patients with benign tumors as controls. To what extent these

[4] Norepinephrine, serum creatinine, serum uric acid, serum cholesterol, and serum urea nitrogen.

patients represent a healthy sample, especially since a percentage of the tumors diagnosed as benign may later turn out to be malignant, is a problem which must be borne in mind.

Demographic surveys of the incidence of heart disease in relation to widowed, divorced, separated, single and married states do not lend unqualified support to the loss-disease hypothesis either, although on balance the evidence is in its favour. Marks [41] has reviewed eight studies potentially relevant to the separation question. These were concerned with heart disease. It was found that four studies gave evidence of higher than average (sometimes substantially higher) rates of disease among widowed, divorced or separated people, one gave evidence of lower than average rates among widowed or divorced, and one gave evidence of lower rates among single, widowed or divorced than among married people (a Swedish sample). The remaining two surveys showed no clear pattern with respect to separation in general, although there was a tendency in both these for widows and widowers to show higher rates.[5] The evidence from these studies taken together thus supports a link between disease and bereavement more strongly than one between disease and other forms of separation not involving death.

What is it possible to conclude from this research? The over-interpretation of findings from studies in the 1950s, which were poorly designed and often lacking control groups, gave rise to something of a reaction against the loss-disease hypothesis which can still be felt today. But reactions have a tendency to swing too far. The body of research is impressive and worth another look. It would certainly be a mistake to place too much emphasis on the results of any one study, taken on their own. Nevertheless, quite similar findings have emerged from very different research initiatives using different ways of assessing 'loss', different subject samples, and concentrating on different diseases. It is as much a mistake to brush aside those studies which omit a control group as to accept uncritically

[5] Several interactions of these effects with age, and one with sex, were also found.

their conclusions. Many contain valuable detailed descriptions of the temporal fluctuation in patients' symptoms in relation to key separation, reunions and substitutions.

It seems likely that too narrow a definition of loss, or insensitivity to its significance to a person, tends to decrease the chance of getting positive results.[6] This may have a bearing on the negative findings with breast cancer. In two out of the three studies where no association between loss and malignancy was found a relatively narrow definition of loss was adopted, and a comparatively insensitive technique of measuring it employed [37, 40]. Nevertheless, a wider view of what counts as a loss experience was taken in the third study [39], but a weakness in the design of this study, to do with the way in which the authors collected information from their subjects, means that the results of this cannot be considered definitive either. An openended interview was used in which subjects were asked to recount any recent experiences they had found distressing. Brown [43] has pointed out that this kind of reliance on subjects' own spontaneous (unsolicited) reports is hazardous, since there are several reasons to expect selectivity and bias in what is said. The fact that people are not the most impartial commentators on events in their own lives, especially events that happened some time in the past, does not need emphasizing. Even the most open and forthcoming individuals are not exempt from normal human strategies of defence, such as the repression of experiences they found painful. Conversely, the significance of quite minor occurrences can become exaggerated out of all proportion. Human memory, in particular the memory of emotionally charged events, is not like a passive store. Its contents become distorted and elaborated with the passage of time. Thus, when someone is asked by an interviewer to recount past events which have distressed him, he cannot be relied on to produce an 'objective' commentary.

Demographic studies, involving large-scale statistical comparisons between groups of people, by their nature go no further than to reveal the incidence of bereavements, divorce, etc., and

[6] This point has been made by several researchers [25, 37, 38, 42, 43].

disregard individual circumstances. It is to be expected that important contextual information will be lost through such an approach. One can be fairly certain, for example, that obtaining a divorce will have little psychological impact on partners who have been living apart for some time. So perhaps it is not surprising that the support which this branch of research offers the loss-disease hypothesis is the weakest of all.

Without a doubt, this group of studies as a whole is highly suggestive of a link between loss and disease. But what exactly is it that is lost? A few authors have tried to answer this question by going deeper into the loss-disease hypothesis and describing what, in their opinion, characterizes the experience which leads to the onset or exacerbation of symptoms in their patients. Their comments afford us a clue. The crucial ingredient of the 'precipitating' event has been variously described as the loss of security [17], difficulty in adjusting to the event [42], and the erosion of self-esteem [18, 48]. Flarscheim's detailed and careful account of the course of symptoms in three pulmonary tuberculosis patients is especially interesting. He writes that 'the loss of a love object *per se* was not necessarily associated with the onset of respiratory symptoms...', (the key factor being) '...the loss of a significant relationship that had enabled them to sustain conformity of behaviour and self-esteem'. (Flarscheim, 1958)

These remarks are important. They suggest that the essential factor may not be the loss of another person in itself but rather the loss of a familiar, well-established pattern of life; a pattern which perhaps was only made possible through another person's company. As Wolff [44] points out, all change involves losing something, and changes demanding the revision of long-held attitudes, beliefs, values and life-styles are those most resisted and those which people find hardest to cope with.

Adjustment to a new job or role

How well people cope with bereavement or separation is, in a sense, how well they adjust to the new situation of being without the lost companion. Closely related to this is the question of the adequacy of people's adjustment to a new position in life, or to use the psychological expression, a new 'role'.

Hinkle[7] observed that among 24 female office employees, those who fitted most comfortably into given niches, and who appeared most suited to the job they were in, enjoyed better overall health. Parens *et al.* [32], in their study of first year student nurses, found that scores on an 'adjustment scale' could predict health over the ensuing eight months. This scale contained questions about the number of social contacts established, satisfaction with these, and contentment with the work and living conditions. The better the adjustment, as measured in this way, the freer a person was from symptoms. Sheldon and Hooper [47] studied marital adjustment, assessing 26 couples over their first year of marriage. Good health was related to good marital adjustment, both being assessed by interviews and questionnaires.

In students requesting treatment for respiratory disorders, the severity of the disorder was found by Jacobs *et al.* [48] to be associated with evidence of poor functioning and being unsettled over the previous year, here again assessed by interviews and questionnaires. 'Role crisis', 'unresolved role conflict', 'alienation' and 'a feeling of absence of self-esteem and failure' were cited by the authors as the main precursors to illness.

Thus, there is reasonable agreement that poor adjustment to a new role is associated with increased incidence of disease. But a certain amount of doubt must remain concerning the direction of causation behind the relations obtained – i.e., whether poor adjustment leads to disease, or vice versa.

Social mobility

Several researchers have been interested to know whether an especially high incidence of disease is to be found among people who change social class during their lifetime. Such transition

[7] See [45, 46].

is referred to by sociologists as 'social mobility', most frequently meaning movement from a lower to a higher social class (upward mobility). There are a variety of reasons why a high rate of disease might be expected in association with a significant change in social status. Someone who finds himself in a new social milieu has to conform to expectations with which he is unfamiliar. Demands on him to revise his old customs may be severe, inducing conflict and strain in the new situation.

Two comprehensive reviews of findings in relation to heart disease reveal a solid body of findings supporting a link between social mobility and disease [41, 49]. Some recent mixed evidence, however, including failures to replicate this association, cautions against drawing oversimplified conclusions too fast. A number of factors seem to be influential in determining whether a relation between mobility and disease is found. Jenkins [50] gives as examples time, place and nature of the disease.

More critical than these factors may be the way in which mobility is conceived and measured. There is a conspicuous lack of agreement over this. Different investigators have used grossly different definitions and methods of assessment of social status, some based on employment, others on income, others on education, etc., together with widely different criteria of what constitutes a change in status. This is certainly one of the main sources of variation in studies, and until a more standard method of assessment is adopted it will remain hard to spot and disentangle the other interacting variables, if there are any. But complex or not, a link between mobility and heart disease is strongly implied by research findings.

Status incongruity

Quite apart from any change in his own personal status, an individual may move in different social circles, and these may make incongruous, or even incompatible, demands on him. This eventuality has become known as 'status incongruity'. The pattern of findings relating incidence of disease to status incongruity is very similar to that on social mobility, and an identical problem arises – that of the many different ways in which status incongruity has been defined and measured.

However, one additional observation is possible. Where status incongruity is defined and measured in terms of a discrepancy in status between a person's parents, what findings there are support a link between status incongruity and disease more consistently than if some other definition is used, such as a difference in status between an individual and his spouse. An unusually high incidence of status incongruity has been discovered among the parents of women with rheumatoid arthritis [51]. Also, it has been noticed that heart disease is especially prevalent among people whose parents belong to different religious denominations [52].

The findings of studies using other measures of status incongruity tend to be complex and interactive, often disputed, and sometimes even negative [53–58].

Geographical mobility

Evidence relating the extent to which people change their place of residence (other than by immigration) to incidence of disease shows somewhat better agreement than do studies of social mobility and studies of status incongruity, possibly because moving home is a less ambiguous business, and thus is easier to identify and record.

Holmes [59] found that tuberculosis rates were higher than normal among ethnic groups who were in the minority in their neighbourhood, and also among people who lived alone and made many occupational and residential moves. He describes these people as 'strangers trying to find a role in the contemporary American scene'.

A study of executives by Christenson and Hinkle [60] revealed that the highest proportion of illnesses of all sorts occurred among those working and living in a social environment perceived as new and unfamiliar.

An interesting investigation of residents of Easter Island is reported by Cruz-Coke *et al.* [61]. Islanders who had migrated to the mainland of Chile to take up urban jobs, and who had then returned, presumably after they had adapted to the new way of life, were compared with those who had stayed behind on the Island. Chronically high blood pressure was found only among the migrants.

Medalie *et al.* [62], in a prospective study, found that there was a high rate of angina pectoris in men who had lived in three or more countries since they started employment.

Immigration

Immigration in itself is not always associated with proneness to disease. Heart disease rates have been reported as both higher and lower than average in foreign-born subjects [41]. Wardwell *et al.* [63], in an analysis of three field studies aimed at relating social variables to the incidence of heart disease, showed that the lowest rates were among the foreign born, with higher rates among the first and subsequent generations to be born in America. The highest rate of all was found to be among first generation Americans with one parent born in Europe and the other in the United States.

These studies illustrate just how complex the relationship between health and immigration is. Sometimes, the findings of studies appear to contradict one another. But some observations on the blood pressure of American doctors and nurses who worked in mission hospitals in China during the 1920s give us a hint as to why this might be. Two independent investigators [64, 65] actually recorded a *drop* in blood pressure to healthier levels coincident with the move to China. The explanation which the authors offer for this refers to the fact that the inmates of mission stations made up a strong, mutually supportive group. They maintained a high level of morale and self-esteem, seeing themselves as working collaboratively towards a valuable goal.

The relevance of these two reports is this. Immigrants coming to live among fellow immigrants, where many of the old familiar traditions are carried on, encounter a much more cushioned form of social discontinuity than do those who are suddenly exposed to an alien community and totally cut off from others with a similar cultural background. Marks [41] considers it well established from sociological studies that the first generation to be *born* in America is normally the one to suffer greatest cultural 'shock', i.e. the one required to make the biggest adaptation from the customs of the parental home to American ways. Foreign born adult immigrants to the United States tend to avoid extreme culture-conflict through engaging in traditional customs within their own smaller ethnic settlements.

Medalie *et al.* [62], studying Israelis, also found the highest incidence of heart attacks to be among first generation Israelis whose parents were born elsewhere. In this study, unlike that of Wardwell *et al.*, second and subsequent generation Israelis showed the lowest rates, with intermediate rates in immigrants.

Studies of immigrants therefore make it clear that simply moving from one country to another does not necessarily cause a deterioration in health. What seems to be important is the pressure to change one's cultural outlook – the exposure to social demands and expectations that are unfamiliar, and that require a knowledge and acceptance of the new community and its culture which the individual does not have. Syme [66] describes the process of going through these changes as 'cultural mobility', and suggests that this is the factor responsible for enhanced disease risk. Moss [67] makes a closely related proposal. In his view disease results from cultural 'alienation' or 'anomie', restricted social involvement, uncertainty, and social incompetence on the part of the newcomer. The converse of this – the situation associated with sustained resistance to disease – is depicted as a condition of rapport and frequent social interchange between the individual and his social environment.

From a review of the evidence, Marks [41] infers that the conflicts arising from exposure to different cultures are experienced more acutely when represented within the parental family than when encountered outside it. A child has to go through a long and complicated process of learning how to relate effectively to his social environment. One of the most influential parts of this socialization process involves the child modelling his behaviour on that of his parents [68]. It is to be expected that contradictory models will result in confused learning, and ultimately in social uncertainty and social incompetence. Perhaps also this helps to account for the fact that status incongruity seems to be most harmful when defined in terms of a difference in status between the subject's parents.

It is likely that a move from one country to another will involve changes in physical variables, such as diet, living conditions and exercise habits. In some studies there have been attempts to take these into account. Even so, it is particularly important not to place too much reliance on any one finding in this area when forming conclusions regarding health. Studies of immigration are also subject to the confounding fact that migration is selective, which is to say that those who migrate from one country to another cannot necessarily be considered representative either of those living in the new or of those living in the old country. For example, some people might migrate *because* they are ill and a change of environment has been recommended by their doctor. But, as is the case with studies of bereavement, in spite of the many variables limiting the ease with which conclusions can be drawn, it would be a mistake to ignore the trends and themes in this research. To do so would be to miss the most useful sort of information it is possible to get from psychosomatic research in natural settings. Several authors have alluded to the consensus of 'evidence', qualifications and conclusions [46, 69, 70].

Rapidly changing social environment

If a society is forced to change its established way of life at such a rate that long held traditions suddenly become redundant and inappropriate to the new social demands, we might expect a similar effect on its members to that on an individual when he moves to an alien cultural setting. A number of anthropological and sociological observations on the effects of intensive urbanization on primitive rural cultures and sub-cultures provide information on the occurrence of disease in such a situation.

Scotch [71] studied Zulus living in urban and rural settings in South Africa. The rural native reserve was ethnologically classified as more culturally stable than the urban setting. Those Zulus in the urban environment were found to have significantly higher average blood pressure levels[8] than the rural Zulu. Dietary factors were not believed to explain the difference. A similar pattern was noted by Hoobler *et al.* in relation to Guatamalan Indians [72].

Tyrola and Cassel [73] have made a study of the effects on heart disease of a ten-year programme of urbanization in North Carolina. The death rate from heart disease was seen to be highest in areas where there was most change, and it tended to increase with accelerating urbanization.

Henry and Cassel [74], in a detailed review of demographic and anthropological comparisons relating to hypertension,[9] conclude that obesity and dietary factors may not be as significant in explaining variations in blood pressure between different populations as social factors. Summarizing the results from eighteen world-wide surveys of average blood pressure levels within different cultures, they suggest that the disruption of the strong cohesion which is endemic to primitive societies may be more significant. This collation of findings clearly shows that blood pressure in 'stable' cultures remains low with advancing age, while that in changing cultures shows an increase which is often dramatic.

Caution regarding the interpretation of these data is again called for. But alternative explanations are thoroughly discussed, and notwithstanding these the authors' conclusion is strongly supported. This is that blood pressure levels at any particular age, and rates of increase with age, are lower ... 'where the culture is stable, traditional forms are honoured and the group members are secure in their roles and adapted to them by early experience.' (Henry and Cassel, 1969)

[8] Age-related.
[9] Chronically high blood pressure.

Some records of blood pressure levels within smaller-scale sub-cultural communities are also summarized by Henry and Cassel and examined in the light of the prevailing social climate. Here too, consistency with this conclusion is striking. The lowest and most stable blood pressures occur predominantly within socially isolated communities carrying on a historically old way of life. High and rising levels are found within groups undergoing social change. The rises within a particular group are invariably simultaneous with an assault on the old way of life due to irresistible pressure for cultural 'development'.

Leaf [75] has made a study of three different, remotely located small populations where it was rumoured the aged members of the community enjoyed exceptional freedom from debilitating illness.[10] His comments reinforce Henry and Cassel's conclusions. He writes:

It is characteristic of each of the areas I visited that the old people continue to be contributing, productive members of their society. The economy in all three areas is agrarian, there is no fixed retirement age and the elderly make themselves useful doing many necessary tasks around the farm or the home ... People who no longer have a necessary role to play in the social and economic life of their society generally deteriorate rapidly. (Leaf, 1973)

Linking up with these observations, Antonovsky [76] has found preliminary support for his proposal that social ties with other people, and with communities in general, are factors which contribute to resistance to disease.

The effect of a changing social environment was explored from a different angle by Cassel [77]. Two groups of lowly paid male shift workers were studied. A comparison was made between those individuals working on shifts whose composition was fixed (i.e. who always encountered the same co-workers),

---

[10] The village of Vilcabamba in Ecuador, the small principality of Hunza in West Pakistan and the highlands of Georgia in the Soviet Caucasus.

and those on shifts whose composition varied. Substantially higher than average levels of serum cholesterol (a chemical whose sustained high level in the blood increases the rise of heart disease) were recorded in the latter group, but not in the former.

Social support

Evidence from many different quarters supports the notion that what might loosely be called 'social support' militates against proneness to becoming ill.

De Araujo *et al.* [78] found the steroid requirements of chronic asthmatics to be significantly less among patients considered to be 'well supported' by their families and friends.[11] Foster *et al.* [80] followed 21 patients on renal dialysis[12] through a period of approximately two years, and found that having at least one parent still alive and being a Roman Catholic were factors associated with survival. 79 percent of the survivors in this sample had established and maintained a nuclear family, contrasted with only 42 percent of those who died, although this difference was not technically significant. Hagburg and Malmquist [81] also found that having 'regular social contacts' was prognostically favourable for the rehabilitation of 23 patients on dialysis.

An investigation by Cobb [35] in which measurements were made of various chemicals in the blood and urine of men being made redundant, was mentioned earlier on in this chapter. The degree of social support[13] offered by the men's families over the terminal period of their employment was also studied. Significant rises in the levels of serum uric acid and serum cholesterol – chemicals known to constitute risk factors for certain diseases – were noted in the group as a whole, but social support appeared to exert a moderating influence. The greater the

---

[11] As measured by the Berle Index [79].
[12] Kidney machines.
[13] Measured on a 13 item scale.

social support offered, the less the elevation in levels of these chemicals was found to be.

One of the strongest and most resilient forms of social support is that provided by religious communities: particularly small, active, close-knit groups. Unfortunately, members of such sects are inclined to observe esoteric customs concerning eating, drinking, smoking and sexual behaviour, which makes causal inferences even more problematical than usual. Syme [82] however recorded a lower death rate from diseases of all kinds in Adventists than among others in the same social milieu. If this difference is not attributable to physical agents, it is consistent with the social support hypothesis.

Evidence concerned with affiliation to one of the major religious denominations also tends to support expectations. Comstock *et al.* [83] have presented a review of findings relating frequency of church attendance to the incidence of various diseases. Hypertension, heart disease, cervical cancer, cancer of the rectum, tuberculosis, articulosclerotic heart deaths, emphysema and cirrhosis of the liver are all conditions that have been documented as less frequent, sometimes substantially so, among regular church-goers. Attempts to eliminate some of the more obvious alternative explanations (e.g. the likely differences in socio-economic status, smoking and drinking habits) were made in several of these studies, but yet again the possible compromising influence of these factors cannot be discounted. Findings showing no link between disease and religion on the other hand are reported for cancer of the colon and rectum. Winklestein and Rekate [84] also failed to find any association with heart disease. However, the criterion of religiosity used in this last study was no more than nominal affiliation with a religious denomination. Evidence of active involvement was not sought. One might therefore surmise that among those subjects who recorded an affiliation with a major religion were a fair number who were neither firmly committed nor actively involved. It is even possible that the socially desirable aspects of belonging to a religious grouping of some kind biased the information supplied by some individuals. Studies of nominal religion are therefore not a good standard for assessing the relation between involvement in a supportive community and disease.

An emergent theme

From the research reviewed so far it is clear that the idea of social factors as one of the potential influences on health is one that must be taken seriously. The substantial body of evidence collected over the past 15 years is forcing a re-assessment of the old idea that psychological risk factors are to be found in physical attributes of people's environments, such as noise or spatial confinement, or even in the classical 'stresses of modern life' syndrome, such as having a demanding job.

Two recently published review articles strongly reinforce the impression that social factors are of primary importance in the psychosomatic sequence. One is specifically concerned with the protective influence on health of social support [85], the other deals with mortality following bereavement, residential moves and retirement [86]. Both contain a considerable amount of evidence not touched on in this chapter, and both authors arrive at conclusions similar to the conclusions reached in the foregoing discussions.

It would be unreasonable to contest the powerful evidence implicating dietary factors, exercise and smoking in the causation of certain specific illnesses. But research under each of the somewhat arbitrary headings in this chapter, especially that involving cross-cultural comparisons, repeatedly suggests a link between social disorientation and general proneness to disease even when diet and smoking are taken into account. Cassel [79] arrives at a similar conclusion. In a review of research into social influences on disease, he mentions a series of studies which indicate that people deprived of a group membership or 'meaningful human contacts', and those living in an area where they are not accepted by the dominant majority, are high risks for certain psychiatric and respiratory diseases.

In drawing conclusions from their anthropological comparisons, Henry and Cassel refer as follows to those factors which appear to be critical in differentiating groups with different rates of hypertension:

> The distinction between these parameters does not depend on the presence or absence of a high state of technology and social sophistication, rather it appears to turn on the issue whether the society or group has an established tradition with a social structure which remains unchallenged during the lifetime of the oldest subjects. (Henry and Cassel, 1969)

Thus, research gives us one fairly clear directive. Most resistant to illness is the socially involved individual: the person who is well adjusted to a stable role within a supportive community.

Social Readjustment Rating Scale (SRRS)

One of the most avidly researched measures of psychological stress is a questionnaire scale devised in America, and associated with the names Holmes and Rahe [87]. It is referred to as the Social Readjustment Rating Scale. It consists of a list of 42 major life events, mainly unpleasant (see Appendix 1), arrived at *ad hoc* and believed by the authors on intuitive grounds to be 'stressful'. Subjects tick an event if it has happened to them over a specified recent period in their lives (e.g. one year or six months). A person's total score is said to represent an index of the amount of change in his life over this period, and is the quantity used to predict the likelihood of his becoming ill in the near future. Such predictions can be tested retrospectively or prospectively. In retrospective studies, the checklist is given to a group of patients whose symptoms have recently appeared, and also to a group of healthy control subjects; and the two groups are differentiated on the basis of their scores. In prospective studies, the checklist is given to a group of healthy individuals, and the likelihood of their becoming ill in the near future is calculated from their scores. Prospective predictions are tested by following up these individuals, over perhaps a five- or ten-year period, and recording the incidence of disease. Clearly the prospective approach provides the stronger test of the questionnaire's power to predict disease, but its disadvantages are that it is time consuming, costly and difficult to administer.

From Appendix 1 it will be obvious that some of the items in the SRRS list represent worse calamities than others. To get an idea of the relative distress value of each item, the list was administered to 400 healthy Americans who were asked to score every event for the amount of 'readjustment' they thought it required. The scores were to range from 0 to infinity, and marriage was arbitrarily assigned a score of 500 as a reference point. There was reasonably good agreement over the scores which should be assigned to the different items; and a weighting for each event, known as its Life Change Unit (LCU) value, was derived by taking the average score for each item and dividing it by 10 for convenience.

A considerable amount of research has gone into assessing the usefulness of a person's total LCU score as a predictor of illness. This has been reviewed by Rahe [4] and by Birley and Connolly [88]. The general conclusion which emerges is that the SRRS can be used to predict illness, both retrospectively and prospectively, but its power to do so is not great.[14] If large samples of individuals are studied, a weak effect of stress or disease, as defined and measured in this way, can be detected. However, no investigator would pretend to be able to predict disease on the basis of a measure of psychological stress alone, no matter how sophisticated this measure was. And as measures of the psychological risk-factor go, it seems likely that the SRRS is a relatively crude one, because of its insensitivity to the circumstances in which the life changes listed take place. For example, 'moving home' may represent more or less of an upheaval depending on a number of factors, such as whether or not it happens frequently, or voluntarily, or in the course of work. Similarly, as I pointed out in the section on loss, 'divorce'

[14] Most of the predictions made from the SRRS are confirmed at a low or marginal level of statistical significance.

may have very little impact if the two partners have been separated for any length of time.

Other criticisms have been levied at the SRRS. Several of the items are ambiguous. In item 7, for instance, what counts as a 'major change in health' (or indeed a 'family member') is not clear. It is uncertain whether 'retirement from work' (item 33) includes semi-retirement, and so on. There is also the possibility that LCU totals correlate more closely with a tendency to report symptoms than with genuine episodes of disease.

Significant advances in the assessment of psychological stress have been made by Brown [43]. Brown has devised an interview procedure in which subjects are asked whether each of a number of events (similar to those listed in the SRRS) has occurred in their recent lives. The topics covered by the interviewer are always the same, but unlike the SRRS the subject is encouraged to give a detailed description of the circumstances leading up to and surrounding each event. It was remarked earlier that people's memories of the distress experienced on account of some past event often undergo distortion as the event becomes distant in time. For this reason, subjective reports of the stressfulness of events are ignored altogether. Interviews are taped, and factual details of events and what led up to them, as they are recounted by the subject, are extracted. These factual details are then rated by trained personnel on a number of different scales. Because the questions put to people, and the way in which information is obtained and scored, are standard – i.e. the same each time – bias from other sources due to selective remembering and distorted reporting of 'stressful' events is reduced.

Brown's structured interview has been researched mainly with psychiatric patients [43], and the findings so far support the contention that it is a more sensitive measure than the SRRS. But it, too, has its drawbacks. The procedures involved are very time-consuming and expensive. To administer the interview and carry out the ratings requires training. Moreover, as with the SRRS, the list of questions put to people, and the ways of rating what is said, are determined in a more or less arbitrary manner. There is no guarantee that the most important questions are being asked. So much relies on the intuition of the authors; and this kind of guesswork, not based on any theory, is bound to result in measures that are somewhat hit-and-miss. Both methods, but especially the SRRS, can be compared with the use of a bulldozer in an archaeological dig. The bulldozer method has its uses; but a more sensitive and direct search – or, as Birley and Connolly [88] put it, 'the trowel, sieve and brush, on carefully selected sites' – is an important adjunct to larger scale approaches.

Animal studies

Do laboratory studies of animals corroborate any of the themes which emerge from human studies? The point has already been made that the 'social' situations experimentally contrived in animal experiments are crude by human standards, and represent at best only very rough approximations to everyday predicaments of people. One problem that has been much researched is whether an animal's susceptibility to disease is affected by its housing conditions. Positive correlations have been reported between conditions of isolation[15] and proneness to develop mammary tumours [89, 90], certain experimentally induced infections [91], and some other diseases [92]. However, when different diseases are studied, higher rates are observed among animals made to live in 'crowded' conditions [93, 94]. Moreover, some studies have failed to find any effect at all attributable to isolation or crowding. Ader [92] puts the mixed results from these experiments down to an erroneous assumption that social conditions will affect all diseases in the same way, and also to vagueness in the use of the terms 'crowding' and 'isolation'. There is no agreement between investigators about how much space an animal requires, and consequently there is divergence over what constitutes 'crowded' living conditions.

In an experiment carried out by Dechambre and Gosse [95],

[15] Housing in single cages.

the enforced isolation of previously grouped mice, *and* the enforced grouping of previously solitary mice, were both found to be conducive to the growth of grafted tumours. This finding opens up another possibility: that it is not so much 'crowding' in itself, or 'isolation' in itself, which affects the likelihood of disease occurring, but change in the accustomed social conditions.

Another experiment, carried out by Henry *et al.* [96], showed that the formal social organization which had been allowed to develop in a colony of mice (involving a hierarchical order of individual dominance, a co-operative nursery and other mutually beneficial arrangements) was disrupted after an extended period of 'force breeding' – the regular removal of newborn pups. A 100 percent incidence of mammary tumour formation was seen to occur simultaneously with the breakdown of order in the previously socialized groups, a rate considerably higher than that observed in two control groups.

Calhoun [97] has developed a method of allowing mice to breed freely in an 'ideal' but spatially restricted environment. Here again, the regular pattern is that initially a highly structured hierarchical social system evolves, with individual animals adopting different co-operative roles within the community. But as soon as the number of mice increases to the point where there are too many animals for too few roles, individuals begin to compete so fiercely for the limited number of roles available that there is a breakdown of the social order, and a consequent near total disintegration of the animals' normal adaptive behaviour. Physiological abnormalities have been discovered in such animals [97], and Henry and his colleagues have identified hypertension and signs of chronic cardiovascular disease under similar conditions of social deterioration [98, 99].

There is an obvious similarity between descriptions of the state of the social environment in these artificial animal 'cities', just before outbreak of disease, and the overall picture which has emerged from the many differently styled studies of humans. In both cases, a high risk of disease is found in individuals who seem to have no place in their immediate social surroundings. Whether this is through their own lack of familiarity with the requirements and conventions of their social environment, or through deprivation of an opportunity to engage in socially sanctioned pursuits, disease-prone individuals are characterized by being unable to become part of the social unit through relating to it in a meaningful way. Thus, in spite of the reservations regarding experiments with animals that are expressed in several places throughout this book, it can be said that the less structured, more 'naturalistic' experiments do bring us a step closer to understanding what is important about social factors in relation to disease. They provide an insight which can be linked up with themes emerging from studies of people.

Early influence

Any discussion of life events in association with illness would be incomplete without mention of the belief shared by many that a person's early experience can affect his susceptibility to disease in later life. It is likely that infantile and childhood experiences mould a person's characteristic style of coping with social change. Several of those investigating the loss-disease issue have discovered, in the history of the patients studied, not only a high incidence of recently experienced losses, but also a greater than normal number of traumatic separations in infancy [13, 20, 37, 100, 101]. It will be recalled from the preceding sections on status incongruity and immigration that the effect of exposure to divergent cultural systems appears to be particularly acute when encountered during childhood. The impression one gets is of a child confronted with two incompatible examples on which to model his own behaviour.

Animal studies have confirmed that certain kinds of early social experience, notably premature separation from the mother, can adversely affect subsequent adaptation in many ways. Early separation can enhance later susceptibility to disease, increase the risk of death, and decrease longevity.

Studies of early 'stimulation', especially the effects of holding, handling and pain on later susceptibility have produced some interesting but confusing findings. In general these findings support the contention that early stimulation is influential, at least in the species studied [92].[16]

That the treatment of the child should affect his later ability to cope with the types of social change which seem so important in relation to disease makes good intuitive sense, and is generally supported by research. The nature of these early influences, however, still remains somewhat obscure.

In conclusion, at least a dozen studies have supported the folk belief that recently bereaved people are more than normally prone to illness of various sorts. Other types of 'loss experience' besides bereavement have been linked to disease onset, and the context in which they occur and their meaning to the subject are factors which appear to be all important. Inadequate adjustment to a new role or position would seem to be associated with poor health. Research has linked social mobility and status incongruity to disease, albeit in a somewhat complex way which is not yet fully understood, maybe partly because of the different meanings it is possible to give to these terms. Geographical mobility, or moving, a much less ambiguous concept, has been shown to relate to disease in a more straightforward way. In assessing the impact of immigration we are brought round to recognizing the cushioning effect of a supporting local immigrant community which perpetuates some of the old customs. High disease risk appears to correlate less with immigration itself than with having to adjust to and integrate into an unfamiliar society: a contingency often experienced most acutely by the children of immigrants. In societies undergoing a heavy programme of change and urbanization, disease and disease risk are highest where the assault on the traditional life-style is greatest. Remarkable parallels to this can be seen in animal studies in which a similar kind of social disruption is produced experimentally. Not surprisingly, the presence of 'social sup-

---

[16] Mainly rodents.

port', vague though this term is, reliably correlates with good prognosis, health and survival.

The limited success of Holmes and Rahe's Social Readjustment Rating Scale encourages the belief that the psychological risk factor for serious illness is something that can be measured. The power of this scale to predict disease is not great, due in part to its insensitivity to the context and meaning of 'life changes'. Brown's interview technique fares better in this respect, but it was suggested that both measures are crude and wasteful of resources because both are the product of guesswork rather than theory.

From a large and varied assortment of findings, we can begin to piece together a picture of the high risk individual. He emerges as someone in the throes of significant social change which for one reason or another leaves him socially paralysed – unable to relate to his changed situation in a meaningful and effective manner.

Personality

Research aimed at linking disease-proneness to personality type has had a much more chequered history than that dealing with 'life events'. In the 1950s, the psychoanalyst Alexander tried to establish that people suffering from particular diseases display characteristic personality traits. Asthma patients, for example, were believed to be characterized by an inhibition of the urge to communicate with others or to cry [1]. But evidence for Alexander's theory has turned out to be insufficient for interest in it to be sustained.

Indeed, for the most part, evidence linking personality patterns to disease has been very disappointing. Overall, research has failed to support the idea that there are disease-prone personalities. Perhaps this is not surprising considering the wide differences in opinion which exist between psychologists and psychoanalysts, and between the various schools within these disciplines, about how personality should be measured. There is not even general agreement about the nature of personality itself. This is undoubtedly one reason for the disenchantment area of enquiry (not only among psychosomatic researchers [2, 3]). Interest in it has steadily declined since its popularity in the 1950s.

Heart disease and 'Type A' behaviour

However, there are exceptions to this, a noteworthy one being evidence linking a particular style of behaviour to heart disease. Very similar sets of traits have been repeatedly identified in coronary prone patients. Heart patients have been described as overly concerned with the need to feel competent and responsible [4], typically hard driving [5], overly committed to their work [6], and excessively committed to their socializing and leisure activities [7, 8]. Bruhn *et al.* [9] have said that they show the 'Sysiphus reaction' – an effortful striving against apparently heavy odds, with little sense of accomplishment or satisfaction.

In 1959, Friedman and Rosenman [10] attempted to sum up the coronary-prone personality in their well known description of the 'Type A behaviour pattern'. This involves at least one of the following characteristics: intense striving for achievement, competitiveness, overcommitment to work, a profound sense of time urgency, impatience and hostility. Jenkins [11, 12] has reviewed research on this and similar descriptions of personality, and finds considerable collective support for its association with proneness to heart disease.

Since Friedman and Rosenman's original description of the Type A individual, the linking of this behaviour pattern to heart disease has become a fairly fashionable field of research. But descriptions by other authors of patients with non-coronary diseases sometimes bear more than a passing resemblance to descriptions of the Type A individual. Abse *et al.* [13] found younger lung cancer patients to be overly conscientious in work attendance. Moos [14], reviewing findings concerned with rheumatoid arthritis, found agreement that arthritic patients tend to be self-sacrificing, perfectionist, and overly conscientious. McClary *et al.* [15] observed an unusual emphasis on activity and independence in patients with disseminated lupus erythematosus. Hinkle [16] concludes from his many studies of the incidence of disease in different natural settings that those most prone to ill health see their environment as more demanding, and their jobs as more unsatisfying, than healthy controls. These findings certainly caution against too narrow a focus, and an exclusive preoccupation with Type A and heart disease. If Type A is a style of behaviour exhibited by the coronary prone individual, as research suggests, it seems that something not too far removed from Type A may also be in evidence among people prone to other illnesses.

In addition to the considerable bulk of evidence confirming that heart patients tend to set themselves rigorous, sometimes even impossible, standards of achievement in their work, other studies have discovered similar perfectionist attitudes in different areas of their lives. Minc [17] has stated that coronary prone patients are more than normally concerned with doing the socially accepted thing. They have been described as highly self-controlled [18, 19], having a strong sense of duty [20], possessing obsessive traits and tending to overcontrol (suppress) emotions [21, 22]. Liesse *et al.* [23] also identified a higher level of rigidity and scrupulousness among heart disease patients than among healthy people. So the possibility must be kept in mind that the Type A style is a much researched special case of a more general disposition to set oneself high and rigid standards. Let us consider this possibility further.

I have cited some evidence pointing to the presence of certain traits similar to Type A characteristics in patients with non-coronary diseases. We also have reports of patients with heart disease which mention forms of rigidity that cannot be described as Type A. Is it possible to complete the picture by discovering other than Type A forms of rigidity in non-coronary patients as well? Abse *et al.* [13] list a number of studies in which traits of 'rigidity' have been discovered in cancer patients. Engel [24], in his extensive studies of ulcerative colitis, makes a point of stressing the rigid standards which these patients tend to have, their severe attitudes to morality, their conscientiousness, orderliness, neatness and punctuality. Hinkle's studies of illness records showed that those most prone to illness were those most inflexibly oriented to their goals, duties and responsibilities [16].

Evidence linking Type A behaviour specifically to heart disease is strong [12] and it is not my intention to contest it. The point to be taken from this discussion, however, is that to concentrate intensively on heart disease and Type A may result in other significant information being obscured.

The suppression of anger

Evidence has been presented, in connection with many different diseases, that people who tend to inhibit their feelings of aggression and hostility have a greater than normal chance of becoming ill [13, 25–28]. Hence, perhaps, the success of 'encounter groups' and other forms of therapy which encourage the patient to 'act out' what he feels. Now, research which has led to the discovery of fight/flight centres in the brain suggests that the expression of aggressive impulses is a normal biologically-based function. This being so, then continual suppression of anger can, in a sense, be regarded as another form of rigidity: an inflexible attitude which repeatedly censors hostile outbursts. Such a tendency has something in common with Type A behaviour and the traits discussed in association with it. All seem to involve a degree of antagonism between normal adaptive biological functions and the censors and restrictions which derive from society.

Before concluding this section, a recent study by Garrity *et al.* [29] bears mention. These authors investigated the hypothesis that certain personality factors increase the risk of illness following major life changes, as assessed by the Holmes-Rahe Social Readjustment Rating Scale. All three personality factors measured in this study[1] were successful in predicting health following life changes, their power to do so being independent of that of the Social Readjustment Rating Scale. The findings were as follows. People characterized by the trait of 'social conformity', indicating a tendency to behave in conventionally accepted ways and to advocate strongly approved social attitudes, were less at risk. More at risk were people characterized by the trait of 'liberal intellectualism', which entails intellectual flexibility, tolerance of ambiguity, tolerance of different points of view from one's own, an understanding of abstract concepts, and criticism of conventional dogma. Also more at risk were those characterized by 'emotional sensitivity',

---

[1] Measured using the 'Omnibus Personality Inventory' (1962).

involving artistic sensitivity and a willingness to express emotions and problems.

On the face of it, these last two findings seem to be at variance with the many reports linking enhaced risk with rigidity and a tendency to inhibit the expression of anger. This serves to illustrate how complex is the study of personality in relation to disease susceptibility. The many different ideas about personality, and the many different styles of measuring it which derive from these ideas, leave a strong element of doubt as to whether one author's use of terms such as 'rigidity' and 'flexibility' is strictly, or even roughly, equivalent to another's.

Subjects in the experiment by Garrity *et al.* were not patients but American college students, and the assessment of health changes was based mainly on the presence or absence of comparatively minor and temporary symptoms, some of which represent little more than day-to-day fluctuations in mood.[2] To assume that one group of personality factors will be linked both with a tendency to report these kinds of symptoms and with susceptibility to serious degenerative conditions is thus a very big step indeed, and at the moment an unwarranted one.

So research into personality is not a clear area. There is no consensus about how personality should be measured, and the findings linking personality to disease are muddled and often seriously contradictory. It is interesting that exactly the same can be said of attempts to discover a 'placebo resonder' – a personality pattern distinguishing those who characteristically respond to dummy treatment. The blame for this, too, almost certainly lies with inadequacies in existing concepts of personality and different ideas about what it is and how it should be measured.

Emotions

Researchers interested in the mental state of people prior to and throughout an illness have reported manifestations of many different emotions and feelings in their patients. A deep-seated sense of frustration, and feelings of dissatisfaction with life's

[2] e.g. 'depression or apathy', 'insomnia', 'lack of appetite'.

achievements are components of many descriptions of the coronary-prone personality [5, 6, 23, 30]. This is especially true of dissatisfactions regarding work. Similar work dissatisfactions have been found in a sample of patients with diverse illnesses [31]. A sense of failure and self-deprecation among patients has been described in various ways: for example, as a tendency to 'self-abasement' in heart patients [30], as 'absence of self-esteem' and 'ego-depletion' in patients with respiratory disorders [32, 33], and as 'devaluation of self' in patients suffering from ulcerative colitis [34]. It has also been noted that a failure of 'positive identification' is prognostically a bad sign in relation to survival on long-term renal dialysis [35].

The several studies made by Engel and Schmale of ulcerative colitis and other conditions have led these authors to accord a central place to what they call the 'giving up' reaction, involving feelings of despair, loss of self-esteem, hopelessness, and 'a disinterest in relating to objects, [and] lack of motivation to change what seems to be unchangeable' [36].

These are some of the more distinct themes. But a variety of different emotions have been recorded among people who are ill. Luborsky *et al.* [27] have reviewed studies of emotional states preceding the onset of symptoms, and concluded that the most frequently reported are: resentment, frustration, depression, anxiety and helplessness, in that order.

Aside from the obvious snag in studying reports of feelings given by ill people – i.e. the possibility that the illness itself will give rise to these feelings, perhaps even at a stage before symptoms appear – there are good reasons why people's reports of how they feel should not be relied on too heavily in research of this nature. Words denoting emotions are known to be applied in a somewhat nebulous fashion. Which of the many available terms a person will select to describe his feelings at any one time can be influenced by a number of factors – some of which are rather surprising. Schachter and Singer [37] have shown that people who are physiologically aroused on account of a high level of adrenalin in their blood may scan their immediate environment for clues as to how to 'interpret' what they feel. In a now classic study, subjects who believed they were participating in an experiment on visual perception were injected with adrenalin. Some were deliberately misinformed about what effects to expect from the injection. When a misinformed subject was shown into a 'waiting room' together with someone whom he believed to be another subject, but who was, in fact, a confederate of the experimenter, he took his cue from the reaction of the 'stooge' subject. If the stooge acted angrily, the real subject labelled his own feelings as anger, but if the stooge acted euphorically, so too did the real subject. This kind of unconscious search for an appropriate label for one's feelings is probably a phenomenon that happens a great deal in everyday life. It is not unusual for a man who has been startled by a tap on the shoulder to exhibit fear, and for this to give way almost instantaneously to anger when he recognizes his assailant. Schachter and Singer's experiment suggests an analysis of this situation along the following lines. After the initial reflexive moment of alarm, although the man realizes that what startled him does not constitute a threat he is nevertheless left with the physiological effects of the adrenalin which has been secreted. Because there are strong norms in most cultures against men appearing frightened, he unconsciously 'interprets' these effects as anger, such an interpretation being more in line with what is socially appropriate.

Which verbal label a person gives to his feelings can therefore be influenced by many things, including the reactions of those he sees around him and the setting in which the report is asked for. This is why it is very dangerous in a theory of psychosomatic disease to place too much emphasis on people's accounts of their feelings.

Thus the decline in interest over recent years in personality and emotion and their place in the psychosomatic scheme is largely due to the kinds of basic conceptual problem outlined in this chapter. One can hardly expect any consensus of findings from research when there is not even agreement between psychologists as to what personality is. Much the same is true of the study of emotions. In the discussion of hypnosis in Chapter 3, the conclusion was reached that the questions conventionally posed regarding the 'authenticity' of hypnotic phenomena turn out to be largely unanswerable when they are given close consideration. I suspect the same may also be true of many of the questions asked about personality and emotions and their relation to illness.

On the other hand, as we saw in the previous chapter, evidence pointing to an association between social upheaval and proneness to becoming ill is strong and reasonably consistent. Given that life events involving social change do put a person at risk, then his resourcefulness in coping with such situations, when they arise, is clearly a factor likely to influence the outcome. It could even tip the balance between health and illness. To look for systematic differences between people in their capacity to adapt to social change would therefore seem, on the face of it, to be a better bet than staying with old ideas about personality. But whether such differences exist and whether they can be reliably measured remains at present an open question.

How are we to make sense of the findings from research on life events, personality and emotions in relation to disease? We saw in Chapter 5 that those working with these problems have to accept the handicap of not being able to conduct controlled experiments, on account of practical and ethical considerations. Only studies which can be called 'descriptive' – those showing a link, or correlation, between disease and some psychological factor – are feasible with people. This makes the task of explanation, or theory building, extremely difficult.

Kuhn [1] has argued that for a theory to be fruitful it must be possible to set up an experimental test, or series of tests, the findings of which could prove *or disprove* the theory. In other words, one of the duties of a theory is to make clear predictions which can be confirmed or refuted by designing the appropriate experiments. The theory that green men inhabit the rooms of houses but vanish when anyone enters, looks in, or tries to detect them, is of no scientific value because there is no way of ever showing it to be false. If no test can conceivably be designed which could show a theory to be wrong, that theory is not a useful construction.

Psychosomatic theory is difficult to develop because descriptive findings are by their nature usually open to more than one interpretation. Probably not one single study with humans, taken on its own, could serve to prove or disprove any given theory. Here the problem does not necessarily lie with the contents of the theory, as it does in the illustration just given. There is nothing to prevent a theory that is *in principle* testable from being advanced. For example, it would be a simple matter to draw up on paper a definitive test of the idea that

recently experienced bereavement results in heightened susceptibility to disease, given limitless facilities and free licence to
control experimentally the lives of a group of people as if they
were a sample of rats. But the undesirability of such a horror-
film venture clearly rules it out.

Some psychologists argue that in view of this situation it is a
mistake to make any theoretical assertions at all. Plainly, this is
an absurd proposal. For what is the ultimate aim of psychosomatic research if it is not to suggest preventive and remedial
measures? To be able to do this not only must we have a good
theory, we must have good *causal* theory. I shall argue that
causal theories can be set up and tested in spite of these
difficulties. Unfortunately, testing them will not depend on just
one, or even a few carefully designed experimental tests. But
we have seen that definite themes emerge from the findings
of differently styled studies, taken *en masse*. Kuhn's criterion can
thus be met by considering together a large number of suggestive findings. Inevitably, this means that the evolution of theory
will be slow. But given that this is virtually the only methodology open to us, there is no other intrinsic reason why it should
not be an acceptable one.

I Psychoanalytic theories

The oldest ways of thinking about psychosomatic disease
were mainly extensions of the Freudian idea that symptoms
could be the symbolic expression of unconscious conflicts and
repressed wishes [2]. Asthmatic wheezing, for example, has
been said to represent the repressed cry of the child following
the withdrawal of affection by the mother [3]. These early ideas
differed fundamentally from contemporary ones. Instead of a
person's psychological state being considered one among many
'risk factors' in a large number of diseases, it was believed that
there were a handful, only, of diseases that were purely
psychosomatic in origin. Alexander's specificity theory [4] was
the first major move to collate such notions. This suggested that
heredity and early experience influenced the infant, and later

the adult personality, in such a way that the individual experienced certain types of conflict especially acutely, and reacted to them by producing psychosomatic symptoms. The resulting symptoms were believed to be symbolically related to the conflict and to the individual's attempts to cope with it. The development of ulcers, for instance, was thought to be related to the frustration or suppression of help-seeking behaviour. The connecting link was seen as the childhood association between the wish to be loved and helped, and the wish to be fed.

A systematic attempt was launched to predict, on the basis of transcribed information from interviews, which one of seven core 'psychosomatic' diseases was present in various samples of patients. The seven diseases studied were: bronchial asthma, rheumatoid arthritis, ulcerative colitis, essential hypertension, neurodermatitis, thyrotoxicosis and peptic ulcer. This met with limited success. Although diagnosis could, in many cases, be predicted correctly from personality profiles, there remained a large incidence of diseases occurring in the absence of the expected personality pattern. Criticisms have also been made of certain aspects of the design of these studies. For these reasons the evidence is generally considered to be insufficiently strong to support Alexander's theory, and interest in it has waned.

The theories of Engel and Schmale [5] and Sandler [6] are examples of more recent 'psychodynamic'[1] formulations. In both these a central role is accorded to subjective feelings which are conceptually distinguished from physiological states. The key concept in Engel and Schmale's theory, for instance, is the 'giving-up' reaction – an experience of hopelessness, helplessness and incompetence to cope with life's demands. This leads to an identifiable bodily response which the authors claim is discernible in many different species,[2] and is associated with increased biological vulnerability and disease.

---

[1] 'Psychodynamic' denotes the active interplay of conscious and unconscious processes (needs, wishes etc.).

[2] They term this 'conservation-withdrawal'.

Roughly speaking, psychoanalytic theories boil down to one or other of two basic propositions. These are (1) that symptoms are brought on by unconscious conflicts, and (2) that symptoms result from distressing subjective experiences. The criticisms of these positions are now well established and go something like this: (1) If a conflict is unconscious (and therefore *a priori* undiscoverable), we cannot find out about it, and so we cannot test the theory. (2) It is not possible to combine subjective and physiological states in the same causal scheme.

The first of these criticisms is self explanatory. The second is a particularly crucial one and perhaps requires some amplification.

I have argued that the ultimate goal of psychosomatic research is to suggest preventive and remedial measures, and that a prerequisite to this goal is an adequate causal theory.[3] This being so, we must take a fresh look at the sequence of causes and effects leading up to the development of symptoms and consider just how psychological influences can be fitted into it. This is not the same as asking whether physiological pathways exist which could transmute activity in the brain into consequences for health. The problem is how we are to conceive of a form of influence variously described as 'psychological', 'mental', 'emotional' ... etc. as producing effects on organic states.

In suggesting, as many psychoanalytic theories do, that particular subjective states (feelings and emotions) can lead to illness[4] a fundamental error is committed. The logical status of words denoting subjective states differs in an important way from that of words denoting organic states and events, and as Ryle has pointed out [7], this precludes their being combined in the same causal account. Put another way, it is beyond our reach as scientists to envisage how a pathological organic condition could be the result of anything other than a prior

[3] It would be logically impossible to conceive preventive and remedial measures in the absence of any causal assertion.

[4] Many psychoanalytic theories do in fact contain this proposition, camouflaged though it often is.

chain of organic causes and effects. To say that it resulted from feelings of 'guilt' or 'despair' simply leaves us in mid air.

This is the body–mind problem at its most acute. Many see it as the most serious drawback to psychosomatic research and theory and there is no doubt it is one of the main reasons for the more considered forms of disenchantment with the subject which is so prevalent among natural scientists. The different categories of concept and the seeming unbreachable gap between them makes the whole idea of psychosomatic influence seem like a non-starter. Its subject matter is regarded as removed from science and its theories as literary rather than scientific constructions.

Psychoanalytic ideas are primarily responsible for this attitude. While they have proved valuable in the clinical diagnosis and treatment of psychiatric illness, without radical changes they cannot provide the basis for a general theory of psychosomatic influence. Their mixed allegorical language, many key concepts of which are imported from ordinary everyday language, is simply not equipped to make clear causal assertions relating psychological state to onset of symptoms. Indeed, it has to be concluded that those theories in which words denoting emotions play a prominent role are not really theories in the true sense at all.

II Psychophysiological theories.

Over the past 15 years there has been a distinct turning away from psychoanalytic formulations and the idea of symbolically expressed unconscious impulses, and a growing interest in the physiological approach. In an effort to get round the problem of relating physical events to mental ones, some writers have abandoned psychological terminology altogether, to concentrate on pure physiology; for example, the effects of removing or electrically stimulating specific area of the brain. Others have dealt with the problem in another way, by focussing on a mental condition and simply identifying it with a physiological one, for example, by proposing that 'psychological stress' = a high level of adrenalin or adrenalin-related substances in the blood. But such a move achieves nothing except to render the psychological concept redundant. If the only way of knowing whether or not 'psychological stress' is present is by measuring blood adrenalin level, then the two terms are synonymous to the extent of being interchangeable, and there is nothing to be gained by retaining the mental term which is now completely defined by a physiological quantity. To disguise the fact that mental terms have been abandoned by keeping them on (or more accurately pensioning them off) as gratuitous synonyms for physiological states is therefore an avoidance rather than a solution of the problem.

The aim of psychophysiology, as it is known, is to relate aspects of an organism's interaction with its environment to physiological states occurring more or less synchronously[5] Emphasis is on the discovery of how physiological states are affected by conditions of the environment. A few studies have been made of people's reactions in real-life situations reckoned intuitively to be stressful, such as parachute jumping and taking exams [9]. But most psychophysiological research is conducted in the laboratory.

As one might expect, those aspects of the environment studied in the laboratory tend to be somewhat simplistic. In experiments using people, minutiae of normal human experience are varied, such as the intensity of experimentally produced pain, the difficulty of a task, and the degree of 'stress' vicariously experienced through watching horrific films [10, 11]. Moreover, the physiological responses measured in human experiments are unavoidably rather gross – short term variations in heart rate, blood pressure, skin conductivity, and the presence of adrenalin-related chemicals in the blood and urine. Lader [12] has emphasized that it is essential not to neglect individual differences both in patterns of physiological

[5] The philosophical basis of this approach ('psychophysical parallelism') is to class subjective experience as a reality whose changes correspond with changes in the state of the nervous system and occur simultaneously with these, but in no way causally interact with them [e.g. 8].

response and in the way that a given aspect of the environment is interpreted. This introduces a high degree of complexity into the design of psychophysiological experiments.

In experiments with animals it is inevitable that those aspects of the environment which are investigated will be somewhat banal by human standards. Some of the 'social' factors studied, for example, are the effects of isolation, grouping, crowding, social disorganization and maternal deprivation.

Now, in setting up such experiments it is clearly desirable to arrive at a description of the relevant features of an organism's environment other than on a purely arbitrary basis. To study the effects of different colours on members of a species not endowed with colour vision is poor planning. The same caution applies when studying the social environment. Some idea of how the animals being used as subjects interpret and code the world around them is essential before making guesses about the things it might be interesting to study.

Amongst psychophysiologists, the most popular way of construing an organism's transactions with its environment is in the language of behaviourism or Skinnerism. Behaviourists talk about the world as composed of 'stimuli'. Under certain conditions the organism is said to make a 'response' to a 'stimulus' which may or may not be followed by a 'reinforcer', or reward. If a reinforcer does follow the response, that response is likely to occur again. This definition of a reinforcer, as that which maintains or increases the likelihood of the response associated with it, is the key principle in the behaviourist system of analysis. The most common simple method of demonstrating this principle involves a rat in a cage, with an indicator light, a lever, and food dispenser. When the light is switched on (the stimulus) depression of the lever (the response) causes food to appear in the food tray (the reinforcer). After a few chance (exploratory) encounters with the lever during periods when the light is illuminated, a hungry rat quickly learns to press the lever more reliably for food. The pattern of responses the animal must make in order to receive the reinforcer (e.g. whether a reinforcer is delivered after every lever press or after a fixed number, or only after some time has elapsed since the last press) is known as the 'schedule of reinforcement'. By varying this and other factors, such as the nature of the stimulus, the style of response required before a reinforcer will be delivered, and the availability of reinforcers,[6] many different types of natural encounters with the environment can be simulated experimentally and their effects on both behaviour and physiology studied.[7] An essential feature of behaviourism is that it is not concerned with planning or intention, or any 'under cover' goings on at all. The only datum of interest is an organism's observable behaviour.

It is easily shown that this kind of analysis is not restricted to the behaviour of rodents or other lower animals. Much human behaviour can be similarly described with a force that is not immediately apparent to those unfamiliar with the essentials of behaviourism. The success of behaviour therapy – application of these principles to the treatment of psychiatric disorders – is currently commanding a great deal of controversial interest [15].

Behaviourism therefore provides us with one way of getting at those aspects of an organism's environment which are significant to that organism, without relying on arbitrary distinctions. The interaction of animal and environment can be described in a terminology which is applicable across all species. But although general in its application, when applied to man this system is seriously limited. The concepts and principles of the behaviourist are based on simple observation of the behaviour of lower animals; mainly the rat. 'Responses' consist in perfected sequences of movements such as pressing a lever.

It is possible, of course, to build up much more complicated sequences than this much as one might train a dog to fetch, carry, and drop a ball. But once a response has been

[6] Withholding reinforcers for a long time may lead to disappearance or 'extinction' of the responses.

[7] The principles of a Skinnerian analysis of behaviour are, of course, much more involved than this brief account would suggest. See, for example, Skinner [13] and Blackman [14].

established through the repeated presentation of reinforcers, an experimenter, or an observer, has no difficulty saying whether or not it has occurred during any specified period of time since it is recognized by a recurring similarity in its observable characteristics – the same or a similar series of limb movements. However, if we are dealing with people and we want to consider, say, the 'response' of 'being considerate', there is a snag since individual 'responses' falling into this category may not appear outwardly similar at all. Helping a blind man across a road and preventing him from crossing are both actions which could be correctly classed as 'considerate', under the appropriate circumstances, but in terms of the movements which an onlooker sees they are not only different but incompatible. In this instance the concept of 'response' is inadequate. It is unable to provide for the social significance of a sequence of behaviour without losing its meaning. Because the things a person does are understood by others through their being seen as purposeful – i.e. as directed towards a goal – an analysis of human behaviour must go beyond the idea of 'responses' of the kind dealt in by behaviourists. Some means of expressing what connects all 'considerate' actions is needed so that they can be regarded as members of the same class, and similarity in external appearance is no basis for this.

The same applies to the concept of a 'stimulus'. When this is a light or a buzzer one stimulus can be recognized as identical to the next on account of the similarity in its visual or auditory qualities. But it is quite impossible to represent, say, 'helplessness', or 'situations which elicit considerate acts', on the same basis. If the social significance of events is an important factor in psychosomatic disease – and the research reviewed in Chapter 5 strongly indicates this is so – it is hard to see how behaviourism can be much of an asset to large scale theory-building in the field of human psychosomatics.

Sociological theories

Can we turn to the ideas advanced by sociologists and social psychologists to bridge the gaps in the psychophysiologist's perspective? Any system making up for the deficiencies of behaviourist explanations would have to incorporate an analysis of how people understand their social world (the world of intentional acts and actions, that is) which is free of any dependence on outward similarity in behaviour. Only when armed with such an analysis shall we be in a position to decide upon those dimensions of interaction between person and environment which might profitably serve as themes in psychosomatic research. What, in fact, do sociological theories have to say about illness?

Many attempts have been made to capture the quality of the disease prone person's relationship to his social surroundings. The high risk individual has been described as alienated from society [16], the subject of 'information incongruity'[8] [18], status incongruity [19], role ambiguity [20] and cultural mobility [21]. His environment has been characterized as unpredictable, lacking social cohesion, not providing social support [see 22] and undergoing rapid cultural revision [23].

All of these generalizations originate from systematic observation. Nevertheless, they are not so much theories as labels for those aspects of a person's social experience which the authors regard as important. Many are couched in a metaphorical or pictorial language, which leaves the way open for considerable ambiguity if they are ever to be translated into identifiable and measurable quantities. Moreover, in none of them is there any basis for conceiving how the individual orders and interprets his social environment, and how the mechanism responsible for such ordering (presumably situated in the higher regions of the brain) could transmit effects having consequences for health.

Moss [18] has worked out a complicated and ingenious

[8] See also Durkheim's [17] account of 'anomie', which is closely related to the first two of these descriptions.

scheme, embodying many of these generalizations, which is perhaps the nearest thing there is to a social theory of disease. The concepts of identification and involvement of a person with a social community, and the opposite of this – his alienation from it – play a central role. The individual's interaction with his social environment is seen as a process of exchange of 'information' between them. One of the main functions of the social community is to supply information to the individual, providing him with a construction of the physical world, and also of the social world – what is normal and expected and what is desirable and undesirable in the society and communities of which he is a part. However, the individual also has private access to this information from other sources; through his direct, first-hand, contact with his physical and social environments, and through contact with other cultures and communities – i.e. other 'networks of information'. Moss postulates that a person's resistance to disease diminishes when he encounters information which is 'incongruous' with that supplied by the social circles in which he moves. If his perception of this incongruity is sufficiently salient and enduring, health is likely to be endangered.

Moss's theory takes the important step of placing emphasis on the social meaning of situations to people. It is not constrained by a narrow behaviourist terminology. However, as is true of many sociological approaches, the central theme – in this case 'information incongruity' – is well defined and its causes and consequences well documented at the societal level, but not at the level of the individual. Its *psychological* implications are largely glossed over. Hence there remains something of a void between the notion of 'information incongruity' and the harmful physiological consequences it is assumed to engender. Rather than admitting this problem, Moss tries to camouflage it by denouncing a causal approach and in its place proposing that social and physiological events 'resonate' with one another. 'Biosocial resonation', as this mysterious process is called, is no more or less than an attempt to have your cake and eat it. As has been said, a viable theory must contain at least one causal assertion, and Moss's theory of illness, for all its elaborate description of social dynamics fails on this essential count.

So sociological and related theories are more descriptive than truly explanatory. Like psychoanalytic theories, they acknowledge the importance of social meaning and in this sense provide richer accounts than do behaviourist theories. But they share a common fault which is a failure to consider how social factors come to have an impact on the individual. This is not a case of straightforward omission; it is due to the absence of a conceptual framework for linking social events with individual (psychological) ones. To be able to do so is imperative in a theory of psychosomatic disease, because becoming physically ill, the end point in the causal sequence, is something which happens to individuals, not societies or groups.

Learned helplessness

It is impossible in one chapter to cover every psychosomatic theory. But a formulation known as the 'learned helplessness model' is currently claiming a great deal of attention and merits separate consideration. Originally conceived by Seligman in an attempt to explain the origins of depression [24], it has recently been extended by Glass to the study of heart disease and the Type A personality [25]. Cast squarely in the behaviourist mould, the basic argument is that life events are experienced as stressful because they threaten an individual's sense of control over his environment. Stressful events are thus defined as 'stimuli' which signal to the individual that there is no relation between his efforts ('responses') and his success at getting what he wants ('rewards'). Type A behaviour is interpreted as a characteristic style of coping in such circumstances – a desperate stepping up of attempts to secure lost 'rewards'. Should the individual fail to regain control through his increased efforts, a period of apathy and depression may ensue, associated with a high risk for illness – specifically coronary disease.

Glass's system is notable for its integration of findings and ideas. The key concept is the concept of 'control', and the potentially harmful consequences of events which deprive a person of control. The definition of control as the power of 'responses' to secure 'rewards' is both the model's strength, and, paradoxically, at the same time, its weakness. It can be imagined just how easy it is to explore the theory in animal experiments where 'responses' and 'rewards' are unambiguously defined by the experimenter in context of the highly contrived environments of the animals acting as subjects. But what is 'control' and what are 'responses' and 'rewards' in the everyday lives of people? Have I exercised 'control' in moving a pot plant from the table to the window-sill? Or in climbing a mountain? Or writing a book? Are these activities 'responses'? If so, what are they responses *to*, and what are the 'rewards'? It is clear that some notion of the goals society and the individual value and uphold is necessary to be able to complete the picture. Once again, we find we need to go beyond the curious world of the behaviourist when considering the activities of man.

Cognitive theories

During the 1960s a certain amount of interest was aroused by so called 'cognitive' theories [e.g. 26]. Cognitive theories concerned themselves with the factors affecting an organism's assessment of situations as threatening or non-threatening, and its choice of coping strategy. To look beyond observable behaviour in this way appeared initially to be something of a radical advance from behaviourist approaches. But the radicalism turned out to be without backbone because cognitive theorists still slavishly adhered to the old 'stimulus', 'response' and 'stress' terminology. In doing so they left themselves wide open to the criticism of behaviourist approaches outlined earlier. In the end, because of this, cognitive theories have achieved little beyond an acknowledgement of the importance of mental evaluation of the dangerousness of encounters, and a description of some of the broad differences in characteristic styles of reaction to threatening events.

Again, it must be said that the account of theories which I have given does not do full justice to all the ideas which have been put forward to explain the findings of research. Many authors besides those mentioned here have written about the psychosomatic sequence and their writings reflect a range of different considerations and interests [e.g. 26–28]. Nevertheless, it is a representative account, and it covers the three main schools of thought on the subject: psychoanalytic, behaviourist and sociological. When theoretical statements are ventured they are almost invariably ventured in the language of one or other of these three schools.

The duties of a theory of psychosomatic influence

Reviewing some of the attempts which have been made to explain psychosomatic findings has highlighted many of the criteria for a workable theory. Broadly speaking these can be divided into practical and logical criteria.

The practical criteria

Plainly, a theory must have the capacity to explain consistency in experimental findings. So it must incorporate the notion of genetic proneness to specific diseases, and it must account for the emergent themes from psychological, sociological and anthropological investigations. In addition, it must relate to observable real-life predicaments in a clear way, and the predictions it makes should not be irrefutable [1, 28]. These are the practical criteria.

The logical criteria

It is the logical criteria binding a psychosomatic theory which, more than anything else, have been neglected in the past. Firstly, any statement accounting for why disease occurs must take the individual as its fundamental unit. Disease is patently something which happens to individuals. Sociological and anthropological theories, because they disregard the way in which social conditions have their impact on the individual, do not have the conceptual apparatus to tackle the focal issue of why a person becomes ill. It is not intended that sociological and anthropological findings should be ignored, but rather that our theory must be a psychological, or person-centred, one.

Second, there must be provision for taking into account the *meaning* of events to people. To achieve this, we must dispense with the overworked terms 'stimulus', 'response' and 'reward' and the restrictions they impose in tying us down to observable behaviour. The focus of the theory must be the world of actions, purposes and intentions, and the mechanism underlying an individual's understanding of this world.

Third, the cause and effect sequence in which we are interested has as its final stage the state of disease. The chain ends in organic pathology, its immediate antecedents being, presumably, the kinds of neural and neuro-hormonal events discussed in Chapter 4. The idea that these can be caused by feelings or emotions must be rejected, for the reasons outlined. The notion that mental activity goes on 'in parallel' with brain activity although the two never actually interact (psycho-physiological parallelism) does not help much either.

I believe the only way round this problem is to construct a plan or 'model' of the events leading up to the onset of symptoms which is two things at the same time. It must be, first, a scheme of psychological or mental activity, and also, *potentially*, a scheme of physiological, or brain, activity. This is to say that the model must be couched in such a way as to be able to lead on to physiological hypotheses should it prove successful in accounting for the facts at a psychological level. [29]

As we shall see, only a model invoking the concepts of underlying structure and social rules is able to fulfil all these conditions.

Surprisingly, advancement in the field of psychosomatics is not being held back by the lack of findings from research. A vast number of findings exist, waiting to be interpreted. The first stage in the interpretation process is to erect the scaffolding onto which possible explanations can be grafted. If the scaffolding is insecure, no explanation, however elegant, will stand up.

A consideration of psychosomatic theories has brought to light particular logical problems in each of the three main theoretical camps, seriously limiting the power of their explanations. We have seen that the conditions a psychosomatic theory must fulfil are as follows:

1. It must account for the findings of psychological, sociological and anthropological research.
2. It must be a psychological (individual-based) theory whose focus is the meaning of actions and events to people.
3. It must be cast in such a form as to be able to lead on to physiological hypotheses.
4. It must not be irrefutable.

Only one style of theory is capable of fulfilling all these conditions – a theory based on the premise that a person's understanding of the social world derives from an underlying structure of relations, and that his own behaviour is the product of a system of social rules. What this means and how it applies to the study of illness will be explained in this chapter.

The case for a structural analysis of human actions

Quite apart from any involvement with psychosomatic disease, structural analyses of human social behaviour in general are currently attracting much attention among psychologists. The recent birth of a new journal publishing papers in this vein,[1]

---

[1] *Journal for the Theory of Social Behaviour* (ed. Harré and Secord).

and the growing number of books in the field, are reflections of a mounting interest. Disenchantment with the traditional experimental method applied to problems in social psychology, together with a feeling that the problems themselves are becoming more and more fragmented as a result of the way in which they are defined and investigated, is one of the negative reasons for the interest in a fundamentally new approach.

People's ordinary everyday language indicates, quite clearly, that actions are understood in terms of intentions: not, as the behaviourists would have it, on the basis of constituent behaviours – outward similarities in limb movements. An action, by definition, is something which is planned and directed towards a goal. If I ask someone why he did something, such as getting into his car and driving into town, he will reply by telling me his motive. He drove into town because he wanted to see his girlfriend, or because he wanted to buy a record.

To understand another's action means to grasp the intention behind it by recognizing the goal towards which it is directed. But a goal can be appreciated only if both actor and observer share the same knowledge about its social significance. Both must be able to see the action as conforming to a pattern, or 'social norm', which is familiar to the members of the community in context of which the action is carried out. For example, if the answer to the question, 'Why did you drive into town?' had been, 'So as to get stuck in a traffic jam', we would be none the wiser.

Exactly the same holds even if the community in question is very small, perhaps consisting of only two individuals: husband and wife, say. The norms shared by marital partners may be highly esoteric. They often are, with the result that many of the things that are done and said between them are not fully understood by others. Nevertheless here too, unless one person's action is recognized as conforming to a conventional, albeit idiosyncratic, pattern, it will not make sense to the other.

Making sense has nothing to do with desirability. An intelligible action may be classed as desirable, or undesirable, or neutral. Its essential characteristic is that it is seen to accord with an acknowledged regularity in that society. Burgling a house, for example, is an action which is widely understood, though not widely approved.

Sometimes people misunderstand one another. This happens because they misread the intention, or goal, behind something the other person does or says. Instead of categorizing the action as conforming to norm X, they wrongly categorize it as conforming to the less desirable norm Y. The misunderstanding is rectified only when they realize their mistake. Often, of course, people justify or excuse themselves for having done something wrong by deliberately misrepresenting the goal behind their own action. They plead that their action was motivated by a more virtuous intention than was really the case.

Consider the two behaviourally incompatible actions: helping a blind man across the road, and preventing him from crossing. This is an instance where both actions are comprehensible as coming from the same norm. We can describe it, crudely, as something like 'being considerate to the disabled'. Here again, for either of these actions to make sense to an onlooker, the onlooker himself must possess a knowledge of this norm. A man from a planet where there are no invalids would not be able to make sense of either action until someone explained to him that this is something which people on Earth do. It is part of our culture.

Thus, people's understanding of other people's actions depends on their being able to assimilate what they see to an underlying knowledge of society's conventions. Because actions are understood on the basis of their social significance, and not on the basis of any similarity in external appearance, we have found it necessary to assume that a certain amount of behind-the-scenes mental activity goes on. Logically, such behind-the-scenes activity must underlie not only a person's perception of the things other people do, but also the things he himself does. It applies both to the perception and to the production of actions.

This is close to what is meant by structuralism. A structural theory is one which assumes the existence of some unconscious organizing system. The unconscious system functions rather like a computer programme, determining and overseeing an end-product.[2] In computers, the end-product is printout, or a visual display. In people it is actions. Although we have no direct access to the 'programme' behind people's actions, we are able to infer its nature through what people do and say – in particular, through the commentaries they are able to provide on their own actions.

Language and meaning

The Swiss linguist, Saussure [3], was one of the first to point out that any study of the meanings of words must invoke the notion of structure. Suppose I am asked to teach the concept of 'clock' to an islander from the remote South Seas, just arrived in England from a rural native settlement where there is no mechanization. I might start by collecting together a dozen or so clocks, showing these to him one by one, each time repeating the word 'clock'. But he will probably be none the wiser, even if I were to persevere with this exercise and show him 100 or 1,000 clocks. The reason is that this method does not inform him of the difference between a clock and, say, a typewriter, or for that matter any other mechanical instrument. I would do much better, after showing him one or two clocks, to show him numerous other different machines pointing out that these are *not* clocks.

This illustrates a very important point – that it is quite wrong to think of language as a set of labels for physical objects. Language is an independent system of relations. A concept gets its meaning not primarily from a one-to-one 'stimulus-response' pairing of syllables with objects, but on account of its context in relation to other concepts.

One cannot have an accurate concept of 'clock' without having a good idea about meters, wheels, televisions, type-

[2] For a more detailed statement of the structuralist position, see Piaget [1] and Levi-Strauss [2].

writers, sawmills, motorbikes, etc., knowing that these things are *not* clocks and knowing the difference (and similarities) between each of these objects and clocks. Thus the meaning of a word derives from its being embedded in a network or 'structure' of other words, not from anything else.

Structures in the understanding of physical objects

Observations on meaning in language, such as those which Saussure made, are really observations on the nature of knowledge and understanding. Saussure's point that the concepts people have about objects are all interrelated, each being endowed with meaning precisely because of this, tells us much about how people understand the physical environment. Essentially, it tells us that the world is understood not on the basis of independent units of information, but on the basis of a much more comprehensive mental scheme. What more can we say about this structure of information? From the way people talk about physical objects, it seems very likely that it is hierarchical in its organization. Consider what happens when a man is confronted with an object he has never seen before. Instantaneously, a number of judgments about it are made. For example, is it big or small; light or dark; soft or hard; moving or still; dangerous or harmless; valuable or worthless.

The most economical way of representing these decisions is in the form of a hierarchy, the general idea of which is illustrated in Figure 4.

At the very top of the hierarchy in this Figure is the general human propensity to form concepts – to categorize things – a propensity which, presumably, is genetically endowed. The uppermost levels in the hierarchy represent very general judgments, such as gross size, texture, and worth. The next levels down consist in slightly finer discriminations. For instance, 'worth' is judged in terms of beauty and value ... etc. At lower levels the judgments become finer still. The resultant concept is thus a function of the collective judgments made about an object right down to the finest levels of all.

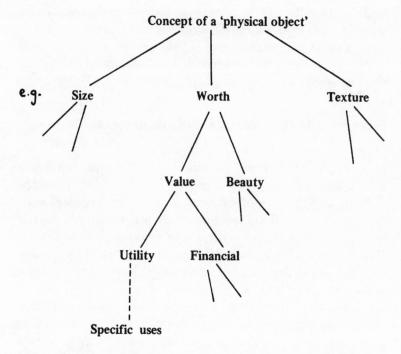

Figure 4   General format of the structure underlying an individual's knowledge of the physical world.

Following a great deal of practice, these decisions are made automatically, without much conscious thought. If the person has expectations about the object he is about to be confronted with, these function as 'pre-sets', enabling many of the decisions in the network to be by-passed. Should his expectations be disconfirmed, the pre-sets have to be aborted and he has to go back to square one.

There is another reason, besides economy, for believing the structure reponsible for a person's interpretation of the physical world to be hierarchical. This is the simple fact that people are able to talk about objects in a variety of different ways, each differing in its generality. For instance, it is quite correct to say that a clock is a time-piece, a measuring device, a machine, and a hard object. Each stage in this chain involves a category which is more general than the last. Likewise, we can say that X is a good thing to have, and that X is useful, and that X is useful in the house, and that X is useful for cooking, and that X is an electric mixer. Thus, what leads us to believe that people's perception of the physical world is handled in this way is simply the existence of different gradations of generality in their ordinary language definitions.

Structures in the understanding of people's actions

Now, a very similar line of argument can be taken with regard to a person's understanding of other people's actions. I have already said that an action is interpreted by its being related to a knowledge of social norms which the observer possesses, largely on account of his having been brought up in the same culture.

Just as the meaning of a physical object depends on that object's relation to others in a mental scheme of things, so too the meaning of an action derives from that action's relation to others which are envisaged. We do not understand something another person does by considering their action in isolation. The action is considered in context of others which could conceivably be taken in the same, or similar, circumstances. As with physical objects, we are pre-set to make a variety of spontaneous decisions, and the decisions we make are a function of our comprehensive knowledge of society. The same arguments compel us to view a person's knowledge of the social world as an integrated structure rather than as fragmented pieces of information. I cannot say 'he did a kind thing', unless I am able to envisage an alternative 'unkind' course of action.

Moreover, here again, it is reasonable to suppose that the underlying mental structure is hierarchical in arrangement. This is illustrated in Figure 5. Here, at the top of the hierarchy is the universal human propensity to impose order on one's own and others' social behaviour. Again, this is assumed to be genetically endowed. Near the top (at level I in the

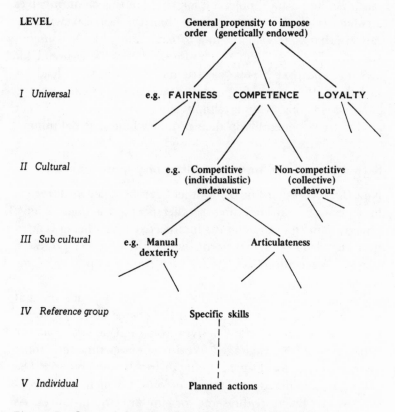

Figure 5 General format of the structure underlying an individual's knowledge of the social world.

Figure) are highly abstract notions such as might be described in our own culture as 'competence', and 'fairness', to take two examples. These are general in the sense that members of most cultures can be said to entertain notions similar to, and equivalent in their generality to, our concepts of 'competence' and 'fairness'.

At level II in this Figure there are derivations from these very general notions – more culture-specific (but still fairly general) definitions of level I abstractions. For instance, 'competence' may be understood primarily in terms of free enterprise and competition in Western urbanized cultures. Similarly, there are likely to be differences in the conception of 'competence' between people living in industrial and people living in rural environments. At level III there are derivatives which are more specific again, involving differences in definitions between smaller (sub-cultural) groups of people. 'Competence', at this level, would be related to a specific area of expertise, and at level IV to a still more specific role or skill within that area of expertise.

The justification for presenting this scheme as a hierarchy is again the capacity of people to supply definitions of actions which differ in their degree of abstractness. Because a person is able to talk about 'competence', for example, in a highly abstract way, and in a highly specific way, and also in many in-between ways, this itself is taken as sufficient evidence that the structure responsible for the encoding of social information is hierarchical. My representation of structures as having five levels, instead of six or ten (see Figure 5) is, of course, arbitrary. But my aim is to show how a structural approach provides the basis for a workable theory of social behaviour, and ultimately for a model of psychosomatic disease. For this purpose we need go no further than an appreciation of the general form of structures.

A structure responsible for interpretation of the social world is thus a system of information about the goals and objectives which society (or a smaller community within society) recognizes. In fact, these goals and objectives are both the expression and the constitution of society, for without them society would not exist.

Rules and the desirability of actions

So far, I have concentrated just on the mechanisms by which actions are interpreted. But very often our interest in things we see being done does not stop there. Having satisfied ourselves that we understand an action, we may go on to evaluate it. We ask ourselves whether we approve of it, disapprove, or don't care. For a person to be able to evaluate other people's actions, and to be able to choose the right course of action for himself, he must have a set of guidelines, or *prescriptive rules*[3]: rules prescribing one course of action rather than another.

Values, beliefs, attitudes, and preferences are all forms of prescriptive rules. One way of conceptualizing prescriptive rules is to regard them as weightings attached to various branches of the structure of norms.

Amanda may be very fussy about the way she dresses, and so buying clothes, to her, represents a series of important decisions. Nicola, on the other hand, may not care what clothes she is seen in. If Amanda goes out and buys some clothes, Nicola will *understand* what she has done but probably will not be interested enough either to approve or to disapprove of the clothes Amanda has bought. Vanessa, however, who is also interested in clothes, will very likely form some sort of an opinion as to whether the clothes Amanda has bought are nice or not. In this example, all three girls possess a knowledge of the norms which exist in our society surrounding clothes, but only Amanda and Vanessa hold prescriptive rules concerning the clothes they wear. Only Vanessa is concerned with evaluating Amanda's action. Only in the case of these two are there weightings in that part of the structural map of society relating to clothes.

Suppose, for the sake of illustration, that structures have a straightforward representation in the brain, and that the structure responsible for understanding the social world is represented by a structure of nerve cells in the cortex having a form roughly the same as the form illustrated in Figure 5. The weightings attached to its various branches might be realized through differential thresholds of firing of the corres-

---

[3] Strictly speaking this class of rule should be referred to as *regulative* rules. This is a more general category, including both *prescriptive* and *permissive* rules – i.e. rules that prescribe and rules that permit courses of action. Collett [4] discusses these various species of rule as they appear in the writings of philosophers.

ponding cell assemblies. Of course, anything as simplistic as this is highly unlikely. Nevertheless, it is interesting to see how a structural formulation of this nature would, *in principle*, lend itself to neural modelling. This cannot be said of any other of the theories which have been put forward in connection with psychosomatic disease.

Thus rules differ from group to group and from individual to individual. Looking at Figure 5, and imagining that rules are weightings attached to the various branches of the hierarchy, the biggest differences between people will be in the lowest levels. Almost everyone would endorse the general notions of 'competence' and 'fairness' in some form, so weightings at the top of the hierarchy can be said to be more or less the same for all. As we proceed down, however, there is progressively more variation between people in the attached weightings. The greatest diversity occurs at the lowest levels of all, marking differences between individuals in their definitions of competence etc., and in the specialized activities to which a criterion of competence is applied.

Rules are responsible for the selection of actions. A structural analysis such as this recognizes several influences on the actions a person chooses to take: the influence of his immediate circle of friends and confidantes (his 'reference groups'), the influence of the broader social circles within which he moves ('sub-cultural' communities), and the influence of the culture, and ultimately the species, of which he is a member. Influence from each of these sources is associated with a particular level in the hierarchy, as is shown in Figure 5.

Must we assume the existence of such a complicated system underlying social behaviour? I have already tried to show that invoking the concept of structure is unavoidable. But is it strictly necessary to assume the existence of rules as well? Why can we not say instead that people learn actions by being trained in the same way that a dog is trained?

Rules in the analysis of language

The capacity of human memory is limited. Consequently it is implausible to suggest that every sentence a person speaks in his lifetime has been learned by him at some prior stage and stored in a huge sentence reservoir. Besides, a person is able to produce an almost infinite number of grammatical utterances, many of which may never have been spoken before by anybody. These are some of the considerations which led Chomsky[5] to suggest that people are equipped with a system of rules which they use automatically and unconsciously in the production of grammatical statements. Chomsky argued that instead of learning actual sentences, English speakers learn a standard set of rules by which sentences can be generated. Understanding of sentences was also said to be handled by this set of rules.

Many linguists are now agreed that there are strong, if not binding, reasons to commend this kind of a theory of grammar [6, 7].

Now, a very similar line of argument can be taken with regard to social behaviour. The range of actions it is possible to envisage, like the range of grammatical utterances, is virtually infinite. Therefore, social behaviour too must be represented as the product of generative rules, that is, rules capable of generating a virtually infinite range of actions. This point of view has been argued much more thoroughly than is possible here by several authors [e.g. 8–10].

So it would seem that this type of analysis of human social behaviour – an analysis incorporating the concepts of structure and rules – is logically unavoidable. Accepting this, what more can be said about the part played by rules in generating actions?

Rules in the genesis of actions

People are biological animals with biological needs, not supermen, and so the things they do are not solely the product of rules but also the result of biological tendencies and limitations.

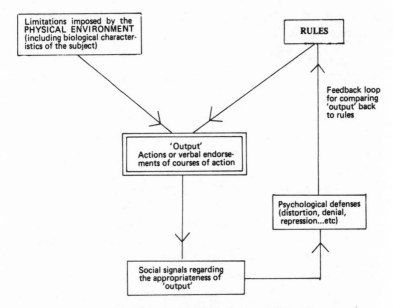

Figure 6   Flow diagram showing the factors which determine 'output', and the comparison of 'output'
back to rules.

Every action a person performs can therefore be assumed to be
the result of (a) rules applied in response to social cues (i.e. in
accordance with the social situation as it is perceived by the
actor), and (b) the limitations imposed by the physical
environment and the biological characteristics of the subject
himself.[4]

People also have the unique capacity to comment on the
things they themselves have done. Very often, their comments
are by way of self-justification. This can be taken to imply
that after an action has been committed, it is referred back
to rules by means of a 'feedback loop'. In this way an
automatic test is made to determine whether or not a committed action is consistent with the rules held. These principles

[4] For our purposes the subject's biological characteristics can be regarded
as part of the 'physical environment'.

are captured in Figure 6, which shows the determinants of actions and the consequences of committing an action.

The process of testing committed actions against rules

An important assumption concerning the process of testing actions against rules is warranted by the findings of psychological research into what is known as 'cognitive consistency' [11]. This is that *the comparison of a committed action with rules does not stop until consistency is registered.*

If a test is made and a discrepancy registered, tests will continue to be made until consistency is eventually registered. For instance, suppose I have committed an action which, on reflection, seems inconsiderate. This means that on comparison back with the rules I hold, a discrepancy is registered between my action and a rule prescribing considerate behaviour. But further analysis of the action and the circumstances under which it was carried out may reveal that I did it under a certain amount of social pressure. Thus, on re-testing, the action will be found to be consistent with rules after all, on grounds of social expediency. It hardly takes psychological research to tell us of the universality of this tendency to justify one's own actions.

But suppose in the above example, the second-time-round appraisal of my action still failed to result in the registration of consistency – that is, suppose I was not able to come up with any satisfactory excuses. In this circumstance, the only way consistency can be achieved (and I have said that consistency is a necessary condition for the comparison process to stop) is by modification of the rule itself so that it is brought into line with the committed action. If I was really unable to find sufficient justification for what I did, even after a great deal of searching, I would then literally *become* a little less considerate as a consequence of my action.

Research on attitude change has confirmed that this happens. It has been found that if a subject makes a commitment he would not normally make (especially when this is done publicly), his own attitude often falls into line with the commitment he has made.[5] Moreover, this effect does not hold up if the subject is able to cite good mitigating excuses for what he did, such as the fact that he was offered a financial incentive, or the fact that strong pressure was put on him. It is as if some explanation for his action has got to be found, and failing all others he opts for the explanation 'I did it because I'm that sort of person'.

So, if the second-time-round and subsequent more detailed appraisals of an action continue to result in inconsistency, rules are modified so as to be brought into line with actions. Modification takes place first at the lowest possible levels (because this effectively involves the smallest amount of change), and then, if re-testing of the action still produces a discrepancy, successively higher-order rules are modified until consistency is eventually achieved. The essentials of this process of successive testings and modifications are captured in a block diagram in Figure 7.

Two further properties of this system can be inferred on logical grounds. The first is that *for rules to exist at all they must be resistant to change.* It is therefore logically necessary to incorporate into this model influences tending to force a match while the comparison process is underway. These are shown in Figure 7 (on the left hand side of the diagram) and are manifested in the many strategies people use to achieve consistency before rules are changed. Into this category come the defensive and distorting tendencies so familiar to psychologists, such as selective perception, repression, and tactics of self-justification.[6]

Secondly, *the habitual[7] performance of purposeful actions has the effect of 'clarifying' rules.* If a committed action is registered as consistent, the rule or rules which it matches may be said to have been clarified in the way that definitions are clarified by

---

[5] The 'forced-compliance' paradigm. See [12]. See also the discussion of this in Chapter 2.

[6] The two processes: matching of an action to rules, and modification of rules, are similar to Piaget's concepts of assimilation and accommodation [13].

[7] Other than sporadic.

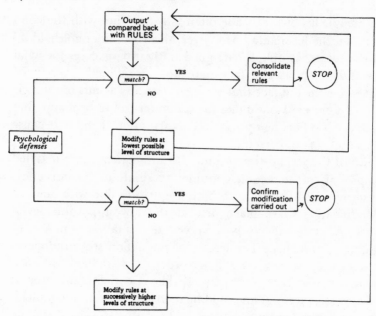

Figure 7   Flow diagram illustrating the process of comparing 'output' (committed actions or verbal endorsements of courses of action) with rules, and the process of testing for consistency.

examples. We have seen that the rules underlying social behaviour are generative. That is, they are capable of prescribing a virtually infinite range of actions. Built into systems of this nature is a certain amount of ambiguity,[8] which is reduced by every example labelled as consistent. The sheer performance of an action and its registration as consistent thus serves to clarify and consolidate a rule (or rules), in the same way as a test case clarifies a new law (or laws).[9]

[8] Or 'conflict', or 'information' (See for example, Berlyne [14]).

[9] In fact, the legal analogy can be taken a step further. Widespread flouting of a law and conflicting judgments concerning it can create pressure for its eventual revision in much the same way as actions registered as discrepant with a rule can provoke changes in that rule. In each case an interim period of resistance to change is to be expected. See also Kuhn's account of historical scientific discoveries, in which he identifies similar recurring patterns in the debunking of accepted ideas and their replacement with new ones [15].

The verbal 'commitment' of actions

People talk about actions as well as perform them. Actual performance is therefore not the only way in which rules can be tested. Actions may be symbolically conceived in fantasy and 'committed' in a weak sense when a person lets others know in conversation what he would or would not do in a given (imagined) set of circumstances. The imaginary circumstances are often based on some current knowledge of someone else's predicament. Indeed, the percentage of people's time spent in casual gossip of this nature, especially that containing a degree of criticism and blame, is remarkably high. ('I would never have done that if I'd been in his shoes ...' etc.) Psychologists have for a long time recognized this kind of exchange between people as one of the most pervasive, if not the most pervasive, feature of ordinary friendly conversation. Festinger [16, 17] called it 'social comparison'. Not only are courses of action discussed in this way, so too are life-styles, attitudes, beliefs and values – the actual rules themselves.

A second important way that rules are consolidated (or modified) is therefore through the process of social comparison, in which mainly actions, but sometimes rules themselves, are discussed conversationally in an evaluative manner. Verbal endorsement of a course of action (or a rule), in the presence of others, is thus analogous to the performance of that action, and so may be thought of as having similar consequences with respect to the consistency-seeking process.[10] Hence, either the real-life performance of actions or their public endorsement (providing this is done voluntarily) is sufficient to instigate the comparison process. I shall refer to both forms of commitment – doing and saying – as 'output', and this is how they are represented in Figures 6 and 7.

---

[10] This statement is in line with evidence that the public expression of attitudes counter to a person's own can bring about a change in that person's attitude towards acceptance of what has been said [11, 18].

A note on consistency

It will be gathered that consistency between an action (posited or committed) and rules is a matter of degree rather than simple agreement or disagreement. Clarification of rules, as I have described it, is, in a sense, a mild form of their modification. Registration of a discrepancy and the large-scale revision of rules which this entails can be associated with changes at higher levels of the structure. On the other hand, 'clarification' can be associated with changes in the lower order derivatives.

Rule-following: the basis for a theory of psychosomatic influence

How does this picture of the individual in interaction with society fit the criteria for a theory of psychosomatic disease summarized at the beginning of this chapter? We have seen that one of the features of a structural model is that it recognizes influences on the individual from several different sources (reference group, sub-cultural communities, etc.). Hence, there is a place in this scheme for psychological, sociological, and anthropological evidence, although the model itself remains a psychological one. It is a psychological model because structures and rules are the unconscious property of individuals. It is able to incorporate accounts from all three disciplines because each of these is identified with a particular level within a structure (see Figure 5).

The concepts of structure and rule also lend themselves to physiological modelling in a unique way. It is reasonable to assume that the formation of planned actions is based on activity in the higher centres of the cortex, in the brain. Now, in order to construct theories and hypotheses about this physiological activity, we must first have a comprehensive psychological model.[11]

[11] As Harré and Secord put it, ... in order to be relevant to the explanation of performance, psychology must necessarily impose its form upon physiological investigations.' (Harré and Secord, 1972, p. 24.)

Suppose I am faced with the task of finding out what is inside a computer without having access to the circuitry itself or to any circuit diagrams. The only way I can go about this is to feed in information and note what comes out as a consequence. If output does not relate to input in a physically simple way, I have to construct models of how information is transformed, and test these models by continuing to observe the relation between input and output. Eventually, I will have a model which correctly predicts output from a knowledge of input. But this model will not be a circuit diagram – it will be more like a model of what is known in the computer world as 'software'. Only when I have proved that my software model is a good one can I go on to construct hypotheses about the circuitry by which the various software routines could be realized. And there may well be more than one way of realizing a particular programme electronically.

In trying to analyse people's social behaviour, I have done something very similar to the above – i.e. constructed a *psychological* model of people's encoding of the social world. The psychological model is like the software model in the above example. The point to be taken is that in instances where the relation between 'input' and 'output' is complex ('input' in our case being a person's perception of his social environment, and 'output' being actions themselves), the intermediary stage of modelling is necessary. Just as we cannot straightaway construct hypotheses about the electronic circuitry in our computer, we cannot, until we have a good psychological model, construct hypotheses about physiological activity underlying social behaviour. A viable psychological model thus provides the starting point for physiological investigations. Obviously whether the psychological model *is* viable or not depends, in the usual way, on its power to account for the facts.

The model of structure and rule-testing which I have outlined is no more than a first attempt at a psychological model. But through evaluating and refining models such as this, it ought to be possible to get to a stage where a generally accepted psychological model provides the springboard for physiological hypotheses.

This is what is meant by the contention that a psychological model 'must be cast in such a form as to be able to lead on to physiological hypotheses'. A model invoking the concepts of underlying structure and social rules lends itself to physiological modelling in a way which none of the conventional psychosomatic theories do.

The first three criteria would thus seem to be met. Consideration of the final criterion – that a psychosomatic theory must lead to predictions which are testable in a clear way – must be left until I have described exactly how this concept of human behaviour as a rule-following activity bears on the issue of psychosomatic disease.

From this sketch of the hypothetical mechanism which underlies the production of actions, it is possible to envisage two opposite states of affairs. On the one hand, there is the 'ideal' situation, where an individual is habitually 'outputting' actions (either in performance or by public endorsement) which, on testing against his system of rules result in a high proportion of good matches, and the minimum of modification. And, on the other hand, there is the situation in which radical modification of rules is often necessary before consistency is achieved. The former will be associated with constant, solid, habitual social behaviour, and probably a sense of personal identity and worth (with each occasion of consistency further clarifying and consolidating rules). The latter, on the other hand, is likely to be associated with inconstant, fitful, and uncertain social behaviour, and a sense of personal ineffectiveness, alienation, and 'loss of identity'.

Disease

How does this system provide the basis for a model of psychosomatic disease? The central thesis of this chapter is now fairly simply stated. It is that an individual's susceptibility to disease is increased when this 'ideal' situation fails to hold.

More precisely, *the likelihood of symptoms appearing is increased in the absence of frequent registrations of consistency.* This may mean either that little or no 'output' is occurring, or that the automatic comparison of 'output' with rules continually results in inconsistency being registered. It is assumed that the form of the resultant disease is a function of heredity, the concentration of impinging antigens and toxins, and other physical 'risk factors'.

From Figure 6, and the assumptions I have made concerning the testing process, it is a comparatively straightforward matter to derive two conditions which must hold if the 'ideal' situation of correspondence between action and rules is to obtain.

(1) the directives laid down by rules should not be incompatible with the physical environment, which includes the limitations imposed by the biological attributes of the subject himself. In other words, rules must be sufficiently pragmatic and malleable to permit actions which satisfy the organism's needs and do not overstep its physical and physiological limitations.

(2) an individual must constantly vindicate rules either by committing or by endorsing actions. More fully this entails:
    either (a) that he habitually engages in purposeful activities[12];
    and/or (b) that he habitually engages in conversation with others (or with one other) in which he declares his commitment to courses of action or to rules (attitudes, values, styles, beliefs etc.) themselves.

'Purposeful activity' is intended here to mean the same as 'social behaviour', and refers to any actively followed pursuit

[12] i.e. any activity with a goal that is understood and shared by others, or at least by one other. This is tantamount to saying that a person's actions must form part of a social communication network as this is described, e.g. by Shibutani [19]. There is also a correspondence between this proposal and Durkheim's concept of a *conscience collective* [20], and the key notions in symbolic interaction theory [21].

[13] The process of social comparison already described.

with an end product (or goal) which is valued and upheld by a group of people.[14] Thieving is classed as a purposeful activity and a social behaviour under this definition, because there is agreement among those who practise it regarding its goals, as well as standards of professionalism concerning how to go about it. So too is gardening, for the same reasons, in spite of the fact that it is often carried on alone. In both these examples, the activity achieves its meaning from a social consensus concerning practice and accomplishment.

Both these conditions (1 and 2) are necessary for 'output' to occur, and for comparison of 'output' with rules to result in the registration of consistency. Provided they are met, it is likely that the individual will be relating to society, or part of it, in a meaningful and effective manner, and that he will experience a sense of personal identity and worth.

The opposite state of affairs is the absence of consistency, whether through repeated inconsistency or comparative lack of 'output'. It is this eventuality which research strongly suggests is linked, in a fundamental way, to enhanced susceptibility. The absence of consistency can be attributed to violation of either or both the two conditions. Some general circumstances can be described which entail a violation of each condition:

Violation of condition 1

  (i) The tenure of extremely severe and inflexible rules inhibiting or restricting the satisfaction of biologically based needs and tendencies;

 (ii) The tenure of extremely severe and inflexible rules demanding a performance which exceeds biological limitations of the organism.

Violation of condition 2(a)

  (i) An abrupt change in a person's social environment, so that a familiar well-practised set of rules is found to be inapplicable to the new social circumstances;

 (ii) A change in a person's social environment, so that the

[14] The 'group' can consist in as few as two people – e.g. husband and wife.

adoption of new unfamiliar rules suddenly becomes necessary.

Violation of condition 2(b)

(i) Severance of a person from a reference group;
(ii) Direct assault on rules themselves (e.g. attitudes, beliefs, values) by objective evidence or through criticism or ridicule.

It must be said straightaway that the 'life events' which spring to mind in connection with the violation of conditions 2(a) and 2(b) represent instances which possibly, but do not inevitably entail the hypothetical state of affairs I am suggesting causes enhanced disease risk. The model can be used to make definite judgments about this, but only when details of the individual circumstances surrounding each event are known. For example, it is expected that bereavement will endanger health if, and only if, the presence of the lost person was a prerequisite either for involvement in purposeful activities, or for social interaction, substitute opportunities for which are not available. The extent of the subject's independent involvements and his access to alternative social contacts (reference groups) are therefore very important factors in assessing the 'risk value' of the loss. In a similar vein, the impact of retirement will be cushioned if the individual has recourse to pursuits and social circles other than those connected with the job itself. Likewise, moving away from friends will entail risk only insofar as they served as an important reference point, and if there are no available substitutes. And so on. To be able to use this model to make predictions about a person's chances of becoming ill, information is required beyond a simple knowledge of whether or not a given life event has occurred.

Some life events that might be linked with violations of conditions 2(a) and 2(b) have already been studied in relation to the onset of various diseases. For example, bereavement, separation, changing jobs, moving home and social mobility.[15] But

---

[15] See Chapter 5.

the model also suggests a fair number of hypotheses that are not so obvious. For instance, insofar as it entails major and abrupt revisions of well-practised rules, getting married must count as a potential influence on health. The same goes for promotion, coming out of prison, retirement, and many other changes which would probably not be classed as 'stressful' on an intuitive definition. Separation from a marital partner or living companion could be deleterious both, if the couple had enjoyed a harmonious and affectionate relationship, and if they had lived together in a chronic state of habitual dissension. The important issue, according to the model, is whether or not this had grown into an integral way of life – i.e. whether the partners had evolved and had become dependent on sets of rules, albeit perhaps antagonistic ones, which were used a great deal in their day to day interaction. There are many literary allusions to relationships which appear to thrive on mutual attribution of blame. The main characters in Edward Albee's *Who's afraid of Virginia Woolf*, husband and wife, turn out to be addicted to a style of life centred around continual insults and recrimination. In Laurie Lee's *Cider with Rosie*, we are told about two old grannies whose main pre-occupation seems to be mutual deprecation. With one of them this is such an obsession that when her opposite number dies, she follows suit in about a fortnight. Such a state of affairs can be translated into the jargon of the social psychologist by saying that the behaviour of each partner functions to some extent as a negative reference point for the other.

This model takes the causal factor in increased susceptibility to disease to be a 'malfunction' in an underlying mechanism. It is therefore assumed that particular emotional states, such as 'helplessness' and 'depression', where they are identified in association with the onset of illness [22], do not play a primary causal role. They are considered, like the organic manifestations of the pathology itself, to be symptomatic of the underlying psychological malfunction rather than to be active in the production of illness. As I have indicated, there are major difficulties in conceiving of how an emotion, in its mentalistic sense, could be logically cast in a causal role.

The main thesis of this chapter, and of this book, can be roughly summarized by saying that a person's resistance to disease remains high provided that his attitudes, beliefs and values are sufficiently compromising, and provided that he is continually 'involved'. 'Involvement' can take two forms: (1) conversation with other people, in which a degree of personal commitment is expressed, and (2) preoccupation in activity, whether carried on alone or in company, which is directed towards a definite goal or end-product, and which entails a modicum of effort. Health is endangered when there is a sudden drop in the extent of one or other of these forms of 'involvement', for whatever reason.

If the ideas embodied in the structural model are a fair representation of the facts, then a somewhat sinister possibility must be entertained. This is that death through illness may actually serve a useful purpose for the human species as a whole. It must be quite clear that 'useful purpose' is meant here in the special sense of Darwin's theory of evolution, as it applies to man.

The selection of members of a species best fitted to survive in a changing environment takes place by genetic mutations causing small variations in an organism's characteristics. Most mutations are disadvantageous, but a tiny minority facilitate survival. Those individuals poorly equipped to survive, either as a result of a harmful mutation or because their faculties are inadequate to cope with an environmental change, simply die out.

Survival of a species by natural selection has no regard for the individual, and numerous highly sophisticated mechanisms have been discovered which serve to protect a species at the expense of its 'weaker' members. For example, when mating, the male praying mantis must jump on to the back of the female in such a way that its legs fall squarely into slots on the female's body. Accurate placement of the male's legs in a single movement protects his life by inhibiting the female from killing and eating him: should the male fail this test and make an incompetent jump, so that his legs miss the slots, the female is stimulated to attack and destroy the male before mating has taken place. Accurate jumping, and the good coordination which this implies, is important during the life of the mantis for trapping prey and avoiding predators. A means of ensuring that only good jumpers can survive to reproduce protects the species and aids its longevity. But this entails the individual being disregarded and frequently selected against.

Most biologists concur that a very important, perhaps the most important, asset to man's survival is his proclivity to organize himself into cooperative groups. Man has lived in groups for at least two million years. A cooperative group or society, however small,[1] because of its pooled resources, has much greater survival potential than a socially unstructured collection of individuals. Now, a cooperative group, by definition, is made up of individuals each of whom has a specific role or function. This is to say that for each individual, criteria of performance (i.e. rules) are reasonably well defined. The more close-knit the community, the more generally endorsed are its objectives and the more clear cut are the rules held by individual members.

Now, I have already described this condition at an individual level as the exemplary state for maintenance of health through the psychosomatic factor.[2] 'Low risk' individuals have been characterized as those who hold clear rules and for whom the opportunity to apply these rules effectively is ever open. 'High risk' individuals, on the other hand, are those who are socially uninvolved: those lacking the wherewithal to relate to a community, even if this means carrying on socially sanctioned pursuits in private. Individuals without this ability contribute nothing to the community's cohesion, and in all probability detract from it in that they draw on its resources without adding to them.

It could therefore be conjectured that psychosomatic disease represents an automatic 'self-destruct' mechanism the purpose of which is to protect the species by selecting against individuals who, as a result of social change, become socially redundant.

A person's mechanism for following rules is the umbilical cord between that individual and society: the interface between

---

[1] Including an association between two people.
[2] See Chapter 8.

the two. If it is correct to say, as I have, that the failure of effective rule-following is the condition which, more than any other, predisposes a person to illness, then it is difficult to ignore the evolutionary implications of such a contingency. Rahe's observation [1] that it is mainly serious and fatal diseases which are found in association with a high incidence of recent life changes is consistent with this speculation.

If psychosomatic disease does have survival value in this way for man, a sophisticated yet paradoxical form of symbiosis could be said to exist. However morally and emotionally repugnant the idea seems, antigens and toxins, so patently harmful to the individual, may nevertheless be advantageous to *species* survival.

The final standard by which a theory is judged is how well it accounts for existing findings, and how well it translates into predictions that can be unambiguously tested. We must be clear then just what the model advanced in Chapter 8 is saying about real life situations. As was pointed out, it does not stipulate that bereavement will always endanger health, nor that divorce, or job change or immigration will invariably do so. Research into each of these possibilities,[1] while relevant to the model, does not strictly speaking constitute a test of it.

The concern of the model is with intentional human behaviour – deliberate actions – and with the state of affairs presumed to hold when the hypothetical mechanism governing the performance of actions becomes confused and ineffective. Enhanced susceptibility to illness has been linked to a condition in which there is a chronic absence of behaviour (or 'output' as I have called it) which corresponds to the desiderata contained in an underlying system of rules. To use a computer analogy again, this circumstance can be regarded as a non-complementarity between the individual's internal social 'programme' and his social environment. We noted that the absence of consistent 'output' can be attributed to two things. Either the rules a person holds are so severe in their demands and so rigid in their form that they periodically clash with the expression of normal biologically based tendencies; or the social environment has changed so that an important opportunity for rule-following no longer exists, and little or no 'output' occurs. 'Output' is the means by which the individual maintains a tie between himself and the community. It involves

[1] See Chapter 5.

personal commitment and takes two forms: actions themselves, or the verbal commitments – the expressions of attitude – which are made so frequently in the company of others.

Conversely, for an individual's general resistance to disease to remain high, I have suggested that the expression of rules through 'output' must continue. The individual must therefore be free of excessively rigid and severe criteria and he must be continually committing himself, actively or verbally. These are the necessary conditions for effective agency, and for maintenance of health through the psychosomatic factor.

So what implications follow for the study of 'life events' and personality?

Life events

To test predictions from the model relating to life events, we might start by pinpointing circumstances which result in a reduction in the extent of a person's active involvement, or a constriction in his social contact. For example, we might look for instances where the opportunity for pursuing customary activities and interests has been suddenly removed, or discouraged as socially deviant or irrelevant. If this happens, and social involvement declines, we can deduce that rules will not be receiving the same degree of clarification and consolidation through the repeated registration of consistency. The ways in which the inappropriateness of behaviour is communicated, and its performance suppressed, need not concern us here.[2] The point to be taken is that although a recently bereaved man, for example, might find himself in this position, before we can say for certain whether his health is at risk we must have more information. We need to know how close he was to his wife, what percentage of the time he spent exclusively in her company, whether he was involved in activities or communities independently of her, and what opportunities are now available for carrying on with these.

[2] See, for example, Schachter [1] for a description of the tactics used by members of a group to induce conformity.

Exactly the same goes for other forms of separation, and for job change, migration, and so on. In each case it is not enough simply to note whether or not one of these life changes has occurred, and to catalogue it on a checklist in the manner of Holmes and Rahe.[3] Neither is it enough to take into account general details of the context of such changes, as Brown attempts to do in his interview and rating method.[4] We need to ask specific questions about the person, his habitual social behaviours, and the disruption in the pattern of these which a life event has caused.

Again, it must be stressed that the term 'social behaviours' does not in this context simply mean things done in the company of others, but anything with a goal that is recognized by other people, or at least by one other.

The specific questions it is necessary to ask are as follows:

1. *Does the subject hold excessively severe and rigid standards?* If so, life events involving social change and reorganization are more than normally likely to leave him in a state where little or no consistency between committed actions and rules is registered. This is on account of the uncompromising quality of the rules themselves, and the likelihood that they will stubbornly persist in prescribing actions that are inappropriate and impractical in the changed circumstances.

2. *Does a given life event remove the opportunity for involvement in purposeful activities?* If so, are there available opportunities for engaging in other substitute forms of activity?

3. *Does a given life event remove the opportunity for social comparison,*[5] by cutting the subject off from a person or group of people in whose company he habitually made verbal commitments and endorsements (i.e. a reference group)? If so, is there access to other social contacts?

---

[3] The Social Readjustment Rating Scale, discussed in Chapter 5.
[4] See Chapter 5, also [2].
[5] The exchange of attitudes, opinions etc., recognized by psychologists to be one of the most pervasive aspects of ordinary friendly conversation.

These questions lead on to a practical technique of measuring the psychological 'risk factor' attached to life events, as I have defined it.

Of the various existing techniques for finding out whether significant social changes have occurred over a specified period, the method developed by Brown [2], and used to predict the onset of symptoms in psychiatric patients, is probably the most sound. Briefly, this is as follows.

Initially, the interviewer devotes some time to establishing a friendly relationship with a subject. He then covers a comprehensive list of commonly experienced life events (see Appendix II) which are believed to require some adaptation, and the subject is asked to say whether each one, or anything similar to it, has transpired in his life over the period of interest. Where this is so, the event in question is carefully dated, and the subject is encouraged to talk freely and openly about the circumstances surrounding it. The questions in the interview are the same for everyone, and only factual information is used. People's accounts of the distress caused by events are ignored, as it is known that such accounts are particularly prone to inaccuracy and distortion. The interviewer thus ends up with a set of reported facts, dates and contextual details.

In Brown's studies, interviews are taped and transcribed; and the transcriptions are then rated on a number of scales by trained, independent raters. This is a time-consuming and costly process. It also has the disadvantage that subjects are required to talk while a tape recorder is running. Some people find this disconcerting and are consequently inhibited in what they say.

There is a great deal to be said for collecting information from people in the way recommended by Brown. However, the rule-following model suggests a quite different method for assessing the stressfulness, or psychological 'risk value', of a given life event. I am currently putting into practice the following method in a study of the recent lives of people who have suffered a first heart attack. The aim is to quantify the impact of life changes experienced by heart patients over the year prior to the initial onset of their symptoms, and to compare the changes experienced by patients with those experienced by healthy control subjects, matched according to age and sex.

A method for assessing the impact of life events

Information about the incidence of life events throughout the pre-morbid year (or equivalent period for control subjects) is collected as suggested by Brown. Interviews with subjects are not recorded, but for every life event which comes to light, two standard question routines are applied.

The aim of the first routine is to discover whether the event resulted in a net change in the amount of time a subject spent in purposeful activities (in hours per week, on average); and the aim of the second routine is to discover whether the event resulted in a net change in the amount of time a subject spent in informal conversation with others (again, in hours per week, on average).[6]

In addition to discovering whether a given life event caused a change in the amount of time habitually spent in one *particular* activity, a further set of probe questions is applied to find out whether this change was counterbalanced by a compensating change in other activities. Similarly, in addition to questions aimed at finding out whether a given 'life event' resulted in the subject seeing less of one *particular* individual, probe questions are asked in order to find out whether the subject saw correspondingly more of others, The series of questions applied in association with each life event discovered is given in Appendix II.

So, for example, if the subject is a keen gardener, and he has moved house during the relevant year, the questions put to him will run like this:

'Did the move result in your doing any more or any less gardening, on average?'

[6] For the purpose of translating this aspect of the model into a workable methodology, it is necessary to assume that all conversation involves verbal commitments of a 'social comparison' nature.

(If the answer was 'less')
'How much less time, in hours per week, on average?' (In this particular case the questions would have to be asked twice – once for summer and once for winter.)

Then a set of questions is asked to determine whether there had been any compensating increase in other activities – i.e.:

'Did you, as a consequence, find you had more time available to do other things?'
(If so)
'What, in particular, did you do in the extra available time?'
'This is rather difficult, but I want you to think back, very carefully, to the time in your life just after *the event*, and try to remember how many hours a week you normally would spend doing this. On average.'
(Where necessary) 'How many hours on an average weekday? And how many on weekends?'

Where necessary, further encouragement is given at this juncture by going through the week on a day-to-day, or even an hour-by-hour basis.

'Now do the same thing for the period in your life just before *the event*.'
'Did you take up anything else, or find that you were doing more of anything else after *the event*?'
(If so – same probes again.)

A similar set of questions is then applied to determine whether there had been any compensating increase in the amount of time devoted to socializing (see Appendix II).
People's accounts are rated by the interviewer on the following two criteria:

    (i) The change caused by a life event in the average amount of time (in hours per week) spent in purposeful activities,[7] irrespective of the nature of the activities themselves;

and (ii) The change caused by a life event in the average

amount of time (in hours per week) spent in conversation with others, irrespective of the identity of the people concerned.

For the purpose of scoring, no distinction is made between time spent in purposeful activities and time spent in conversation with others. The end-product is therefore a single score, representing the number of hours per week increase or decrease in both these forms of social involvement.

Increases in average hours per week involvement of either sort count as positive scores, and decreases as negative scores. When the necessary information has been collected from subjects in this manner, all scores relating to specific events, activities, and areas of socializing, as well as scores relating to compensating changes (changes in other areas), are summed up to give a single final index.

Carrying out this procedure is sometimes difficult, and there has to be a certain amount of flexibility in the question routine itself. Some individuals have to be coaxed to provide a sufficient amount of detail concerning their day-to-day activities, and changes in there, in order that the necessary ratings can be made. But with encouragement, and if all else fails by obtaining hour-by-hour accounts, this detail can be extracted.

Certain arbitrary conventions have to be applied. For example, temporary, or reversible changes (such as school holidays) are ignored altogether. Changes in either form of social involvement that are not clearly attributable to a life event are ignored. Time spent in the company of others, where it is clear that little or no conversation of a 'social comparison' nature took place, is also ignored. (Here, when there is any doubt, the subject is asked whether the individual concerned

---

[7] A 'purposeful activity' was taken to include any actively followed pursuit to which criteria of desirability can be applied. Such criteria may apply either to performance itself (as in a sport or playing a musical instrument) or to the outcome of an activity which forms part of a larger scale project (as in working for exams or gardening). Ambiguous instances were resolved in the way suggested by Harré and his co-workers; that is, by asking the subject himself for the reason behind his preoccupation (see, for example, Marsh, Rosser and Harré. *The rules of disorder*. London: Routledge, 1978).

was someone with whom he often exchanged opinions or points of view.)

Occasionally, multiple changes follow a particular life event, so that it becomes very difficult for the subject to respond to the standard question routines. In such instances, an alternative approach is used, and the subject is asked about changes in the amount of time he had available to do nothing. The actual question put to the subjects is;

> 'How much more (or less) time did you find you had available after *the event* to relax – to sit and do nothing, or read, or watch T.V. or whatever, on average?'

He is then questioned further to find out exactly what 'doing nothing' entails in his case. It is important to ensure that this itself does not involve planning, or recreational activities with a goal, such as playing cards.

This interview and rating procedure is thus heavily structured, so as to be as standard as possible without losing access to essential information. It will be clear that the emphasis of the rating procedure is less on identifying 'life events' themselves than on determining their effect on a person's social involvement. Moreover, it is the net amount of such involvement rather than its nature which is considered to be important. So, for example, if someone who has retired spends the extra 40 hours per week he now has free watching television, he is given a score of − 40 on this particular issue. But if he uses the extra 40 hours home decorating and rebuilding his car, he gets a score of 0 (assuming, that is, there are no changes in what he does with the remainder of his time). Similarly, if a man's wife has left him, and the time he used to spend in her company he now spends with his friends, here too the score will be 0.

Thus the nature of the events themselves is almost irrelevant. Brown's questionnaire and interview technique is used purely as a 'way in' – a standard means of getting people to talk about things which may have altered their pattern of living.

Built into this rating procedure is the proviso for taking into account so called 'substitute activities' and 'social support' – factors which past research has shown to be significant in influencing proneness to becoming ill and likelihood of survival.

As a research instrument, this technique can be applied both retrospectively and prospectively. In a retrospective design, a group of people who are sick and a group of people who are healthy are interviewed as described. Their lives prior to the initial onset of symptoms (and the equivalent period in the lives of the healthy controls) are studied, and comparisons are made between the two groups. We might expect to find greater social upheaval, as defined and measured in this way, among those in the sick group than among the healthy controls.

The preliminary results from the retrospective study of heart patients are encouraging. The interview procedure itself has proved practicable and relatively easy to administer. It also shows signs of being able to differentiate between heart patients and controls more sensitively than other techniques for assessing the 'stress' from life events, such as the Holmes–Rahe Social Readjustment Rating Scale.

However, there are many weaknesses in retrospective research of this nature. The prospective approach provides a much sounder basis for testing predictions. In this, a group of healthy individuals, perhaps people about to be screened for signs of a specific illness, are seen and interviewed in exactly the same way. They are then followed by the researcher over a set period (usually between one and five years), and a record is kept of their health during this time. In this way the psychological assessment can be used actually to forecast which individuals are most likely to become ill in the future. The assessment technique is thus evaluated on the basis of how accurate its forecast turns out to be.

Personality

The model suggests two general hypotheses about personality and proneness to disease. The first concerns the defensive strategies which are brought into play to force a match between 'output' and rules, so that an individual can represent (or more accurately, misrepresent) something he has done or said as consistent with the rules he holds. These strategies manifest themselves in the distorting, denying and rationalizing man-oeuvres people unwittingly use to justify their behaviour to themselves. Thus, for example, a plainly deceitful action may be seen as quite morally acceptable with a little help from some selective remembering of the circumstances leading up to it.

People differ in their defensive style – the characteristic way they clear themselves of blame. Some are inclined to repress things, while others resort to their skill with language and 'explain things away'. Apart from such differences in style, people also differ in their overall capability to defend them-selves. Another way of putting this is to say that the criterion for what constitutes consistency between 'output' and rules is characteristically less strict in some individuals (the well defended ones) than in others. This being so, remembering that defences act in favour of consistency, we might expect people with a strong defensive capability to show a lower than average susceptibility to illness.

Several lines of evidence support this hypothesis. A large number of studies have linked unsuccessful psychological defences to rapid progression of cancer and autoimmune con-ditions [3]. Strong[8] psychological defences have been associated with good prognosis for survival on kidney machines [4], and with low levels of body chemicals, such as corticosteroids, known to constitute risk factors for various diseases [5, 6]. Lazarus has reviewed a number of findings supporting this latter con-clusion [7].[9]

One particular style of defence merits special attention.

---

[8] But not pathologically so.

[9] Kissen [8], and Bahnson and Bahnson [9], in a series of studies of the personalities of cancer patients, have found evidence that these patients tend to deny and repress unpleasant emotions to a greater extent than is normal. However, it does not follow that a person who represses and denies un-comfortable feelings is one who is 'strongly defended' in the sense intended here.

Occasionally, actions that are socially discrepant, even to the extent of being publicly condemned, are sustained by a belief on the part of the actor that he is imbued with a special unique authority. The individual sees his own eccentric activities as conforming to directives removed from those upheld in his immediate social environment. Consequently, he is able to carry on extraordinary, perhaps even disapproved activities, yet remain relatively impervious to the attacks, criticisms, and other techniques society has for inducing conventionality. Consistency between actions and rules is achieved by assigning an absolute value to what is done through the inferred approval of a (probably non-existent) 'higher' authority. St. Joan, for example, reputedly knew the things she was doing to be 'right' through the voices she 'heard'.

Of the conventional psychological descriptions of personality, the one which closest fits this description is the 'paranoid' or 'schizoid' type. Characteristic of these traits is a discrepancy between the individual's beliefs and reality. The psychiatric condition of paranoid schizophrenia entails a failure to relate thoughts and action to the real world.[10] Fantasies and hallucinations, if these occur, are indistinguishable from real life situations and perceptions. The paranoid tendency exhibits itself in the person's conviction that he is being controlled or usurped by a non-existent force. Delusions of grandeur or of persecution are frequent symptoms, and the belief that he is a special agent of God is not uncommon.

Is there any evidence to suggest that abnormal resistance to disease is to be found among individuals with firmly held delusional beliefs of this nature?

Huxley *et al.* [10], discussing the possibility that there is a strong genetic component in schizophrenia, summarize the findings of a number of studies by saying:

Overt schizophrenics are extremely resistant to surgical and

[10] Schizophrenia is not, as popular myth would have us believe, characterized by a 'split personality'. The 'split', if there is one, is between the individual's mental world and reality.

wound shocks (and recover more rapidly), to visceral perfora-
tion, to high doses of histamine (correlated with fewer mast
cells in the skin), insulin, thyroxine and other physiologically
active substances, to pain, to arthritis, to many allergies and
probably to many infections (with the exception of tuberculosis, which they are prone to). One of us has seen a
schizophrenic recover successfully from the most appalling
burns which would have killed any normal person in hours
or minutes.[11]

The impression we get from this extract however is not
invariably supported. Survey reports, while sometimes confirming a low rate of physical illness among psychiatric patients,
sometimes reveal exactly the reverse. Babigian and Odoroff
[11], for example, studied death rates in a large psychiatric
population and found the relative risk of death for psychiatric
patients to be two-and-a-half to three times that for the general
population. The chronically ill, the aged and the alcoholic
contributed to this difference, but even when these individuals
were removed the relative risk remained one-and-a-half times
that of the general population. It is also important to bear
in mind that the psychiatric patients in this and similar surveys
comprise a very heterogeneous population, and include de-
pressives, neurotics, schizophrenics, patients with organic brain
syndrome, suicide cases and probably drug addicts. Even the
sub-samples of 'schizophrenics' are likely to include patients
with a variety of different disturbances: psychiatric diagnosis is
known to be very variable. The problems of relating incidence
of physical disease to incidence of mental illness by means of a
survey are considerable. It is noteworthy that Innes and Millar
[12], in an investigation of psychiatric referrals in Scotland,
found the raised death risk for psychiatric patients to be
largely accounted for by organic psychoses.

[11] Alternative explanations of these findings must of course be borne in
mind, particularly the possibility argued by Huxley et al., that schizophrenia
and differential susceptibility to various diseases are both derivatives of the
same genetic factor.

So large scale studies of psychiatric patients do not get us very far. Much more useful in relation to the hypothesis under consideration are smaller scale approaches. One group of studies in particular provides an intriguing clue as to what might lie behind these ostensibly conflicting reports.

Weblin [13] noticed that the onset of schizophrenia frequently coincided with a remission in asthmatic symptoms. Similar observations have also been made by other authors. Clow and Prout [14] reported an amelioration of mental disorder in 100 hospital mental patients during periods of physical illness; and Appel and Rosen [15] observed the same 'alternation' between somatic and psychiatric (in this case paranoid and schizoid) symptoms in three out of four intensively studied patients, two of whom were suffering from ulcerative colitis and one from rheumatoid arthritis.

An interpretation of these findings favoured by some authors [e.g. 16, 17] is that proneness to mental illness and proneness to physical illness *do* in fact go hand in hand, but succumbing to one functions in some way as a protection against the other. Recall that in the rule model, psychological defences are represented as a device for achieving consistency between actions and rules, before rules are changed (Figure 6). A certain amount of repression, distortion and denial is quite normal, and probably absolutely necessary, as I have said, for healthy adaptive functioning. The idea that psychiatric states, especially those involving a profound distortion of reality, are an exaggerated form of defence against insoluble problems and conflicts is by no means a new one. Could mental illness and physical illness then be alternative reactions to the same problem; the same underlying 'malfunction'? If so, we would expect events in people's lives preceding episodes of psychiatric illness to be similar in nature to life events found prior to the onset of physical illness.

Kuo [18], in a recent study of Chinese immigrants to America, has found evidence that social isolation and poor adjustment to the American way of life were associated with poor mental health. These factors appeared more critical in affecting mental health than other more conventionally attested forms of 'stress'.

In a recent study of alcoholics twelve months after a course of treatment, Orford *et al.* [19] found that 'marital cohesion' played a large part in contributing to favourable outcome from treatment. 'Marital cohesion' can be defined roughly as the degree of togetherness, mutual cooperation and unity between husband and wife.

Studies carried out by Leff and his associates have also confirmed that the onset and relapse of schizophrenia are affected by similar life events to those found in association with physical illness [20]. In a study of patients being treated for schizophrenia and depression, Vaughn and Leff [21] discovered that future relapse could be predicted on the basis of the amount of criticism to which patients were subjected by their relatives. The greater the number of critical comments a patient received, the poorer were his chances of remaining well. In terms of the rule model, criticism, especially when it comes from people who are close to the subject, is antagonistic to the achievement of consistency, and can be construed as an assault upon rules themselves.

In Brown's meticulously conducted studies of schizophrenia and depression in London, it was found that the factor best able to predict[12] depressive illness was 'the experience of loss' [2, 22]. This is meant in a broad sense, to include separations, the threat of separation or bereavement (e.g. the potentially fatal illness of someone close), an unpleasant revelation about someone close which challenged the subject's opinion of that person (e.g. news about a husband's unfaithfulness), enforced change of residence, redundancy, and material deprivations and disappointments.

The closeness of these findings to those discussed in relation to physical illness is readily apparent. It is conceivable then, that the genesis of psychiatric and physical symptoms each represents an alternative response to an underlying pathology in psychological functioning, the essence of which I have tried to

[12] The predictions in this study were retrospective.

capture in the rule model and the assumptions surrounding it.

The second hypothesis about personality derives from the assumption that disease proneness is related to the long-term tenure of objectives[13] so severe and uncompromising in their demands on the individual as to be unrealistic – that is, incapable of implementation owing to the limitations imposed by the physical environment and the biological characteristics of the individual himself. It is important not to confuse this state of affairs with the tenure of firmly held goals which the individual sees himself as living up to, whether his attribution of success is grounded in reality or fantasy. An important factor is therefore an individual's own ideas concerning the fulfilment of his aims.

There are several lines that can be taken to investigate this hypothesis. One is to ask whether people having extreme standards of one sort or another are more prone to disease than others with humbler criteria for living. The high pressure, achievement oriented Type A person comes to mind. Perhaps this is the description of someone who holds definitions of competence and achievement which are so extreme that he constantly sees himself as failing to live up to them. The reason is quite simply that a level of performance is demanded which normal human limitations do not permit, owing to the need to rest and take other steps to satisfy organismic needs. It could be that when these natural tendencies manifest themselves, the Type A individual construes them as laziness and inadequacy, and therefore failure. If this analysis is anywhere near the mark, we might expect coronary-prone Type As characteristically to construe their efforts as falling short of the desired standard.

Reports from many sources confirm that coronary-prone individuals tend to feel unsatisfied with their achievements [23–26]. Arlow [27] presented evidence that the heart patient is 'inwardly convinced that he is a sham and cannot accept success. This inner insecurity and sense of weakness remains unaffected by realistic achievements.' Cathey et al. [28] state

[13] Derived from rules.

that all the heart patients in their study felt that the work they had undertaken was too difficult and that they had failed in achieving their life's goals. Miller [29] found that heart patients scored higher than average on a measure of 'overcontrol',[14] which was said to indicate that they are excessively concerned with the need to feel competent and responsible. Wardwell *et al.* [30], write that heart patients reveal an 'unstable self-concept', and Siltanen *et al.* [31] have presented evidence showing the existence of an unusually great discrepancy in heart patients between how they see themselves and how they would like to be.

It was noted in Chapter 6 that other inflexible styles of behaviour besides Type A have been reported in heart patients. Furthermore, some findings were discussed which pointed to the presence of rigidity of the Type A variety, as well as rigidity which cannot be called Type A in patients with non-coronary diseases. There is therefore a considerable body of evidence, consistent with the model, suggesting that Type A behaviour is a special instance of a more general characteristic: a tendency to hold rigid and extreme standards of one sort or another.

Emotions

What does the model have to say about emotions? Illness is assumed to result from a 'malfunction' in a hypothetical internal mechanism, not from any emotional state or states. Nevertheless, there is nothing to rule out the possibility that specific feelings may also result from this underlying malfunction. Such a contingency is illustrated in Figure 8.

It will be clear from Figure 8 that the model does not lead to hypotheses and predictions about emotional states in the same way as it does for life events and personality. However, one can speculate that the two conditions responsible for a chronic absence of consistency also give rise to certain

[14] As assessed by the Minnesota Multiphasic Personality Inventory (MMPI).

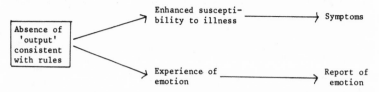

Figure 8 Emotions as an additional consequence of the 'underlying malfunction'

unpleasant emotions. The first condition – tenure of rules which are incompatible with the physical environment – might reasonably be expected to engender feelings of frustration and failure, owing to the repeated encountering of obstacles in the way of goals. The second – deprivation of an opportunity to corroborate rules – might be expected to evoke feelings of personal worthlessness, ineffectiveness, inadequacy, loss of identify, hopelessness, alienation and loneliness.

As we have seen, there are real problems in interpreting people's reports of emotions, which makes these ideas almost impossible to research. But broadly speaking, the findings of studies confirm these expectations.[15]

[15] See the discussion of emotions in relation to disease in Chapter 6.

Clearly, it would be premature at this stage glibly to proceed with recommendations about care of the sick. It must be emphasized that the model I have put forward is no more than a first attempt at organizing the evidence in a particular manner. Nevertheless, should the ideas developed in the preceding three chapters turn out to be along the right lines, many practical implications would follow. Here then are some pointers to what could be done, and some comments about what is bad in contemporary opinion, convention and policy regarding treatment, on the assumption that the ideas in the model are substantially valid – even though at present this assumption is unwarranted. It is important to establish that setting up theories of this nature is not just building castles in the air. Such theories have far-reaching practical consequences.

At the heart of this model of psychosomatic influence is the concept of *agency* – personal commitment – and the assumption that the absence of this is related, in a crucial way, to enhanced susceptibility to illness. Two kinds of personal commitment have been discussed. One is the real life voluntary commitment to activities with a purpose or goal; the other is the verbal declaration, in conversation, of attitudes, opinions, beliefs and values etc. These are the ways in which an individual relates to society, and also the ways in which he sustains a sense of personal identity and worth. The hypothesis has been put forward that a person's general level of resistance to disease is affected by the extent of his habitual involvement in one or other of these classes of activity, and that as this involvement declines, for whatever reason, the likelihood of his becoming ill increases correspondingly.[1]

According to the model, there is nothing to choose between these two categories of personal commitment. Both are regarded as sub-divisions of the same psychological process. A housewife who does nothing but gossip all day, and a hermit who hardly ever sees another person but spends all his time making violins, both adequately fulfil the criterion for active involvement.

For a start, then, it could be surmised that someone dedicated to a single pursuit, such as his work, or doing things for another individual, so that this occupies almost all of his time and excludes any other activity, is at greater risk than someone with a variety of different interests, or someone whose social contact is more diversified. Obviously, the danger in a monadic commitment will be greatest where there is a chance of it being suddenly terminated, for instance by enforced retirement, or death.

Consider a hypothetical comparison between two men on the verge of retirement. Suppose one is a keen family man, amateur musician and member of a local sports club; and suppose the other has no family and no hobbies or interests outside his work. Obviously, the former is the one more protected from the condition I have associated with a deterioration in health because his habitual involvement in outside work interests means that he possesses sets of rules which will still be operative after he has retired. The latter's experience, on the other hand, has equipped him with comparatively specialized rules, few of which are appropriate to the world outside his job. When the opportunity to carry on with his work no longer exists, he faces an adaptation which initially amounts to a substantial restructuring of his internal 'social programme'. He is an extreme example of someone at risk.

It is no use pretending that people can be routinely endowed

[1] Provided, of course, a reduction in the extent of his involvement in one class of activity is not counterbalanced by an increase in his involvement in the other. What is important is a change in the net amount of personal involvement, where this includes both categories of commitment. See Chapter 10.

with families, friends and interests. But it will be apparent that there are many things that can be done, both by an individual himself, and by those around him, to avoid a situation of exclusive preoccupation with one isolated interest, especially where there is a chance that the opportunity for indulging it will be cut off. No two people's interests and social lives are the same, and it would be trite to attempt to catalogue preventive and remedial measures 'cookbook' style. It has been stressed that the rule-following model is generative, which is to say it can be applied to individual cases each time generating an analysis pertinent only to that specific case.[2] Because every personal predicament is unique, it follows that an analysis of it, and any implications stemming from such an analysis, must themselves be unique. To ask for a universal list of suggestions about how to minimize the risk to health from the psychological factor would be a little like asking for a comprehensive list of all the sentences it is conceivably possible to construct.

But in general, to 'prepare psychologically' for such changes means to equip oneself with a knowledge of the rules that will become appropriate to the new style of life, and if possible to familiarize oneself with them by practising or 'rehearsing' them a little. In this way, a person can inoculate himself against the potentially harmful consequences of foreseeable events involving social change.

Many of the recommendations for preventive action which follow from this principle are little more than common sense, and are already adhered to by people in an intuitive manner. For example, the wife of an executive may express concern that her husband will not have 'enough to do' when he retires. However, this and related concerns run a great deal deeper than such intuitions would credit, as we have seen. The folk beliefs which are part of every culture undeniably contain a certain amount of valid information. The problem lies in separating this information from the superstitions, prejudices and natural human distortions that are equally a cultural

[2] An 'ideographic' analysis.

endowment. Research has made it clear that many of the conditions intuitively believed to be 'stressful', such as high noise levels, poor working conditions or a heavy work load, do not seem to entail anything like the threat to health that do changes calling for a re-establishment of a person's orientation to his social environment. Moreover, there are certain instances where recommendations based on the model are at variance with social convention and common sense: the abrupt chances conventionally expected when people get married, for example. Release from prison too, notwithstanding its positive aspects, represents a transition from a highly structured and rule-bound routine in a highly cohesive community, to an unpredictable, perhaps rejecting, outside world. In some circumstances this must be an extremely taxing adaptation, carrying with it serious implications for physical health. The same is true to a lesser extent of coming out of other institutions. Even our attitudes towards people recovering from sickness are by no means free of dogma. The relentless pressure so often applied to 'take it easy', and 'not to do too much' – sound enough advice in many instances – may be counterproductive if carried too far. Arranging things so that everything is done for such a person, and depriving him of opportunities for active involvement when he is physically strong enough, may be the worst kind of 'help' it is possible to give. It would be quite wrong to proceed with pat recommendations without detailed knowledge about a specific case, but in every instance the best tactic would seem to be one of informed compromise.

The least manageable of all social changes are those that occur without any prior warning. Deaths, in particular, are not always expected. In such instances a decisive factor may be whether the survivor has the inclination and the energy to become caught up in new interests. Interestingly, there have been many published and broadcast accounts of people who have coped with the loss of someone close by determining to realize a difficult ambition.

The role of family and friends, both as providers of social

support, and as a source of encouragement to a person to think in terms of new commitments, is of course, a vitally important one. To encourage someone who has experienced a major loss to become actively involved in new interests may however not be an easy task, especially if that person is conscious that pressure is being brought to bear.

A psychology experiment carried out in 1959 by Festinger and Carlsmith [1], using ideas taken from cognitive dissonance theory,[3] is worth quoting in this context, since it highlights one of the key factors in trying to influence other people's attitudes and interests. The subjects in this experiment were American college students, some of whom were paid a token amount of money ($1) and some of whom were paid a much larger sum ($20) for complying with a request. They were aksed to tell other students that an extremely boring and tedious task they had just finished was interesting. Later on, and quite independently (ostensibly as part of an 'official survey'), they were asked for their own personal opinions about the interest value of the task. Those who had been given the token payment rated the task as more interesting than those who had been paid the larger amount. The interpretation offered by the authors of these findings was that to tell a lie for $20 was considered justifiable by most of the students ('Anyone would agree to do this, if they were offered $20'), but to tell a lie for $1 was not. Consequently those in the $1 group were 'compelled' to view their own attitudes as closer to what they had said than those in the $20 group. The point to be taken from this experiment, and others which have produced similar findings [2], is that a person's attitudes and interests *can* be shaped by coercing him to do things, providing he does not regard what he does as the result of coercion. A large volume of research on conformity [3] has made it clear that subtle pressure from a group can induce an individual to do all kinds of things, including things that are discrepant with his attitudes. How-

[3] See Chapter 2.

ever, as soon as he becomes aware of an attempt to influence him, any enduring effect is lost.[4]

Similar manipulations are possible in a less structured way in an everyday context. We do not have to look far for instances where these principles are knowingly or unknowingly applied. The trick of getting someone to do something, and then letting them think their action was self-initiated, is a time-worn one. Attitudes can follow on from actions produced in this way, so that there is the real possibility of interests being stimulated or awakened by skilfully placed, well camouflaged, inducement to activity. Even applied to the severest cases of apathy and depression, techniques which get people active (and it does not matter if the actions initially provoked are of the most minor and insignificant nature, such as preparing a meal or playing a game of cards) may lay the foundations for larger-scale involvement later on.

I have outlined just a few general principles which can be applied at a personal level to avert the psychological condition which has been linked to enhanced susceptibility. Most important of all, insight into the nature of the psychological 'risk factor' can alert a person to predictable changes which could have consequences for health. It can also suggest advance preventive measures, and can point to advantageous courses of action in the changed circumstances. The same knowledge can be applied by 'outsiders' to warn an individual of predicaments he does not foresee, and to offer him support and encouragement.

Meditation and bio-feedback
Absent from this discussion is any consideration of the personality component in disease risk, and the therapeutic value of relaxing and meditative techniques such as yoga, bio-feedback and hypnosis. These are currently attracting a con-

[4] This is reminiscent of influence through suggestion and hypnosis, the effectiveness of which also seems to depend on a temporary suspension of a person's critical faculty (See Chapter 3). The issue of attributed agency, and its relation to the social constraints which are operative, is quite a complicated one, and is discussed by Totman [4].

siderable following. It is not my intention to decry such techniques in any way, or to dispute their efficacy. Neither is there any reason to suppose they are in conflict with the ideas embodied in the rule-following model. Indeed, it is possible to speculate that meditative states induce a temporary plasticity in the neural structures responsible for rule-following, thereby facilitating adaptive modifications of rules. The risk which I have suggested is associated with the tenure of rigid and extreme criteria may thus be ameliorated to a certain extent by regularly practising one of these forms of mental transformation.

The reason for this omission is simply that several well informed discussions of such procedures and the benefits accruing from them can be found elsewhere [5–8].

Public policy

If correct, the ideas put forward in this book have a number of implications for social policy-making.

The hospital environment: restorer of health or perpetuator of disease? The impersonality of contemporary medical treatment in Britain, especially that administered through the National Health Service, needs no further describing. What repercussions does this have for the health of those being treated? According to the rule model, it has its dangers. There is an obvious sense in which the formality and mechanization in treatment function to alienate an individual, not only from his own friends and acquaintances, but also from familiar patterns of everyday life in general.

The orderly hospital environment with its liturgical routines requires the subordination of real world personae and the learning of a highly specialized structure of relations and priorities, embedded in which is the role of 'patient'. The word 'patient' itself, like 'subject', betrays an attitude of depersonalization. The question of why it should be necessary for a person's ordinary world 'self' to be suppressed to such an extreme degree is probably quite a complicated one, and it is not clear that 'the smooth running of the establishment' constitutes a full explanation. Nevertheless, the fact remains that this is done, and done effectively. The important mitigating instance is, of course, the nurse (or doctor) who takes time off from her routine administrations to chat to a patient on a friendly basis. In some hospitals this is encouraged, but in others, particularly where there is a chronic shortage of staff, 'too much' talking to patients (which in real terms often means very little) is frowned on. Paradoxically, what is possibly one of the most influential aspects of the healing process is often discouraged, or at best accorded only a low priority.

On the other hand, the highly structured and secure quality of the hospital environment breeds a small minority of 'professional patients': people who, possibly as a result of having few outside commitments, interlock with hospital routine and accept, piecemeal, the life-style of a patient. A psychoanalyst might say that such an individual 'introjects' the role of patient so that it becomes an integral part of his concept of himself. In the language of the rule-following model, the hospital ward offers the individual new opportunities for rule-following, beyond those available elsewhere. Having 'over-adjusted' to this environment, he functions more adaptively within it than outside it. His condition improves, and eventually he is discharged into a world widely discrepant with the highly specialized set of rules he has come to hold.

So perhaps it is not surprising that there are numerous case reports, and indeed hundreds of everday examples of a pattern in which, independent of the effects of medication, symptoms disappear after a spell in hospital, reappear soon after discharge, and disappear again after re-admission, and so on. It is a mistake to talk about this self-perpetuating situation as 'malingering' since the evidence reviewed and summarized in this book suggests that the fluctuations in symptoms are likely to reflect changes in the state of a real, organically based condition.

What is it possible to do in cases like this? It would seem there is only one way to break the vicious circle, and this is for the individual to become involved in activities and social contacts that are unrelated to the hospital. Without some continuity between the hospital staff and those caring for him at home, putting this into practice is extremely difficult. It is a feature of the Health Service in Britain that when a patient is discharged from hospital, the hospital physicians relinquish most of their responsibility for him. Unavoidably, a drop in the amount of contact with a patient, and a divestment of interest in him, accompany this relinquished responsibility. The degree to which general practitioners and social workers are in touch with hospital staff varies, but usually the amount of collaboration is not great. The members of each profession tend to work within the boundaries of that profession, and there is little overlap. There is die-hard observance of the creed that responsibility for a patient should be 'handed over' from one authority to another, and that at all costs no one must tread on anyone else's toes.

Secrecy in hospitals regarding a patient's diagnosis often amounts to little less than a religion. There are of course instances where secrecy is undeniably in the patient's best interest. But a blanket policy of secrecy – secrecy for its own sake – is undoubtedly one of the main causes of the segregation between medical and non-medical personnel, not least the patient's friends and relatives. Ideally, a patient's health should be the shared concern of hospital doctors, general practitioners, nurses, social workers, and his friends and family. And of course himself. There is a long way to go before the gaps between these categories can be bridged so that objectives are seen by all parties as the same, and genuine collaboration takes place. One of the major obstacles to bridging the gaps remains the fact that to some extent at least they are defended in the interests of professional protectiveness: to ensure the perpetuation of status and elitism.

Hospital vs. home
In discussing the best forms of care for terminally ill patients, Morison [9] comments:

Unfortunately most insurance plans, including the otherwise enlightened National Health Service in Britain, have tended to emphasize hospital care to the detriment of adequate support for proper care in the home. Recent studies of home care for seriously ill patients suggest that in many cases it can be not only more satisfactory emotionally than hospital care but also considerably less costly. (Morison, 1973)

Hywel Davies, an American cardiologist, has recently put forward very similar views [10]. Davies argues that in many cases the coronary patient may stand a better chance of survival if not moved from his home into the alien surroundings of a hospital.

It would certainly seem that there is a strong case for sending patients home at the earliest possible opportunity. On this point attitudes have probably changed for the better over recent years, due in part perhaps to the increasing demand for hospital beds and facilities. During the 1950s and 1960s in Britain, hospitals had a curious tendency to 'hang on' to patients for needlessly extended periods of time — a practice which is not quite extinct even now. The argument for doing this, on the face of it, is a very reasonable one: a level of skilled treatment and monitoring of patients is possible in a hospital ward which is rarely available in the home. But it is essential to bear in mind that the psychological disadvantages of a prolonged stay in hospital might outweigh the gains of this superior physical attention so that the net rate of improvement is actually slower in hospital than at home. In a minority of cases, health could even deteriorate as a result of extended separation from the familiar home environment. But the temptation to advocate a swing from one extreme to the other must be resisted. Advantage comes from being aware of both contingencies, so that the correct compromise can be worked out in each individual case.

Visitors
The visitors a person sees in hospital are likely to be a major

source of psychological support to him, and consequently a major source of benefit to his physical health. A patient's contact with his close friends and family represents a 'lifeline', often the only one which exists, between the powerful constitution of the hospital and familiar 'real-world' rules.

In being able to talk to familiar people in a familiar style the patient has in effect an opportunity to exercise real world rules. Joking about events in the ward reduces the hospital society from the cosmic proportions it has assumed to something more like a curiosity. Some of the sting can thus be taken out of the alienation from normal patterns of activity. Visitors enable a temporary reversal of the transformation from person to patient.

A notable example of an institution where considerable importance is attached to visiting is St. Christopher's hospital near London, which caters for terminally ill patients. At St. Christopher's, visiting by people of all ages is considered to be beneficial, and visitors are encouraged to carry on everyday activities when they are with patients.

Generally speaking then, visiting would seem to have highly favourable consequences for health. But here again, it is a question of striking a balance between the advantageous psychological consequences of talking to visitors, and the detrimental physical effects which may come from too much stimulation and activity where this might be exhausting.

The passive vs. the participating patient

Sometimes it is feasible for long-stay patients to participate in the administration of the ward, if they so wish. Another possibility for helping patients to sustain a sense of involvement while they are in hospital, and one likely to be more motivating, is the issue of their own treatment and welfare. Once again, medical tradition goes against this. For various reasons, some of them justifiable, the general tendency is to treat patients as passive objects. Helplessness is enforced – sometimes with ruthless efficiency. Many would argue that in view of the way hospitals are organized, nothing short of a complete rethinking of the medical services can change this. But free choice, and a person's experience of it, are nebulous quantities. What is important, in a sense, is not so much the degree of choice the patient *in fact* has, but whether or not he *feels* instrumental in affecting what happens to him.[5] (Recall the experiments on pain and insomnia described in Chapter 2.) There are countless ways of structuring administrations, from the prescription of nighttime sedatives to major operations, so that a person is made to feel he has some control over the decisions taken, and some investment in what is going on. Even a consciously articulated decision to 'leave everything to those in charge' represents a definite commitment.

Physical vs. psychological

In each of the areas of medical practice I have touched on, there is an element of conflict between physically based procedures, whose effects on health are well documented and immediate, and procedures which affect health indirectly and less accessibly – through their psychological consequences. The question that has to be faced when an individual case is under consideration is where the best balance is struck. The point I have tried to bring out is that because the influence on health from the psychological factor is less readily apparent than that from physical factors, and because the medical services are historically geared to thinking about treatment in an overt, physical way, the psychological factor is underestimated and insufficiently provided for in medical policy making. If the ideas summarized in the rule-following model are valid, then ultimately treatment of organic conditions by physical means serves more to alleviate symptoms than to remove their cause.

This is one way in which spiritual healing wins out over conventional medicine. Instead of offering physical inter-

[5] Indeed, it is not clear that a distinction between the concept of 'free choice' and that of 'an individual's experience of free choice' can sensibly be made. Whether or not an actor is seen by an outside observer to be constrained in what he does, is, in a sense, quite a different issue from that of whether the action can be said to be free. Previously I have argued that 'free choice' means the same thing as 'the experience of free choice' [4].

vention, a spiritual healer is able to give a person the un-spoken possibility of a comprehensive new form of involvement – a whole new spectrum of rules, in the form of the attitudes, beliefs, values and customs which are the healer's creed. Those who are already believers receive an affirmation of the rules they hold, and perhaps encouragement to find new ways of expressing and acting on this faith. By committing himself to the treatment procedures in the first instance, an individual implicitly makes an investment in the attached doctrine. From this moment on, the stage is set so that a mutually reinforc-ing interplay can take place. Temporary remissions in symp-toms, perhaps occurring as a result of metabolic or cyclic biological fluctuations, are attributed to the healing administra-tion, serving as 'objective' confirmation or 'proof' of the validity of the doctrine. The strengthening of belief leads to improved health via the mechanism outlined in Chapter 8, in turn providing further consolidation of the psychological commit-ment.[6] And so on. Thus, the 'cures'[7] effected by religious denominations may be more profound and more enduring than those achieved by conventional physical techniques. At the end of the day, the recipient is equipped not just with patched up health, but with a re-affirmation of the rules he lives by, and consequently a re-inspired orientation to life in general.

Work

A person's work occupies a major part of his waking existence. Most people work for an employer, so that what they do is to a large extent laid down by others. What implications can be drawn concerning psychological gains and dangers in the planning of jobs? Common sense tells us that involvement in work is heightened if there is scope for personal decision making. But different individuals prefer different amounts of licence in their work. One man's preferred level of manoeuv-rability in the planning and carrying out of what has to be

[6] This sequence was suggested in Chapter 3.
[7] e.g. so called 'miracle cures'.

done may represent an unacceptable load of responsibility to another. Nevertheless, there is an ideal position on the continuum for every individual, so that he feels he is exercising freedom to choose, but this latitude for choice is not experienced as overwhelming.

At one extreme is a worker who, day after day, carries out an identical operation at the same point on a production line. Contrast this with the work of a craftsman, who is responsible for each stage in the manufacture of a product, no two of which are ever the same. Clearly, the degree of interest, involvement and satisfaction will be greatest in the second case.

But variation is not important in itself. It is important only as a means of preserving the identity of individual endeavour. In modern manufacturing plants turning out large quantities of a standard product, it is very difficult to see how this can be done. But as a general principle, maximizing the degree of personal decision-making in jobs, within the limits of individual tolerance, enables individual investment of skill and effort to be reflected (or more to the point, to be *seen* by the individual to be reflected) in the end-product. In the language of the model, this is providing an opportunity for testing and corroborating rules corresponding to 'efficiency', 'competence', expertise', 'imagination' and so on.

Retirement

Leaf [11], in a paper concerned with ageing, writes:

> The pattern of increasing early retirement in our own society (America) takes a heavy toll of our older citizens. They also find that their offspring generally have neither any room nor any use for them in their urban apartment. These are economic determinants that cannot be reversed in our culture today. Their devastating effect on the happiness and life-span of the elderly could be countered at least in part by educational programs to awaken other interests or avocations to which these people could turn in zest when their

contribution to the industrial economy is no longer needed. The trend toward shorter worker hours and earlier retirement makes the need for such education urgent. (Leaf, 1973)

As I have said, a man faced with retirement, who has worked in the same job for many years, whose work has been a source of satisfaction to him and whose primary opportunity for social contact is provided through it, is a prime example of someone at risk. This is especially true of someone with few interests and companions outside his work. Where retirement means a sudden switch from full-time employment to no employment at all, the adaptation required is enormous. An extensive, highly developed, regularly activated set of rules becomes redundant literally overnight.

One way in which this situation could be averted is by making the change a gradual one. A policy of phased retirement, so that at very least an individual retires in two stages, from working five days a week to working two or three, would significantly modify the impact of the change which becomes necessary, and hence reduce the risk to health. The intermediate stage would have both practical and motivational value, in that the necessity to structure the non-working day in some manner would become apparent, and ways of doing so could be tried out.

The employees of a large number of firms are automatically made to retire at a given age, although they may well be functioning at a high level of competence up until the date of termination. Where appropriate, to make continued use of such people on an occasional consultative basis might also ameliorate some of the harmful effects of total retirement.

Conclusion

It has not been my intention in this chapter to make prescriptions: only to spell out a few practical implications of the rule-following model, should this prove to be an acceptable representation of existing evidence. Many of the suggestions are no more than common sense. Many amenities are a reality at the moment. There are day centres and organized projects for the elderly. There is some, but perhaps not enough, provision for members of immigrant communities to enjoy cultural continuity by carrying on certain of the customs followed in their countries of origin.

But it is essential to remember that the element of personal choice is a necessary ingredient for such provisions to be effective. To compel a person to undertake activities against his will is profitless. From a policy-making angle, all that can be done is to ensure that sufficient opportunities for involvement are available.

If an individual is healthiest and feels most alive when caught up in projects, or when there are others around with whom he can exchange opinions, the best of both worlds is had by those working with others towards the fulfilment of a shared objective. Ideally placed are the members of a dissident or crusading group united against a tyrannical opponent, for in this instance above all others will the common cause be clearly reflected, unanimously endorsed, and energetically defended. And in this instance will the rules of individual performance be most sharply defined. Why else do people reminisce so enthusiastically about the wars they have been involved in? And about their schooldays? And why else do people recall so vividly their roles in collaborative enterprises and decorate their walls with photographs of rows of their fellow conspirators?

APPENDIX I

The Holmes–Rahe 'Social Readjustment Rating Scale'

An individual is given this list and required to indicate whether each of the events below has occurred over a specified recent period in his life. L.C.U. values[1] are shown to the right of each item.

Item	L.C.U. Values
Family:	
1 Death of spouse	100
2 Divorce	73
3 Marital separation	65
4 Death of close family member	63
5 Marriage	50
6 Marital reconciliation	45
7 Major change in health of family	44
8 Pregnancy	40
9 Addition of new family member	39
10 Major change in arguments with wife	35
11 Son or daughter leaving home	29
12 In-law troubles	29
13 Wife starting or ending work	26
14 Major change in family get-togethers	15
Personal:	
15 Detention in jail	63
16 Major personal injury or illness	53
17 Sexual difficulties	39

[1] See Chapter 5.

18	Death of a close friend	37
19	Outstanding personal achievement	28
20	Start or end of formal schooling	26
21	Major change in living conditions	25
22	Major revision of personal habits	24
23	Changing to a new school	20
24	Change in residence	20
25	Major change in recreation	19
26	Major change in church activities	19
27	Major change in sleeping habits	16
28	Major change in eating habits	15
29	Vacation	13
30	Christmas	12
31	Minor violations of the law	11

Work:
32	Being fired from work	47
33	Retirement from work	45
34	Major business adjustment	39
35	Changing to different line of work	36
36	Major change in work responsibilities	29
37	Trouble with boss	23
38	Major change in working conditions	20

Financial:
39	Major change in financial state	38
40	Mortgage or loan over $10,000	31
41	Mortgage foreclosure	30
42	Mortgage or loan less than $10,000	17

(From Rahe, R. H., 1972. Table 1.)

APPENDIX II

Standard questionnaire used by the interviewer to assess the incidence of events in people's lives involving social change and reorganization.

The interview consists in a set of standard questions. The probe routines which follow are applied when any 'life event' is discovered, as appropriate. (See Chapter 10)

The interview

'Here are some questions about things which happen to people during the normal course of their lives. Some of them may have happened to you over the past eighteen months. It may be that something similar but not quite the same as certain of the things mentioned are relevant in your particular case, in which case I would like you to tell me about these. Please be frank, and try to give as much detail about everything as possible. Everyone's experiences are different, and we want to know as much about yours as you can tell us. All the records are treated absolutely confidentially by us. The important thing is not to let me put words in your mouth – I just want to know the facts as they really are. The more factual you can be, and the more accurate, the more help it is to us. Now, all the things I shall ask you refer just to the past eighteen months in your life. We're not interested in anything that may have happened before this. If you're not quite sure about exactly when something happened, tell me about it, and we'll try to pinpoint exactly when it was. O.K.?'

I *Job*

1. Have you retired/lost your job/changed your job/employment/school?

2. Have you been given a new position in the same employment, e.g. promotion?
3. Have you been working with the same people, or have they changed at all over the past eighteen months?
4. Has anyone you have worked closely with left?
5. Any time away from work for any reason – sickness, strike? (Extent)
6. Any difficulties at work with supervisors/colleagues/juniors?
7. Have any of these things happened to anyone close to you? (Who?/nature)

II *Residence*

1. Have you moved home over the last eighteen months?
2. Have you immigrated to this country?
3. Are you expecting to move?
4. How do you get on with the neighbours and those living close by? Any problems? Any instance of falling out with people who used to be good friends?

III *Major personal changes*

1. Have you married over the past eighteen months?
2. Have you become engaged over the past eighteen months?
3. Have you separated/divorced from your husband/wife over this time?
4. Have you recently made any special new friendships or relationships with any particular person?
5. Have you recently broken off any close friendships or relationships?
6. *For single people* – Did you have a boyfriend/girlfriend whom you lost?
7. Have you reconciled with your wife/girlfriend/boyfriend/fiancé or anyone after splitting up?
8. Has anyone close to you died during this time?

9. Have you yourself had any serious illness or nervous trouble or accidents? Have you been seriously depressed?

10. Have you had any important news about anyone you know? Any unexpected news?

    Sometimes people learn unexpected things about others close to them, such as discovering their child has been stealing at school, or their husband/wife has been having an affair, or their boyfriend/girlfriend has been seeing someone else.

    Any surprising news of any sort? Unpleasant *or* pleasant?

IV *Family*

1. Have any of the things I have asked you about happened to any of your family or close friends over the last eighteen months?

2. Have you had any newcomers to the family? (Babies/grandchildren/in-laws/others – have they been resident with you?)

3. Any pregnancies in the family (Fiancé/girlfriend?) Any miscarriages?

4. Has anyone in the family left home?

5. Have you had any major differences of opinion with any of your family or close friends? Any rows or difficulties?

6. So there have been just the .... of you living at home over the last eighteen months?

For those living with spouse

6. Have you and your husband/wife been living at home during the past eighteen months?

If negative reply to 6

7. Have you been separated for any length of time during this time?

V *Changes in relations with friends/groups*

1. Has anything happened over this time which has caused you to see much more or much less of any of your close

friends or relatives – or anyone you talk to a lot and perhaps confide in?

2. Have you been mixing much more or much less with any group of people – family or friends over this time?

3. Are you a member of any organized clubs, groups, societies or communities? (religious groups)

4. Have you become a member of any organized groups over this time?

5. Have you left or broken off from any organized clubs, societies or communities?

6. Have you taken up any new hobbies, interests or pastimes? Have you been spending more time involved in your customary hobbies, interests etc.? (Reason)

7. Have you given up any hobbies, interests or pastimes? Have you been spending less time involved in any of these things? (Reason)

8. Any other significant changes in the general pattern of your social life? (Nature/reason) Would you say the average amount of time you spend socializing has stayed about the same over this time? On average? Or has there been any increase in your social life? Or any decrease? Overall?

VI *Miscellaneous*

1. Any crises or emergencies in your family, or among your close friends which we've not talked about? Anything at all involving you, or affecting you in any way?

2. Have you had any changes in salary or wealth? (e.g. won the pools/gone bankrupt)

3. Generally, have you made any changes in your day-to-day routine other than the things we've talked about?

4. Have you had a pet die over this time, or been taken away?

5. Has your contact with people you don't normally meet increased at all?

6. Has anyone at home started school or college?

7. Have you been in any institutions, or come out of one?

8. *If over 38 and female.* Have you had any problems associated with the change in life (Menopause)?)

9. Have you experienced any 'conflicts of loyalties' over this time?

10. Has anything happened over this time which gave you a great deal of pleasure or satisfaction? (Nature)

11. You'll have gathered by now that we're interested in things which have happened to you that involve changes in your life. Especially your day-to-day activities, and your social life. Anything upsetting *or* exciting. Can you think of anything else at all that we've not mentioned? PAUSE. Anything at all?

Question Routine I: Work and non-work activities

(*To be applied for each 'life event' identified, if relevant*)

Aim: To discover whether a life event resulted in a net change in the amount of time the subject was involved in goal-directed activities,[1] on average. Also, to discover whether there was a compensating increase, or decrease (a) in the amount of time spent in alternative goal-directed activities,[1] and (b) in the amount of time spent in the company of others.

'Did it result in your doing more (or less) of X during the week, on average?' (If so) 'How many more (or less) hours per week, on average?'*

if more | if less

Apply probes A(i) and A(ii) | Apply probes B(i) and B(ii)

* A standard technique of extracting this information, as it is described in 'Probes' section, was applied.

[1] As a rule of thumb, a 'goal-directed' activity can be taken as anything which could be said to be done well or badly.

Question Routine II: Contact with others

(*To be applied for each 'life event' identified, if relevant*)

Aim: To discover whether a life event resulted in a net change
in the amount of time the subject spent in the company of others. Also, to discover whether there was a
compensating increase, or decrease, (a) in the amount of
time spent with different individuals, and (b) in the
amount of time spent in goal-directed activities.[1]

'Did it result in your seeing any more (or any less) of
the person (or people) concerned' (or, where appropriate, 'Did it result in your spending any more (or
any less) time socializing generally?') (If so) 'How
much more (or less) of them did you see, in hours per
week, on average?'* (or, 'how much more (or less)
time, in hours per week, on average?').*

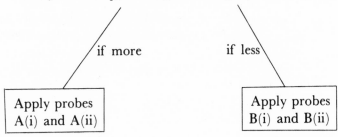

if more → Apply probes A(i) and A(ii)

if less → Apply probes B(i) and B(ii)

Probes: Batch A. Compensating decreases in activities and socializing

(*To be applied as detailed in Question Routines I and II*)

A(i) 'Did you as a consequence, find you had less time
available to do other things?'
(If so)
'What, in particular, did you give up?'
'This is rather difficult, but I want you to think back,
very carefully, to the time in your life just before *the event*,
and try to remember how many hours a week you normally spent doing this. On average.'

(Where necessary) 'How many hours on an average weekday? And how many over the weekend?'

(Where necessary, further encouragement is given at this juncture by going through the week on a day-by-day, or even an hour-by-hour basis)

'Now do the same thing for the period in your life just after *the event.*'

'Did you give up, or do less of, anything else after *the event?*'

(If so – same probes again)

A(ii) 'Did you, as a consequence, find you spent less time socializing?'

(If so)

'What part of your social life, in particular, did you give up?'

'This is rather difficult, But I want you to think back, very carefully, to the time in your life just before *the event*, and try to remember how many hours a week you normally spent with him/her/them. On average.'

(Where necessary, further encouragement is given at this juncture by going through the week on a day-by-day, or even an hour-by-hour basis)

'Now do the same thing for the period in your life just after *the event.*'

'Did you see less of anyone else, or of any other group of people, after *the event?*'

(If so – same probes again)

Probes: Batch B. Compensating increases in activities and socializing (*To be applied as detailed in Question Routines I and II*)

B(i) 'Did you, as a consequence, find you had more time available to do other things?'

(If so)

'What, in particular, did you do in the extra time that was available?'

'This is rather difficult, but I want you to think back, very carefully, to the time in your life just after *the event*, and try to remember how many hours a week you normally spent doing this. On average.'

(Where necessary) 'How many hours on an average weekday? And how many over the weekend?'

(Where necessary, further encouragement is given at this juncture by going through the week on a day-by-day, or even an hour-by-hour basis)

'Now do the same thing for the period in your life just before *the event*.'

'Did you take up, or do more of, anything else after *the event*?'

(If so – same probes again)

B(ii) 'Did you, as a consequence, find you spent more time socializing?'

(If so)

'Who did you see more of)'

'This is rather difficult, but I want you to think back, very carefully, to the time in your life just after *the event*, and try to remember how many hours a week you normally spent with him/her/them. On average.'

(Where necessary) 'How many hours on an average weekday. And how many over the weekend?'

(Where necessary, further encouragement is given at this juncture by going through the week on a day-by-day, or even an hour-by-hour basis)

'Now, do the same thing for the period in your life just before *the event*.'

'Did you see any more of anyone else, or any group of people, after *the event*?'

(If so – same probes again)

REFERENCES

CHAPTER 1

[1] DOUGLAS, M. (Ed.) (1970) *Witchcraft: confessions and accusations*. London: Tavistock.

[2] FABREGA, H. and MANNING, P. K. (1973) An integrated theory of disease: Ladino–Mestizo views of disease in the Chapanis Highlands. *Psychosomatic Medicine*, *35*, 223–239.

CHAPTER 2

[1] GOODY, E. (1970). In M. Douglas (Ed.) *Witchcraft confessions and accusations*. London: Tavistock.

[2] SHAPIRO, A. K. (1959) The placebo effect in the history of medical treatment implications for psychiatry. *American Journal of Psychiatry*, *116*, 298–304.

[3] HOUSTON, W. R. (1938) Doctor himself as therapeutic agent. *Annals of Internal Medicine*, *11*, 1416–1425.

[4] ROSE, L. (1971) *Faith healing*, Penguin Books.

[5] ROSE, L. (1954) Some aspects of paranormal healing. *British Medical Journal*, Dec. 2, 1329–1332.

[6] SHAPIRO, A. K. (1964) Etiological factors in the placebo effect. *Journal of the American Medical Association*, *187*, 712–714.

[7] FESTINGER, L. (1957) *A theory of cognitive dissonance*. Evanston, Illinois: Row, Peterson.

[8] TOTMAN, R. G. (1973) An approach to cognitive dissonance theory in terms of ordinary language. *Journal for the theory of social behaviour*, *3*, 215–238.

[9] MacIntyre, A. C. (1958) *The unconscious.* London: Routledge and Kegan Paul.

[10] Zimbardo, P. G. (1969) *The cognitive control of motivation.* Illinois: Scott Foresman.

[11] Dixon, N. F. (1971) *Subliminal perception: the nature of a controversy.* London: McGraw-Hill.

[12] Christie, M. J. (1975) The psychosocial environment and precursors of disease. In P. H. Venables and M. J. Christie (Eds) *Research in psychophysiology.* London: Wiley.

[13] Totman, R. G. (1976a) Cognitive dissonance and the placebo response. *European Journal of Social Psychology, 5,* 119–125.

[14] Totman, R. G. (1976b) Cognitive dissonance in the placebo treatment of insomnia – a pilot experiment. *British Journal of Medical Psychology, 49,* 393–400.

[15] Totman, R. G., Reed, S. E. and Craig, J. W. (1977) Cognitive dissonance, stress and virus-induced common colds. *Journal of Psychosomatic Research, 21,* 55–63.

[16] Dunlop, D., Henderson, T. and Inch, R. (1952) A survey of 17,301 prescriptions on form E.C. 10. *British Medical Journal,* Feb. 1, 292–295.

[17] Rickels, K. and Hesbacher, P. T. (1973) Over-the-counter daytime sedatives: a controlled study. *Journal of the American Medical Association, 223,* 29–33.

[18] Beecher, H. K. (1962) Plain, placebos and physicians. *The Practitioner: Symposium on Anaesthesia and Analgesia, 189,* 141–155.

[19] Lowinger, P. and Dobie, S. (1969) What makes placebos work? A study of placebo response rates. *Archives of General Psychiatry, 20,* 84–88.

[20] Haas, H., Fink, H. and Hartfelder, G. (1963) The placebo problem. *Psychopharmacology Service Centre Bulletin,* 1–65.

[21] Jacobs, P. H., Tromovitch, T. A., Lucas, G. and Puzack, H. P. (1963) Effect of chloroquine and placebo on warts. *Archives of Dermatology, 87,* 89–90.

[22] SHURE, N. (1965) The placebo in allergy. *Annals of Allergy,* *23,* 368–376.

[23] CROUNSE, R. G. (1965) The response of acne to placebos and antibiotics. *Journal of the American Medical Association, 193,* 906–910.

[24] THRIFT, C. D. and TRAUT, E. F. (1966) Further studies of placebo management of skeletal disease. *Illinois Medical Journal, 129,* 683–685.

[25] LICHTENSTEIN, E., POUSSAINT, A. F. *et al.* (1967) A further report on the effects of the physician's treating of smoking by placebo. *Diseases of the Nervous System, 28,* 754–755.

[26] NODINE, J. H., SHULKIN, H. W. *et al.* (1967) A double-blind study of the effect of ribonucleic acid in senile brain disease. *American Journal of Psychiatry, 123,* 1257–1259.

[27] SINGER, D. L. and HURWITZ, D. (1968) Placebos in management of diabetes. *New England Journal of Medicine, 278,* 742.

[28] CARNE, S. (1961) The action of chorionic gonadotrophin in the obese. *Lancet,* Dec. 9, 1282–1284.

[29] GOODMAN, N. G. (1969) Triiodothyronine and placebo in the treatment of obesity. A study of fifty-five patients. *Medical Annual, 38,* 658–662.

[30] RUDZKI, E., BORKOWSKI, W. and CZUBALSKI, K. (1970) The suggestive effect of placebo on the intensity of chronic urticaria. *Acta Allergica (Kobenhaven) 25,* 70–73.

[31] KOLVIN, I., TAUNCH, J. *et al.* (1972) Enuresis: a descriptive analysis and a controlled trial. *Developmental Medicine and Child Neurology, 14,* 715–726.

[32] CARTER, D. B. and ALLEN, D. C. (1973) Evaluation of the placebo effect in optometry. *American Journal of Optometry, 50,* 94–103.

[33] BEECHER, H. K. (1955) The powerful placebo. *Journal of the American Medical Association, 159,* 1602–1606.

[34] MEDICAL TIMES (Editorial) (1963) The toxic placebo. Side and toxic effects reported during the administration of placebo medicine. *Medical Times, 91,* 778.

[35] VALINS, S., ADELSON, R., GOLDSTEIN, J. and WEINER, M.

(1971) The negative placebo effect – consequences of overselling a treatment. *Paper presented at the International Association for Dental Research.*

[36] VINAR, O. (1969) Dependence on placebo: a case report. *British Journal of Psychiatry, 115,* 1189–1190.

[37] FINDLEY, T. (1953) The placebo and the physician. *Medical Clinics of North America, 37,* 1821–1826.

[38] ELKES, J. and ELKES, C. (1954) Effect of chlorpromazine on the behaviour of chronically overactive psychotic patients. *British Medical Journal,* Sept. 2, 560–565.

[39] WAYNE, E. J. (1956) Placebos. *British Medical Journal,* July 2, 157.

[40] KOTEEN, H. (1957) Use of a 'double-blind' study investigating the clinical merits of a new tranquilizing agent. *Annals of Internal Medicine, 47,* 978–989.

[41] PARK, L. C. and COVI, L. (1965) Non-blind placebo trial: an exploration of neurotic patients' responses to placebo when its inert content is disclosed. *Archives of General Psychiatry, 12,* 336–345.

[42] LUCAS, C. J. (1962) *Unpublished address to Finchley Pharmaceutical Society.*

[43] GRENFELL, R., BRIGGS, A. H. and HOLLAND, W. C. (1961) A double-blind study of the treatment of hypertension. *Journal of the American Medical Association, 176,* 124–128.

[44] JANET, P. M. (1925) *Psychological healing, a historical and clinical study.* Transl. E. and C. Paul, London.

[45] FRANK, J. D. (1972) *Persuasion and healing.* Baltimore and London: John Hopkins University Press.

[46] LEDER, S. (1969) Psychotherapy: placebo effect and/or learning? *International Psychiatry Clinics, 6,* 114–133.

[47] SHAPIRO, A. K. (1970) Placebo effects in psychotherapy and psychoanalysis. *Journal of Clinical Pharmacology, 10,* 73–78.

CHAPTER 3

[1] ORNE, M. (1962) On the social psychology of the psychological experiment. *American Psychologist, 17,* 776–783.

[2] MASON, A. A. (1955) Surgery under hypnosis. *Anaesthesia, 10,* 295–299.

[3] BOWERS, K. S. (1976) *Hypnosis for the seriously curious.* Monterey, California: Wadsworth.

[4] HILGARD, E. G. (1975) Hypnosis. *Annual Review of Psychology, 26,* 19–44.

[5] FROMM, E. and SHOR, R. E. (Eds) (1972) *Hypnosis: research developments and perspectives.* Chicago: Aldine-Alderton.

[6] SUTCLIFFE, J. D. (1961) 'Credulous' and 'sceptical' views of hypnotic phenomena: experiments on esthesia, hallucination, and delusion. *Journal of Abnormal and Social Psychology, 62,* 189–200.

[7] KNOX, V. J., MORGAN, A. H. and HILGARD, E. R. (1974) Pain and suffering in ischemia. *Archives of General Psychiatry, 30,* 840–847.

[8] MELZACK, R. (1973) *The puzzle of pain.* Penguin Books.

[9] EWIN, D. M. (1974) Condyloma acuminatum: successful treatment of four cases by hypnosis. *American Journal of Clinical Hypnosis, 17,* 73–78.

[10] CLAWSON, T. A. and SWADE, R. H. (1975) The hypnotic control of blood flow and pain: the cure of warts and the potential for the use of hypnosis in the treatment of cancer. *American Journal of Clinical Hypnosis, 17,* 160–189.

[11] SINCLAIR-GIEBEN, A. H. C. and CHALMERS, D. (1959) Evaluation of treatment of warts by hypnosis. *Lancet,* Oct. 3, 480–482.

[12] BEAHRS, J. O., HARRIS, D. R. and HILGARD, E. R. (1970) Failure to alter skin inflammation by hypnotic suggestion in five subjects with normal skin reactivity. *Psychosomatic Medicine, 32,* 627–631.

[13] BARBER, T. X. (1972) Suggested ('hypnotic') behaviour:

the trance paradigm versus an alternative paradigm. In E. Fromm and R. E. Shor (Eds) *Hypnosis: research developments and perspectives*. Chicago: Aldine-Alderton.

[14] HELLIER, F. F. (1951) The treatment of warts with X-rays. Is their action physical or psychological? *British Journal of Dermatology, 63*, 193–194.

[15] MAHER-LOUGHLAN, G. P. (1976) Hypo-autohypnosis in treating psychosomatic illness. In O. W. Hill (Ed.) *Modern trends in psychosomatic medicine – 3*. London: Butterworths.

[16] LUPARELLO, T. J., LEIST, N., LOURIE, C. H. and SWEET, P. (1970). The interaction of psychologic stimuli and pharmacologic agents on airway reactivity in asthmatic subjects. *Psychosomatic Medicine, 32*, 509–513.

[17] HILGARD, E. R. and TART, C. T. (1966) Responsiveness to suggestions following waking and imagined instructions and following induction of hypnosis. *Journal of Abnormal Psychology, 71*, 196–208.

[18] ULLMAN, M. (1959) On the psyche and warts: I. Suggestions and warts: a review and comment. *Psychosomatic Medicine, 21*, 473–488.

[19] VACCHIANO, R. B. and STRAUS, P. S. (1975) Dogmatism, authority, and hypnotic susceptibility. *American Journal of Clinical Hypnosis, 17*, 184–189.

[20] TOTMAN, R. G. (1973) An approach to cognitive dissonance theory in terms of ordinary language. *Journal for the theory of social behaviour, 3*, 215–238.

[21] ARONSON, E. (1968) Dissonance theory: progress and problems. In R. P. Abelson, E. Aronson *et al.* (Eds) *Theories of cognitive consistency: a source book*. Chicago: Rand McNally.

[22] PLATONOV, K. I. (1959) *The word as a physiological and therapeutic factor*. Moscow: Foreign Languages Publishing House.

[23] SMITH, E. E. (1961) The power of dissonance techniques to change attitudes. *Public Opinion Quaterly, 25*, 626–639.

[24] ZIMBARDO, P. G., WEISENBERG, M., FIRESTONE, I. and

LEVY, B. (1965) Communicator effectiveness in producing public conformity and private attitude change. *Journal of Personality, 33,* 233–255.

[25] DIXON, N. F. (1971) *Subliminal perception: the nature of a controversy.* London: McGraw-Hill.

[26] ZUCKERMAN, M. (1960) The effects of subliminal and supraliminal suggestion on verbal productivity. *Journal of Abnormal and Social Psychology, 60,* 404–411.

CHAPTER 4

[1] BERLYNE, D. E. (1960) *Conflict, arousal and curiosity.* New York: McGraw-Hill.

[2] ROUTTENBERG, A. (1968) The two-arousal hypothesis: reticular formation and limbic system. *Psychological Review, 75,* 51–80.

[3] SELYE, H. (1956) *The stress of life.* New York: McGraw-Hill.

[4] LEIDERMAN, P. H. and SHAPIRO, D. (1965) *Psychobiological approaches to social behaviour.* London: Tavistock.

[5] CIBA FOUNDATION SYMPOSIUM 8 (1972) *Physiology, emotion and psychosomatic illness.* Elsevier: Associated Scientific Publishers.

[6] SELYE, H. (1951–1956) *Annual report on stress.* Montreal: Acta Inc., 1951; Selye, H. and Horava, A. 1952, 1953; Selye, H. and Heuser, G. 1954, M. D. Public (New York) 1955–1956.

[7] SAWREY, W. L. and WEISZ, J. D. (1956) An experimental method of producing gastric ulcers. *Journal of Comparative Physiological Psychology, 49,* 269–270.

[8] MAHER, B. A. (1966) *Principles of psychopathology.* New York: McGraw-Hill.

[9] SELIGMAN, E. P. (1975) *Helplessness.* San Francisco: Freeman.

[10] SOLOMON, G. F. (1970) Psychophysiological aspects of rheumatoid arthritis and auto-immune disease. In O. W.

Hill (Ed.) *Modern trends in psychomatic medicine – 2*. London: Butterworths.

[11] DE MOLINER, A. F. and HUNSPERGER, R. W. (1962) Organization of the subcortical system governing defense and flight reactions in the cat. *Journal of Physiology, 160,* 200–213.

[12] GRAY, J. A. (1972) The structure of the emotions and the limbic system. In CIBA Foundation Symposium 8. *Physiology, emotion and psychosomatic illness.* Elsevier: Associated Scientific Publishers.

[13] FONBERG, E. (1972) Control of emotional behaviour through the hypothalamus and amygdaloid complex. In CIBA Foundation Symposium 8. *Physiology, emotion and psychosomatic illness.* Elsevier: Associated Scientific Publishers.

[14] MALAMUD, N. (1967) Psychiatric disorder with intracranial tumors of the limbic system. *Archives of Neurology, 17,* 113–124.

[15] CARROL, B. J. (1976) Psychoendocrine relationships in affective disorders. In O. W. Hill (Ed.) *Modern trends in psychosomatic medicine – 3*. London: Butterworths.

[16] JERNE, N. K. (1973) The immune system. *Scientific American, 229 (1),* 52–60.

[17] AMKRAUT, A. and SOLOMON, G. F. (1975) From the symbolic stimulus to the pathophysiologic response: immune mechanisms. *International Journal of Psychiatry in Medicine, 5,* 541–563.

[18] KORNEVA, E. A. (1967) The effect of stimulating different mesencephalic structures on protective immune response patterns. *Fiziologicheskii zhurnal SSSR IM. I. M. Sechenova, 53, 42.* See also Solomon, G. F. (1970) op. cit.

[19] CAIRNS, J. (1975). The cancer problem. *Scientific American 233(5),* 64–78.

[20] PREHN, R. T. (1969) The relationship of immunology to carcinogenesis. *Annals of the New York Academy of Sciences 164(2),* 449–457.

[21] SOUTHAM, C. M. (1969) Discussion. Emotions, im-

munology and cancer. How might the psyche influence neoplasia? *Annals of the New York Academy of Sciences,* *164(2),* 473–475.

[22] KATZ, J., GALLAGHER, T. *et al.* (1969) Psychoendocrine considerations in cancer of the breast. *Annals of the New York Academy of Sciences, 164(2),* 509–516.

[23] LURIA, A. R. (1966) *Higher cortical functions in man.* London: Tavistock.

[24] GIBSON, J. J, (1966) *The senses considered as perceptual systems.* London: Allen and Unwin.

[25] DIXON, N. F. (1971) *Subliminal perception: the nature of a controversy.* London: McGraw-Hill.

[26] LIPOWSKI, Z. J., LIPSITT, D. R. and WHYBROW, D. C. (Eds) (1977) *Psychosomatic Medicine – current trends and clinical applications.* New York: Oxford University Press.

CHAPTER 5

[1] MILLER, N. E. (1969) *Automatic learning: clinical and physiological implications.* London: International Congress of Psychology.

[2] LUM, L. C. (1976) The syndrome of habitual chronic hyperventilation. In O. W. Hill (Ed.) *Modern trends in psychosomatic medicine – 3.* London: Butterworths.

[3] SHAPIRO, D. and SURWIT, R. S. (1977) Operant conditioning: a new theoretical approach in psychosomatic medicine. In Z. J. Lipowski, D. R. Lipsett and P. C. Whybrow (Eds) *Psychosomatic medicine: current trends and clinical applications.* New York: Oxford University Press.

[4] RAHE, R. H. (1972) Subjects' recent life changes and their near-future illness reports. *Annals of Clinical Research, 4,* 250–265.

[5] DOHRENWEND, B. S. and DOHRENWEND, B. P. (Eds) (1974) *Stressful life events: their nature and effects.* New York: Wiley.

[6] JENKINS, C. D. (1976) Recent evidence supporting psychologic and social risk factors for coronary disease. *New*

England Journal of Medicine, 294, 987–995, 1033–1039.

[7] HILL, O. W. (Ed.) (1976) *Modern trends in psychosomatic medicine – 3.* London: Butterworths.

[8] LIPOWSKI, Z. J., LIPSITT, D. R. and WHYBROW, D. C. (Eds) (1977) *Psychosomatic Medicine – current trends and clinical applications.* New York: Oxford University Press.

[9] MADDISON, D. and VIOLA, A. (1968) The health of widows in the year following bereavement. *Journal of Psychosomatic Research, 12*, 297–306.

[10] PARKES, M. (1970) The psychosomatic effect of bereavement. In O. W. Hill (Ed.) *Modern trends in psychosomatic medicine – 2.* London: Butterworths.

[11] LE SHAN, L. L. and WORTHINGTON, R. E. (1956a) Loss of cathexes as a common psycho-dynamic characteristic of cancer patients: an attempt at statistical validation of a clinical hypothesis. *Psychological Reports, 2*, 183–193.

[12] LE SHAN, L. L. and WORTHINGTON, R. E. (1956b) Some recurrent life history patterns observed in patients with malignant disease. *Journal of Nervous and Mental Disorders, 124*, 460–465.

[13] LE SHAN, L. L. (1966) An emotional life history pattern associated with neoplastic disease. *Annals of the New York Academy of Sciences, 125(3)*, 780–793.

[14] GREEN, W. A., YOUNG, L. and SWISHER, S. H. (1956) Psychological factors and reticuloendothelial disease II Observations on a group of women with lymphomas and leukemias. *Psychosomatic Medicine, 18*, 284–303.

[15] GREEN, W. A. and MILLER, G. (1958) Psychological factors and reticuloendothelial disease: IV. *Psychosomatic Medicine, 20*, 124–144.

[16] LITZ, T. (1949) Emotional factors in the etiology of hyperthyroidism. *Psychosomatic Medicine 11*, 2–8.

[17] CHAMBERS, W. N. and REISER, H. F. (1953) Conjestive heart failure. *Psychosomatic Medicine, 15*, 39–60.

[18] FLARSCHEIM, A. (1958) Ego mechanisms in three pulmonary tuberculosis patients. *Psychosomatic Medicine, 20*, 475–483.

[19] LEVIN, K. K. (1959) Role of depression in the production of illness in pernicious anaemia. *Psychosomatic Medicine*, *21*, 23–27.

[20] PHLIPPOPOLOUS, G. S., WITTKOWER, E. D. and COUSINEAU, A. (1958) The etiologic significance of emotional factors in onset and exacerbation of multiple sclerosis. *Psychosomatic Medicine*, *20*, 458–474.

[21] LINDEMANN, E. (1950) cited in Engel, G. L. (1955) Studies of ulcerative colitis III. The nature of the psychologic process. *American Journal of Medicine*, *19*, 231–256.

[22] McCLARY, A. R., MEYER, E. and WEITZMAN, E. L. (1955) Observations on the role of the mechanism of depression in some patients with disseminated lupus erythematosus. *Psychosomatic Medicine*, *17*, 311–321.

[23] MILLET, J. A. P., LIEF, H., and MITTELMANN, B. (1953) Raynaud's disease. Psychogenic factors and psychotherapy. *Psychosomatic Medicine*, *15*, 61–65.

[24] FRENCH, T. M. (1939) Psychogenic factors in asthma. *American Journal of Psychiatry*, *96*, 87–101.

[25] SCHMALE, A. H. (1959) Relation of separation and depression to disease. I. A report on a hospitalized medical population. *Psychosomatic Medicine*, *20*, 259–277.

[26] MUTTER, A. Z. and SCHLEIFER, M. J. (1966) The role of psychological and social factors in the onset of somatic illness in children. *Psychosomatic Medicine*, *33*, 333–343.

[27] BONFILS, S. S. and DE M'UZAN, M. (1974) Irritable bowel syndrome vs. ulcerative colitis: psychofunctional disturbance vs. psychosomatic disease? *Journal of Psychosomatic Research*, *18*, 291–296.

[28] ENGEL, G. L. (1955) Studies of ulcerative colitis III. The nature of the psychologic process. *American Journal of Medicine*, *19*, 231–256.

[29] ADLER, H. M. and HAMMETT, V. B. (1973) The doctor-patient relationship revisited. An analysis of the placebo effect. *Annals of Internal Medicine*, *78*, 595–598.

[30] LOMBARD, H. L. and POTTER, E. (1950) Epidemiological aspects of cancer of the cervix. *Cancer*, *3*, 960–969.

[31] SCHMALE, A. H. and IKER, H. P. (1966) The psychological setting of uterine cervical cancer. *Annals of the New York Academy of Sciences, 125(3),* 807–813.

[32] PARENS, M. D., McCONVILLE, B. J. and KAPLAN, S. M. (1966) The prediction of frequency of illness from the response to separation. *Psychosomatic Medicine, 28,* 162–171.

[33] THEIL, H. G., PARKER, D. and BRUCE, T. A. (1973) Stress factors and the risk of myocardial infarction. *Journal of Psychosomatic Research, 17,* 43–57.

[34] KASL, S. V. and COBB, S. (1970) Blood pressure changes in men undergoing job loss: a preliminary report. *Psychosomatic Medicine, 32,* 19–38.

[35] COBB, S. (1974) Physiologic changes in men whose jobs were abolished. *Journal of Psychosomatic Research, 18,* 245–258.

[36] IMBODEN, J. B., CANTER, A. and CLUFF, L. (1963) Separation experiences and health records in a group of normal adults. *Psychosomatic Medicine, 35,* 433–441.

[37] MUSLIN, H. L. and PEIPER, W. (1962) Separation experience and cancer of the breast. *Psychosomatics, 3,* 230–236.

[38] MUSLIN, H. L., GYARFAS, K. and PEIPER, W. J. (1966) Separation experience and cancer of the breast. *Annals of the New York Academy of Sciences, 125(3),* 802–806.

[39] GREER, S. and MORRIS, T. (1975) Psychological attributes of women who develop breast cancer: a controlled study. *Journal of Psychosomatic Research, 19,* 147–153.

[40] SCHONFIELD, J. (1975) Psychological and life experience differences between Israeli women with benign and cancerous breast lesions. *Journal of Psychosomatic Research, 19,* 229–234.

[41] MARKS, R. (1967) A review of empirical findings. In S. L. Syme and L. G. Reeder (Eds) *Social stress and cardiovascular disease. Milbank Memorial Fund Quarterly, 45.*

[42] MEI-TAL, V., MEYEROWITZ, S. and ENGEL, G. L. (1970) The role of psychological process in a somatic disorder: multiple sclerosis. *Psychosomatic Medicine, 32,* 67–86.

[43] BROWN, G. (1974) Methodological research on stressful life events. In B. S. Dohrenwend, and B. P. Dohrenwend (Eds) *Stressful life events*. New York: Wiley.

[44] WOLFF, H. H. (1977) Loss: a central theme in psychotherapy. *British Journal of Psychology, 50*, 11–19.

[45] THURLOW, H. J. (1967) General susceptibility to illness: a selective review. *Canadian Medical Association Journal, 97*, 1397–1404.

[46] HINKLE, L. E. (1974) The Effect of exposure to culture change, social change and changes in interpersonal relationships on health. In B. S. Dohrenwend and B. P. Dohrenwend (Eds) *Stressful life events*. New York: Wiley.

[47] SHELDON, A. and HOOPER, D. (1969) An enquiry into health and ill-health and adjustment in early marriage. *Journal of Psychosomatic Research, 13*, 95–101.

[48] JACOBS, M. A., SPILKEN, A. Z., NORMAN, M. M. and ANDERSON, L. S. (1970) Life stress and respiratory illness. *Psychosomatic Medicine, 32*, 233–243.

[49] JENKINS, C. D. (1971) Psychologic and social precursors of coronary disease. *New England Journal of Medicine, 284*, 244–255, 307–317.

[50] JENKINS, C. D. (1976) Recent evidence supporting psychologic and social risk factors for coronary disease. *New England Journal of Medicine, 294*, 987–995, 1033–1039.

[51] COBB, S., SCHULL, W. J., HARBURG, E. and KASL, S. V. (1969) The intrafamilial transmission of rheumatoid arthritis: an unusual study. *Journal of Chronic Diseases, 22*, 193–194.

[52] LEHR, I., MESSINGER, H. B. and ROSENMAN, R. H. (1973) A sociobiological approach to the study of coronary heart disease. *Journal of Chronic Diseases, 26*, 13–30.

[53] SYME, S. L., HYMAN, M. M. and ENTERLINE, P. E. (1965) Cultural mobility and the occurrence of coronary heart disease. *Journal of Chronic Diseases, 26*, 13–30.

[54] COHEN, J. B. (1974) Sociocultural change and behaviour patterns in disease etiology: an epidemiological study of coronary disease among Japanese Americans. *Ph.D. disser-*

tation in Epidemiology, School of Public Health, University of California at Berkely.

[55] SHEKELLE, R. B., OSTFELD, A. M. and PAUL, O. (1969) Social status and incidence of coronary heart disease. *Journal of Chronic Diseases, 22,* 381–394.

[56] HORAN, P. M. and GRAY, B. H. (1974) Status inconsistency, mobility and coronary heart disease. *Journal of Health and Social Behaviour, 15,* 300–310.

[57] SHEKELLE, R. B. (1976) Status inconsistency, mobility and CHD: a reply to Horan and Gray. *Journal of Health and Social Behaviour, 17,* 83–87.

[58] BENGTSSON, C., HALLSTROM, T. and TIBBLIN, G. (1973) Social factors, stress experience, and personality traits in women with ischaemic heart disease, compared to a population sample of women. *Acta Medica Scandinavica (Suppl.) 549,* 82–92.

[59] HOLMES, T. H. (1956) Multidiscipline studies of tuberculosis. In P. J. Sparer (Ed.) *Personality, stress and tuberculosis.* New York: Int. University Press.

[60] CHRISTENSON, W. N. and HINKLE, L. E. (1961) Differences in illness and prognostic signs in two groups of young men. *Journal of the American Medical Association, 177,* 247–253.

[61] CRUZ-COKE, R., ETCHEVERRY, R. and NAGEL, R. (1964) Influences of migration on blood pressure of Easter Islanders. *Lancet,* March 28, 697–699.

[62] MEDALIE, J. H., KAHN, H. A. *et al.* (1973) Myocardial infarction over a five year period. I Prevalence, incidence and mortality experience. *Journal of Chronic Diseases, 26,* 63–84.

[63] WARDWELL, W. I., HYMAN, M. and BAHNSON, C. B. (1964) Stress and coronary disease in three field studies. *Journal of Chronic Diseases, 17,* 73–84.

[64] FOSTER, J. H. (1927) Blood pressure of foreigners in China. *Archives of Internal Medicine, 40,* 38–45.

[65] TUNG, C. L. (1927) Relative hypotension of foreigners in China. *Archives of Internal Medicine, 40,* 153–158.

[66] SYME, S. L. (1967) Implications and future prospects. (Editorial) In S. L. Syme and L. G. Reeder. *Social stress and cardiovascular disease. Milbank Memorial Fund Quarterly*, 45.

[67] MOSS, G. E. (1973) *Illness, immunity and social interaction.* New York: Wiley.

[68] BANDURA, A. and WALTERS, R. H. (1963) *Social learning and personality development.* New York: Holt, Rinehart and Winston.

[69] SMITH, T. (1967) A review of empirical findings. In S. L. Syne and L. G. Reeder, (Eds) *Social stress and cardiovascular disease. Milbank Memorial Fund Quarterly*, 45.

[70] CASSEL, J. C. (1970) Physical illness in response to stress. In S. Levine and N. A. Scotch (Eds) *Social stress.* Chicago: Aldine.

[71] SCOTCH, N. A. (1960) Preliminary report on the relation of sociocultural factors to hypertension among the Zulu. *Annals of the New York Academy of Sciences, 84*, 1000–1009.

[72] HOOBLER, S. W., TEJADA, G., GUZMAN, M., and PARDO, A. (1965) Influence of nutrition and 'acculturalization' on the blood pressure levels and changes with age in the highland Guatemalan Indians. *Circulation, 32, 4, Oct. Supplement II*, 116.

[73] TYROLA, H. A. and CASSEL, J. T. (1964) Health consequences of culture change: the effect of urbanization on coronary heart mortality in rural residents. *Journal of Chronic Diseases, 17*, 167–177.

[74] HENRY, J. P. and CASSEL, J. C. (1969) Psychosocial factors in essential hypertension. Recent epedemiologic and animal experimental evidence. *American Journal of Epidemiology, 90*, 171–200.

[75] LEAF, A. (1973) Getting Old. *Scientific American, 229*, 44–52.

[76] ANTONOVSKY, A. (1972) Breakdown: a needed fourth step in the conceptual armamentarium of modern medicine. *Social Science and Medicine, 6*, 537–544.

[77] CASSEL, J. C. (1964) Social science theory as a source of

hypotheses in epidemiological research. *American Journal of Public Health, 54,* 1482–1488.

[78] DE ARAUJO, G., VAN ARSDEL, P. P. *et al.* (1973) Life changes, coping ability and chronic intrinsic asthma. *Journal of Psychosomatic Research, 17,* 359–363.

[79] BERLE, B. B., PINSKY, R. H., WOLF, S. and WOLF, H. G. (1952) Berle index: a clinical guide to prognosis in stress disease. *Journal of the American Medical Association, 149,* 1624–1628.

[80] FOSTER, F. G., CHON, G. L. and McKEGNEY, F. P. (1973) Psychobiologic factors and individual survival on renal hemodialysis, a two year follow-up. *Psychosomatic Medicine, 35,* 64–82.

[81] HAGBURG, B. and MALMQUIST, A. (1974) A prospective study of patients in chronic hemodialysis – IV. Pre-treatment psychiatric and psychological variables predicting outcome. *Journal of Psychosomatic Research, 18,* 315–319.

[82] SYME, S. L. (1970) Lecture given at SUNY, Buffalo, 1970. Cited by G. E. Moss in *Illness, immunity and social interaction.* New York: Wiley, 1973, p. 156.

[83] COMSTOCK, G. W. and PARTRIDGE, K. B. (1972) Church attendance and health. *Journal of Chronic Diseases, 25,* 665–672.

[84] WINKLESTEIN, W. and REKATE, A. C. (1964) Age trend of mortality from coronary artery disease in women and observations on the reproduction patterns of those affected. *American Heart Journal, 67,* 481–488.

[85] COBB, S. (1976) Social support as a moderator of life stress. *Psychosomatic Medicine, 38,* 300–314.

[86] ROWLAND, K. F. (1977) Environmental events predicting death for the elderly. *Psychological Bulletin, 82,* 349–384.

[87] HOLMES, T. H. and RAHE, R. H. (1967) The social readjustment rating scale. *Journal of Psychosomatic Research, 11,* 213–218.

[88] BIRLEY, J. L. T. and CONNOLLY, J. (1976) Life events and physical illness. In O. W. Hill (Ed.) *Modern trends in psychosomatic medicine – 3.* London: Butterworths.

[89] ANDERVONT, H. B. (1944) Influence of environment on mammary cancer in mice. *Journal of the National Cancer Institute*, 4, 579–581.

[90] MUHLBOCK, O. (1951) Influence of environment on the incidence of mammary tumors in mice. *Acta International Union Against Cancer*, 7, 351.

[91] ADER, R. (1967) The influence of psychologic factors on disease susceptibility in animals. In M. L. Conalty (Ed.) *The husbandry of laboratory animals*. London: Academic Press.

[92] ADER, R. (1976) Psychosomatic research in animals. In O. W. Hill (Ed.) *Modern trends in psychosomatic medicine – 3*. London: Butterworths.

[93] FRIEDMAN, S. B., GLASGOW, L. A. and ADER, R. (1969) Psychological factors modifying host resistance to experimental infections. *Annals of the New York Academy of Sciences*, *164(2)*, 381–393.

[94] LA BARBA, R. C. (1970) Experiential and environmental factors in cancer. *Psychosomatic Medicine*, *32*, 259–276.

[95] DE CHAMBRE, R. D. and GOSSE, C. (1973) Individual versus group caging of mice with grafted tumors. *Cancer Research*, *33*, 140–144.

[96] HENRY, J. P., STEPHENS, P. M. and WATSON, F. M. C. (1975) Force breeding, social disorder and mammary tumor formation in CBA/USC mouse colonies: a pilot study. *Psychosomatic Medicine*, *37*, 277–283.

[97] CALHOUN, J. B. (1973) Death squared: the explosive growth and demise of a mouse population. *Proceedings of the Royal Society of Medicine*, *66*, 80–88.

[98] HENRY, J. P., MEEHAN, J. P. and STEPHENS, P. M. (1967) The use of psychosocial stimulation to induce prolonged systolic hypertension in mice. *Psychosomatic Medicine*, *29*, 408–432.

[99] HENRY, J. P., ELY, D. L. *et al.* (1971) The role of psychological factors in the development of articulerosclerosis in CBA mice: observations on the heart, kidney and aorta. *Atherosclerosis*, *14*, 203–218.

[100] BAHNSON, C. B. (1969) Psychophysiological complementarity in malignancies: past work and future vistas. *Annals of the New York Academy of Sciences 164(2)*, 319–334.

[101] SCHMALE, A. H., MEYEROWITZ, S. and TINLING, D. C. (1970) In O. W. Hill (Ed.) *Modern trends in psychosomatic medicine – 2*. London: Butterworths.

CHAPTER 6

[1] ALEXANDER, F., FRENCH, T. M. and POLLOCK, G. H. (1968) *Psychosomatic specificity*. Chicago: University of Chicago Press.

[2] MISCHEL, W. (1968) *Personality and assessment*. New York: Wiley.

[3] HARRÉ, R. (Ed.) (1976) *Personality*. Oxford: Blackwell.

[4] KINNANE, J. F. and SUZIEDELIS, A. (1964) *Sources of interpersonal anxiety in the physically handicapped*. Unpublished report submitted to the Vocational Rehabilitation Administration, Washington D.C. (See also Caffrey, B. (1967) op. cit.)

[5] ROMO, M., SILTANEN, P., THEORELL, T., and RAHE, R. H. (1974) Work behaviour, time urgency and life dissatisfaction in subjects with myocardial infarction: a cross cultural study. *Journal of Psychosomatic Research, 18*, 1–8.

[6] VAN DIJL, H. (1975) Myocardial infarction patients and work attitudes – an empirical study. *Journal of Psychosomatic Research, 19*, 197–202.

[7] RUSSEK, H. I. (1958) Editorial stress and the etiology of coronary artery disease. *American Journal of Cardiology, 2*, 129–134.

[8] THEIL, H. G., PARKER, D. and BRUCE, T. A. (1973) Stress factors and the risk of myocardial infarcation. *Journal of Psychosomatic Research, 17*, 43–57.

[9] BRUHN, J. G., PAREDES, A., ADSETT, C. A., and WOLF, S. (1974) Psychological predictors of sudden death in myocardial infarction. *Journal of Psychosomatic Research, 18*, 187–191.

[10] FRIEDMAN, M. and ROSENMAN, R. H. (1959) Association of specific overt behaviour pattern with blood and cardiovascular findings. *Journal of the American Medical Association*, *169*, 1286–1296.

[11] JENKINS, C. D. (1971) Psychologic and social precursors of coronary disease. *New England Journal of Medicine*, *284*, 244–255, 307–317.

[12] JENKINS, C. D. (1976) Recent evidence supporting psychologic and social risk factors for coronary disease. *New England Journal of Medicine*, *294*, 987–995, 1033–1039.

[13] ABSE, D. W., WILKINS, M. M. *et al.* (1974) Personality and behavioural characteristics of lung cancer patients. *Journal of Psychosomatic Research*, *18*, 101–113.

[14] MOOS, R. H. (1964) Personality factors associated with rheumatoid arthritis: a review. *Journal of Chronic Diseases*, *17*, 41–55.

[15] McCLARY, A. R., MEYER, E. and WEITZMAN, E. L. (1955) Observations on the role of the mechanism of depression in some patients with disseminated lupus erythematosus. *Psychosomatic Medicine*, *17*, 311–321.

[16] HINKLE, L. E. (1974) The effect of exposure to culture change, social change and changes in interpersonal relationships on health. In B. S. Dohrenwend and B. P. Dohrenwend (Eds) *Stressful life events*. New York: Wiley.

[17] MINC, S. (1965) Psychological factors in coronary heart disease. *Geriatrics*, *20*, 747–755.

[18] BONAMI, M. and RIMÉ, B. (1972) Approche exploratoire de la personalité precoronarienne par analyse standardisée de données projectives thematiques. *Journal of Psychosomatic Research*, *16*, 103–113.

[19] THOMAS, C. B. and GREENSTREET, R. L. (1973) Psychobiological characteristics in youth as predictors of five disease states: suicide, metal illness, hypertension, coronary heart disease and tumor. *John Hopkins Medical Journal*, *132*, 16–43.

[20] MERTENS, C. and SEGERS, M. J. (1971) L'influence des facteurs psychologiques dans la genese des affections

coronariennes. I Données bibliographiques. *Bulletin de l'Académie Royale de Medécine de Belgique, 11,* 155–199.

[21] RIMÉ, B. and BONAMI, M. (1973) Specificité psychosomatique et affections cardiaques coronariennes: essai de verification de la theorie de Dunbar au moyen du MMPI. *Journal of Psychosomatic Research, 17,* 345–352.

[22] DONGIER, M. (1974) Psychosomatic aspects in myocardial infarction in comparisom with angina pectoris. *Psychotherapy and Psychosomatics, 23,* 123–131.

[23] LIESSE, M., VAN IMSCHOOT, K., MERTENS, C. and LAUWERS, P. (1974) Characteristiques psychologiques et reactions physiologiques au stress de sujets normaux et coronariens. *Journal of Psychosomatic Research, 18,* 101–113.

[24] ENGEL, G. L. (1955) Studies of ulcerative colitis III. The nature of the psychologic process. *American Journal of Medicine, 19,* 231–256.

[25] SCOTCH, N. A. and GEIGER, H. J. (1963) The epidemiology of essential hypertension: a review with special attention to psychologic and sociocultural factors: II. *Journal of Chronic Diseases, 17,* 167–177.

[26] LUBORSKY, L., DOCHERTY, J. P. and PENICK, S. (1973) Onset conditions for psychosomatic symptoms: a comparative review of immediate observation with retrospective research. *Psychosomatic Medicine, 35,* 187–204.

[27] STRAKER, N. and TAMERIN, J. (1974) Aggression and childhood asthma: a study in a natural setting. *Journal of psychosomatic research, 18,* 131–135.

[28] GREER, S. and MORRIS, T. (1975) Psychological attributes of women who develop breast cancer: a controlled study. *Journal of Psychosomatic Research, 19,* 147–153.

[29] GARRITY, T. F., SOAMES, G. W. and MARX, M. B. (1977) Personality factors in resistance to illness after recent life changes. *Journal of Psychosomatic Research, 21,* 23–32.

[30] SILTANEN, P., LAUROMA, M. *et al.* (1975) Psychological characteristics related to coronary heart disease. *Journal of Psychosomatic Research, 19,* 183–195.

[31] PARENS, M. D., McCONVILLE, B. J. and KAPLAN, S. M. (1966) The prediction of frequency of illness from the response to separation. *Psychosomatic Medicine, 28*, 162–171.

[32] FLARSCHEIM, A. (1958) Ego mechanisms in three pulmonary tuberculosis patients. *Psychosomatic Medicine, 20*, 475–483.

[33] JACOBS, M. A., SILKEN, A. Z., NORMAN, M. M. and ANDERSON, L. S. (1970) Life stress and respiratory illness. *Psychosomatic Medicine, 32*, 233–243.

[34] BONFILS, S. S. and DE M'UZAN, M. (1974) Irritable bowel syndrome vs. ulcerative colitis: psychofunctional disturbance vs. psychosomatic disease? *Journal of Psychosomatic Research, 18*, 291–296.

[35] HAGBURG, B. and MALMQUIST, A. (1974) A prospective study of patients in chronic hemodialysis – IV. Pretreatment psychiatric and psychological variables predicting outcome. *Journal of Psychosomatic Research, 18*, 315–319.

[36] SCHMALE, A. H., MEYEROWITZ, S. and TINLING, D. C. (1970) In O. W. Hill (Ed.) *Modern trends in psychosomatic medicine – 2.* London: Butterworths.

[37] SCHACHTER, S. and SINGER, J. E. (1962) Cognitive, social and physiological determinants of emotional state. *Psychological Review, 69*, 379–399.

CHAPTER 7

[1] KUHN, T. S. (1962) *The structure of scientific revolutions.* Chicago, Illinois: University of Chicago Press.

[2] FREUD, S. (1926) *Inhibitions, symptoms and anxiety.* Standard Edition 20. London: Hogarth Press.

[3] PINKERTON, P. and WEAVER, C. M. (1970) Childhood asthma. In O. W. Hill (Ed.) *Modern trends in psychosomatic medicine – 2.* London: Butterworths.

[4] ALEXANDER, F., FRENCH, T. M. and POLLOCK, G. H. (1968) *Psychosomatic specificity.* Chicago: University of Chicago Press.

[5] ENGEL, G. L. and SCHMALE, A. H. (1972) Conservation-withdrawal: a primary regulatory process for organismic homeostasis. In CIBA Foundation Symposium 8. *Physiology, emotion and psychosomatic illness.* Elsevier: Associated Scientific Publishers.

[6] SANDLER, J. (1972) The role of affects in psychoanalytic theory. In CIBA Foundation Symposium 8. *Physiology, emotion and psychosomatic illness.* Elsevier: Associated Scientific Publishers.

[7] RYLE, G. (1949) *The concept of mind.* London: Hutchinson.

[8] LADER, M. (1972) Psychophysical research and psychosomatic medicine. In CIBA Foundation Symposium 8: *Physiology, emotion and psychosomatic illness.* Elsevier: Associated Scientific Publishers.

[9] BASOWITZ, H., PERSKY, H., KORCHIN, S. J. and GRINKER, R. R. (1955) *Anxiety and stress: An interdisciplinary study of a life situation.* New York: McGraw-Hill.

[10] HARDY, J. D., WOLF, H. G. and GOODELL, H. (1952) *Pain sensations and reactions,* Baltimore: Williams and Wilkins.

[11] LAZARUS, R. S., SPEISMAN, J. C., MORDKOFF, A. M. and DAVISON, L. A. (1962) A laboratory study of psychological stress produced by a motion picture film. *Psychological Monographs, 76, No. 34. Whole No. 553.*

[12] LADER, M. (1970) Psychosomatic and psychophysiological aspects of anxiety. In O. W. Hill (Ed.) *Modern trends in Psychosomatic Medicine – 2.* London: Butterworths.

[13] SKINNER, B. F. (1972) *Beyond freedom and dignity.* London: Jonathon Cape.

[14] BLACKMAN, D. (1974) *Operant conditioning: an experimental analysis of behaviour.* London: Methuen.

[15] LEITENBERG, H. (1976) (Ed.) *Handbook of behaviour modification and behaviour therapy.* New Jersey: Prentice-Hall.

[16] BENNETTE, G. (1969) Psychic and cellular aspects of isolation and identity impairment in cancer: a dialectic of alienation. *Annals of the New York Academy of Sciences, 164(2),* 352–364.

[17] DURKHEIM, E. (1951) *Suicide: a study in sociology.* Transl. J. A. Spaulding and G. Simpson. Glencoe, Illinois: Free Press.

[18] Moss, G. E. (1973) *Illness, immunity and social interaction.* New York: Wiley.

[19] SHEKELLE, R. B., OSTFELD, A. M. and PAUL, O. (1969) Social status and incidence of coronary heart disease. *Journal of Chronic Diseases, 22,* 381–394.

[20] FRENCH, J. R. P. (1973) Person role fit. *Occupational Mental Health, 3,* 15–20.

[21] SYME, S. L., HYMAN, H. M. and ENTERLINE, P. E. (1965) Cultural mobility and the occurrence of coronary heart disease. *Journal of Chronic Diseases, 26,* 13–30.

[22] KIRITZ, S. and Moos, R. H. (1974) Physiological effects of social environments. *Psychosomatic Medicine, 36,* 96–114.

[23] HENRY, J. P. and CASSEL, J. C. (1969) Psychosocial factors in essential hypertension. Recent epedemiologic and animal experimental evidence. *American Journal of Epidemiology, 90,* 171–200.

[24] SELIGMAN, E. P. (1975) *Helplessness.* San Francisco: Freeman.

[25] GLASS, D. C. (1977) *Behaviour pattern, stress, and coronary disease.* New York: Wiley.

[26] LAZARUS, R. S. (1966) *Psychological stress and the coping process.* New York: McGraw-Hill.

[27] GRINKER, R. R. (1973) *Psychosomatic concepts.* New York: Jason Aronson.

[28] LIPOWSKI, Z. J. (1975) The patient, his illness and environment. In S. Arieti and M. F. Reiser (Eds) *American Handbook of Psychiatry, 2nd ed., Vol. 4.* New York: Basic Books.

[29] HARRÉ, R. (1976) The constructive role of models. In L. Collins (Ed.) *Social issues in the seventies.* London: Tavistock.

CHAPTER 8

[1] PIAGET, J. (1968) *Structuralism*. London: Routledge and Kegan Paul.

[2] LEVI-STRAUSS, C. (1968) *Structural Anthropology*. Allen Lane, The Penguin Press: Harmondsworth.

[3] SAUSSURE, F. de (1916) *Cours de linguistique général*. Paris: Payot.

[4] COLLETT, P. (1977) (Ed.) *Social Rules and Social Behaviour*. Oxford: Blackwell.

[5] CHOMSKY, N. (1965) *Aspects of the theory of syntax*. Cambridge, Mass.: MIT Press.

[6] POSTAL, P. M. (1964) Underlying and superficial linguistic structure. *Harvard Educational Review, 34,* 246–266.

[7] LYONS, J. (1977) *Chomsky*. Sussex: The Harvester Press Ltd.

[8] WINCH, P. (1958) *The idea of a social science*. London: Routledge and Kegan Paul.

[9] KELVIN, P. (1969) *The bases of social behaviour*. London: Holt, Rinehart and Winston.

[10] HARRÉ, R. and SECORD, P. F. (1972) *The explanation of social behaviour*. Oxford: Blackwell.

[11] ABELSON, R. P., ARONSON, E., McGUIRE, W. J., NEWCOMB, T. M., ROSENBERG, M. J. and TANNERBAUM, P. H. (Eds) (1968) *Theories of cognitive consistency: a source book*. Chicago: Rand McNally.

[12] KIESLER, C. A., COLLINS, B. E. and MILLER, N. (1969) *Attitude change: a critical analysis of theoretical approaches*. New York: Wiley.

[13] FLAVELL, J. A. (1963) *The development psychology of Jean Piaget*. Princeton: Van Nostrand.

[14] BERLYNE, D. E. (1957) Uncertainty and conflict: a point of contact between information theory and behaviour theory. *Psychological Review, 64,* 329–339.

[15] KUHN, T. S. (1962) *The structure of scientific revolutions*. Chicago, Illinois: University of Chicago Press.

[16] FESTINGER, L. (1950) Informal social communication. *Psychological Review*, 57, 271–282.

[17] FESTINGER, L. (1954) A theory of social comparison processes. *Human Relations*, 7, 117–140.

[18] BEM, D. J. (1968) Dissonance reduction in the behaviourist. In R. P. Abelson, E. Aronson *et al.* (Eds) *Theories of cognitive consistency: a source book*. Chicago: Rand McNally.

[19] SHIBUTANI, T. (1967) Reference groups as perspectives. In J. Manis and B. Meltzer (Eds) *Symbolic interaction: a reader in social psychology*. Boston: Allyn and Bacon.

[20] DURKHEIM, E. (1953) *Sociology and philosophy*. Transl. D. F. Pocock. Glencoe, Illinois: Free Press.

[21] CARDWELL, J. D. (1971) *Social psychology: a symbolic interaction perspective*. Philadelphia: Davis.

[22] LUBORSKY, L., DOCHERTY, J. P. and PENICK, S. (1973) Onset conditions for psychosomatic symptoms: a comparative review of immediate observation with retrospective research. *Psychosomatic Medicine*, 35, 187–204.

CHAPTER 9

[1] RAHE, R. H. (1972) Subjects' recent life changes and their near-future illness reports, *Annals of Clinical Research*, 4, 250–265.

CHAPTER 10

[1] SCHACHTER, S. (1951) Deviation, rejection and communication. *Journal of Abnormal and Social Psychology*, 46, 190–207.

[2] BROWN, G. (1974) Methodological research on stressful life events. In B. S. Dohrenwend, and B. P. Dohrenwend (Eds) *Stressful life events*. New York: Wiley.

[3] SOLOMON, G. F. (1969) Emotions, stress, the central nervous system, and immunity. *Annals of the New York Academy of Sciences, 164(2)*, 335–343.

[4] HAGBURG, B. and MALMQUIST, A. (1974) A prospective study of patients in chronic hemodialysis – IV. Pretreatment psychiatric and psychological variables predicting outcome. *Journal of Psychosomatic Research, 18*, 315–319.

[5] KATZ, J., GALLAGHER, T. *et al.* (1969) Psychoendocrine considerations in cancer of the breast. *Annals of the New York Academy of Sciences, 164(2)*, 509–516.

[6] COBB, S. (1974) Physiologic changes in men whose jobs were abolished. *Journal of Psychosomatic Research, 18*, 245–258.

[7] LAZARUS, R. S. (1977) Stress and coping in adaptation illness. In Z. J. Lipowski, D. R. Lipsitt, and P. C. Whybrow (Eds) *Psychosomatic medicine: current trends and clinical applications.* New York: Oxford University Press.

[8] KISSEN, D. M. (1966) The significance of personality in lung cancer in men. *Annals of the New York Academy of Sciences, 125(3)*, 820–826.

[9] BAHNSON, M. B., and BAHNSON, C. B. (1969) Ego defenses in cancer patients. *Annals of the New York Academy of Sciences, 164(2)*, 546–559.

[10] HUXLEY, J., MAYR, E., OSMOND, H. and HOFFER, A. (1964) Schizophrenia as a genetic morphism. *Nature, 204*, 220–221.

[11] BABIGIAN, H. M. and ODOROFF, C. L. (1969) The mortality experience of a population with psychiatric illness. *American Journal of Psychiatry, 126*, 470–480.

[12] INNES, G. and MILLAR, W. M. (1970) Mortality among psychiatric patients. *Scottish Medical Journal, 15*, 143–148.

[13] WEBLIN, J. E. (1963) Psychogenesis in asthma; an appraisal with a view to family research. *British Journal of Medical Psychology, 36*, 211–225.

[14] CLOW, H. E. and PROUT, C. T. (1946) Study of modification of mental illness by intercurrent physical disorders in 100 patients. *American Journal of Psychiatry, 103*, 179–184.

[15] APPEL, J. and ROSEN, S. R. (1950) Psychotic factors in psychosomatic illness. *Psychosomatic Medicine, 12*, 236–243.

[16] DOUST, J. W. L. (1952) Psychiatric aspects of somatic immunity. *British Journal of Social Medicine, 6*, 49–67.

[17] ROSS, W. D., HAY, J. and McDOWALL, M. F. (1950) The incidence of certain vegetative disturbances in relation to psychosis. *Psychosomatic Medicine, 12*, 179–183.

[18] KUO, W. (1976) Theories of migration and mental health: an empirical testing on Chinese Americans. *Social Science and Medicine, 10*, 297–306.

[19] ORFORD, J. and OPPENHEIMER, E. *et al.* (1976) The cohesiveness of alcoholism-complicated marriages and its influence on treatment outcome. *British Journal of Psychiatry, 128*, 318–339.

[20] LEFF, J. (1977) Environmental influences on schizophrenia. *Paper presented to the Society for Psychosomatic Research*, Oct. 20, 1977.

[21] VAUGHN, C. E. and LEFF, J. P. (1976) The influence of family and social factors in the course of psychiatric illness: a comparison of schizophrenic and depressed neurotic patients. *British Journal of Psychiatry, 129*, 125–137.

[22] BROWN, G. W. and HARRIS, T. (1978) *Social origins of depression*. London: Tavistock.

[23] FRIEDMAN, M. (1964) Behaviour pattern and its pathogenic role in clinical coronary artery disease. *Geriatrics, 19*, 562–567.

[24] CAFFREY, B. (1967) A review of empirical findings. In S. L. Syme and L. G. Reeder (Eds) *Social stress and cardiovascular disease. Milbank Memorial Fund Quarterly, 45*.

[25] THEORELL, T. and RAHE, R. H. (1972) Behaviour and life satisfactions of Swedish subjects with myocardial infarction. *Journal of Chronic Diseases, 25*, 139–147.

[26] ROMO, M., SILTANEN, P., THEORELL, T., and RAHE, R. H. (1974) Work behaviour, time urgency and life dissatisfaction in subjects with myocardial infarction: a cross cultural study. *Journal of Psychosomatic Research, 18*, 1–8.

[27] ARLOW, J. A. (1945) Identification in coronary occlusion. *Psychosomatic Medicine, 7,* 195–209.

[28] CATHEY, C., JONES, H. B. *et al.* (1962) The relation of life stress to the concentration of serum lipids in patients with coronary artery disease. *American Journal of the medical Sciences, 244,* 421–441.

[29] MILLER, C. K. (1965) Psychological correlates of coronary artery disease. *Psychosomatic Medicine, 27,* 257–265.

[30] WARDWELL, W. I., BAHNSON, C. B. and CARON, H. S. (1963) Social and psychological factors in coronary heart disease. *Journal of Health and Human Behaviour, 4,* 154–165.

[31] SILTANEN, P., LAUROMA, M. *et al.* (1975) Psychological characteristics related to coronary heart disease. *Journal of Psychosomatic Research, 19,* 183–195.

CHAPTER 11

[1] FESTINGER, L. and CARLSMITH, J. M. (1959) Cognitive consequences of forced compliance. *Journal of Abnormal and Social Psychology, 58,* 203–210.

[2] KIESLER, C. A., COLLINS, B. E. and MILLER, N. (1969) *Attitude change: a critical analysis of theoretical approaches.* New York: Wiley.

[3] SECORD, P. F. and BACKMAN, C. W. (1964) *Social psychology.* New York: McGraw-Hill.

[4] TOTMAN, R. G. (1973) An approach to cognitive dissonance theory in terms of ordinary language. *Journal for the theory of social behaviour, 3,* 215–238.

[5] BRENER, J. (1976) The clinical application of biofeedback techniques. In O. W. Hill (Ed.) *Modern trends in psychosomatic medicine – 3.* London: Butterworths.

[6] PELLETIER, K. R. (1977) *Mind as healer, mind as slayer. A holistic approach to preventing stress disorders.* New York: Delta.

[7] LIPOWSKI, Z. J., LIPSITT, D. R. and WHYBROW, D. C. (Eds) (1977) *Psychosomatic Medicine – current trends and*

clinical applications. New York: Oxford University Press.

[8] SCHWARTZ, G. E. and BEATTY, J. (Eds) (1977) *Biofeedback: theory and research*. London: Academic Press.

[9] MORISON, R. S. (1973) Dying. Scientific American, 229, 54–62.

[10] DAVIES, H. (1977) *Modern Medicine. A doctor's dissent*. London: Abelard.

[11] LEAF, A. (1973) Getting Old. *Scientific American, 229*, 44–52.

INDEX

INDEX